Target
BERLIN

TARGET BERLIN

MISSION 250: 6 MARCH 1944

JEFFREY L. ETHELL
AND
ALFRED PRICE

ARMS AND
ARMOUR

CE

940.544 ETH

C212250999

Published in Great Britain
in 1989 by Arms and Armour Press, Artillery House,
Artillery Row, London SW1P 1RT.

Distributed in the USA by Sterling Publishing Co. Inc.,
2 Park Avenue, New York, NY 10016.

Distributed in Australia by
Capricorn Link (Australia) Pty. Ltd, P.O. Box 665,
Lane Cove, New South Wales 2066, Australia.

Front cover illustration © Keith Ferris, 1984.

First published 1981
by Jane's Publishing Company Ltd.

Designed by Peter Matthews; maps and diagrams by
Peter Endsleigh Castle, FRSA, AMRAeS.

British Library Cataloguing in Publication Data:
Ethell, Jeffrey
Target Berlin – 2nd ed.
1. Germany. Berlin. Air raids by United States Army
Air Force, 8th, 1944 (March)
I. Title   II. Price, Alfred, *1936–*
940.54'21
ISBN 0-85368-915-6

Typesetting by Method Limited, Essex and Typesetters
(Birmingham) Ltd; photograph sections camerawork by M&E
Reproductions, North Fambridge, Essex; printed and
bound in Great Britain by Mackays of Chatham, Kent.

CONTENTS

ILLUSTRATIONS

Photographs follow pages 52 and 116

Dedicated to Betty and Jane, who had to live through it too.

INTRODUCTION

On Monday 6 March 1944 the US 8th Air Force for the first time mounted a full-scale daylight attack on Berlin, capital of the Third Reich. As a result of the hard-fought battles on the way to the target, over it and during the return flight, 69 US four-engined bombers and 11 escorting fighters failed to regain their bases; in no other day's fighting, before or after, would the 8th Air Force lose a greater number of aircraft. This book describes the day's events as seen through the eyes of more than 160 Americans and Germans in the air and on the ground.

AUTHORS' NOTE

In this book the times stated are in British Summer Time (one hour ahead of Greenwich Mean Time) in use in Britain and by the US Army Air Forces based there on 6 March 1944. This coincided with the Middle European Time in use in Germany and in the Luftwaffe.

In the case of the witnesses the ranks, ages, positions and surnames (of ladies who later married) are those on 6 March 1944. For simplicity, in the body of the text the US ranks of First and Second Lieutenant are given as 'Lieutenant'; and Staff Sergeant, Technical Sergeant and Master Sergeant are given as 'Sergeant'.

Many US aircraft involved in the action carried names and these, where known, are given. No comprehensive list linking names with aircraft serial numbers was ever made, however; and about a third of the aircraft had no names at all, usually because they were newly delivered and their crews had no time to name them or chose not to do so.

All distances stated are in statute miles, aircraft speeds are given in miles per hour (true), weights in US tons and fuel tankages are given in US gallons.

Where possible German words have been anglicized in the text; thus Günther is written as Guenther, Müller as Mueller and Bär as Baer. German unit designations have been translated to their closest English equivalent: Fighter Geschwader for Jagdgeschwader, Destroyer Geschwader for Zerstoerergeschwader, Fighter Division for Jagddivision and Air Fleet for Luftflotte. Because no exact English terms exist for them, unit descriptions such as Staffel, Gruppe and Geschwader (plurals Staffeln, Gruppen and Geschwader) remain in German. Also German rank titles have been retained (a list of comparative ranks is given in Appendix A).

In several publications the abbreviations Bf 109 and Bf 110 are used, respectively, for the Messerschmitt 109 and 110 (Bf for Bayerische Flugzeugwerke). In official Luftwaffe documents, however, the abbreviations 'Bf' and 'Me' both appear frequently; so both are correct. In this book the less cumbersome abbreviation 'Me' is used.

PROLOGUE

Noon on Monday 6 March 1944, 21,000 feet over the small town of Haseluenne in northern Germany. Oberleutnant Wolfgang Kretchmer's was one of several Focke-Wulf 190s of Fighter Geschwader 1 that had just flashed through the formation of B-17s of the 13th Combat Wing after a massed head-on attack. Glancing back at the receding enemy Kretchmer was satisfied with the results; one bomber had reared up out of control, some were trailing smoke, others were losing height obviously in trouble. The German pilot returned his eyes to the front to find that somehow his comrades had all disappeared. He was alone. Undaunted, Kretchmer pulled his fighter around in a tight turn and sped after the enemy bombers, determined to have another go at them.

The sight of the B-17s going down, the red flares and frenzied radio calls for help from the survivors drew in P-47 escorts from all directions. As he arrived at the scene Colonel 'Hub' Zemke, commander of the 56th Fighter Group at the head of a flight of eight Thunderbolts, caught sight of Kretchmer's FW 190 below. Zemke silently admired the German pilot's bravery in attempting a lone attack on so many bombers. But he was there to prevent such things. He ordered one section of four P-47s to cover him then led his own section of four down to attack. Using maximum power the Thunderbolts hurtled after the unsuspecting prey.

Too late Wolfgang Kretchmer realized his predicament. He glanced back to check his tail before opening fire at one of the bombers and was horrified to see Zemke's Thunderbolt looming large behind him. Instinctively Kretchmer yanked the Focke-Wulf into a tight turn to the left, but as he did so he saw the muzzle flashes from the P-47's eight machine guns and his aircraft shuddered under the impact of the hits. The rounds struck the German fighter all over the wings and fuselage and as he pulled away in a fast climb Zemke saw it go down trailing dense black smoke.

The Focke-Wulf was done for. With flames from the ruptured fuel lines at the front of the cockpit sweeping back over his head and shoulders, Kretchmer knew he had to get out quickly, before the fire reached the fuel tanks under his seat and the fighter exploded. Keeping his eyes tightly closed he pulled the lever to jettison the canopy. But there was no expected 'whooosh' and sudden roar of air to indicate it had gone. Cursing his luck and still keeping his eyes closed, Kretchmer felt for the handle to wind back the canopy. Six turns should have been sufficient to open it fully; but after eight or nine there was still no change in the noise around him. It seemed he was doomed to go down with his blazing fighter. Resigned to imminent death, he turned his head to avoid the worst of the flames and squinted to one side to see what had gone wrong. Then he suddenly realized: the canopy had gone! He was not trapped after all! Kretchmer threw off his straps and with a strength born of desperation struggled into the howling slipstream. As he fell clear of the Focke-Wulf he yanked his ripcord, felt a bone-jarring jerk as the parachute opened, then moments later was unceremoniously dumped on the ground.

At her father's farm on the outskirts of Quakenbrueck 15-year-old Elfriede Kleybocker emerged from the air raid shelter to see Kretchmer's arrival. With her mother, father and two brothers she ran to help. Still dazed after his narrow escape Kretchmer staggered to his feet and released his parachute; a sudden stabbing pain in his right thigh announced he had been hit there by splinters. The wounded pilot looked in a sorry state. His face and hands had been badly burned, his pants had gone and all he had on below the waist were his boots and the tattered remains of his underpants. Somebody went to the house and returned with a blanket which was draped around Kretchmer like a skirt. It was an unimpressive garb for an officer in the Luftwaffe of the Third Reich but the best that could be provided in the circumstances. Shortly afterwards an ambulance arrived to take the wounded pilot to hospital.

Wolfgang Kretchmer recovered well from his wounds and now his facial burns have almost disappeared. His flying days over, he works as an architect at Haan. After the war he kept in contact with the Kleybockers and attended Elfriede's marriage. Hub Zemke's flying career is also long over, he now farms in California. Brought into contact by the authors of this book, the two pilots have exchanged a cordial correspondence and it is hoped they will soon meet. The bitterness of war is over. Only the memories remain, of men who shared the common bond of wartime flying and its attendant dangers.

CHAPTER 1

MONDAY 6 MARCH 1944

00.01 to 7.45am

Total war is not a succession of mere episodes in a day or a week. It is a long-drawn-out and intricately planned business, and the longer it continues the heavier are the demands on the character of the men engaged in it.

General George Marshall

March 6 1944; the Second World War, which had opened in September 1939 accompanied by hopes it would be 'over by Christmas', was almost at the close of its fifth winter and the end seemed as far away as ever. By now the conflict was truly global in its extent, with bitter actions being fought at distant places unheard of before or since. In the Pacific US forces were struggling against the stubborn Japanese defense to secure Los Negros in the Admiralty Islands. And a bombing campaign was in progress to neutralize Japanese bases at Rabaul and in the Marshall and Caroline Islands. In Burma British and Indian troops had halted the Japanese offensive in the Arakan and were preparing to push the enemy out of positions around Buthidaung and Letwedet. In Russia the Soviet Army had launched a powerful offensive on the southern part of the front near Shepetovka and was pushing forwards into the Ukraine against stiff German resistance. In Italy the German defenders had been able to block the Allied advance northwards and had also sealed off the bridgehead at Anzio just south of Rome. In the North Atlantic a relentless battle was in progress between U-boats and escorts around the eastbound convoy HX 280, with losses on both sides. And over Europe the Allied round-the-clock strategic bombing offensive against Germany was gaining in strength, with US heavy bombers attacking by day and their British counterparts by night.

In its issue of 6 March the *New York Times* gave its main headline to the Soviet offensive in the Ukraine 'Russians Gain on 112-Mile Front, Near Main Ukraine Escape Line' it stated, 'Nazi Plight Grave'.

Red Army forces under the command of Marshal Gregory K. Zhukoff in a two-day offensive on the First Ukrainian Front have smashed twelve German divisions and driven forward fifteen to thirty-one miles on a 112-mile front, capturing more than 500 inhabited points. . . .

Other war reports dealt with the latest US air attacks on targets in occupied Europe, under the headline 'Liberators Blast Nazi Air Center at Cognac, Bergerac Fields'.

> Keeping up their steady hammering of enemy targets, the United States Strategic Air Forces sent out Liberator and Marauder bombers today in day-long, heavy strikes at German military installations in southwestern and northern France. The attacks were close on the heels of the blows last night by Royal Air Force Mosquito formations at Berlin and undisclosed objectives in western Germany....

Alongside this news, however, the *New York Times* carried a report on an article entitled 'Massacre by Bombing' which had appeared in the pacifist magazine *Fellowship* endorsed by several church leaders including Dr Harry Emerson Fosdick.

> Twenty-eight clergymen and other leaders issued an appeal yesterday protesting against continued 'obliteration' bombings of German cities and calling upon Christians 'to examine themselves concerning their participation in this carnival of death' and to acquaint themselves with 'the realities of what is being done in our name in Europe...'

The other main US home news item concerned whether or not the 5 cent fare on the New York transport system should be increased to 10 cents. Mayor La Guardia had commented 'The question is, should the city of New York continue on a five-cent fare, which had developed it into the greatest city in the world, or should it increase the fare.' La Guardia said it was his 'considered judgement' that a popular referendum on the matter would result in a vote of at least three-to-one against such an increase.

On the commodity markets gold was priced at $35 per ounce, crude oil $1.11 a barrel and wheat $1.86⅜ a bushel. On Broadway the musical 'Oklahoma' was about to run its 400th performance; the Radio City Music Hall was showing 'Up In Arms' with Danny Kaye and the Rivoli theater was showing 'Song of Bernadette'.

In Germany the 6 March issue of the *Volkischer Beobachter*, official newspaper of the National Socialist party, also carried news of hard-fought battles on the Eastern Front. But in this case the official communiqué was dated the previous day and mentioned only fighting in the northern part of the front which had taken place three days before that. Under the headline 'Heavy Soviet Losses Near Vitebsk' it described fighting along the Smolensk - Orsha highway.

> The enemy losses in just this sector of the front amounted to 3,000 dead, 51 tanks, 54 anti-tank guns, 50 machine guns and 1,000 hand weapons including 11 anti-tank rifles. In two days of fighting at the bridgehead at Nowiki the Bolsheviks lost 700 men killed and taken prisoner. The greater part of these losses occurred in the sector to the southeast of Vitebsk, where during an attack on two of our positions by five divisions the Bolsheviks were thrown back after an action lasting six days.

The newspaper also published a suitably vague account of the US daylight bombing attack on Germany the previous Saturday.

> During mid-day on 4 March North American bomber formations carried out terror

attacks on some places in western Germany. These caused some damage to residential areas and casualties among the civilian population, particularly in the cities of Cologne and Bonn. Numerous churches, hospitals and public buildings were hit. A weak bomber formation with fighter escort succeeded in penetrating to the Berlin area but our air defenses prevented it carrying out a concentrated attack. Forty-one enemy aircraft, including 21 four-engined bombers, were destroyed.

Since all German newspapers were closely controlled by Dr Goebbels's propaganda ministry, no stories were permitted which even hinted that the country and the war were not being conducted perfectly. In conformity with the official line, the *Volkischer Beöbachter* carried a gloating report on the recent breakdown of Anglo-American diplomatic relations with Argentina following the Army coup there nine days earlier:

> The world is given an excellent example of the Anglo-American blackmail methods when it comes to dealing with small states. Now we see what Roosevelt and his cronies really mean by their often extolled term 'self determination'. Washington could not have given South Americans a clearer indication of what to expect from its 'good neighbor' policy; it is no more than an attempt to extend its Jewish-Imperialist area of sweated-labor under the motto: 'If you do not wish to be my brother I shall beat your head in!'

For relief from the war stories and political commentaries the German reader could escape to the entertainment pages. There was a review of Handel's opera 'Caesar' running at the Concert Hall at Kassel starring Alfred Borchardt in the title role; and the musical comedy 'Der Rosenkavalier' being shown at the Innsbruck State Theater to celebrate the 80th birthday of Richard Strauss. Also there was a list of films in production at the Bavarian Film Company. Among these were the love film *Ich brauche Dich* (I need you) with Marrianne Hoppe and Willy Birgel and the musical comedy *Es lebe die Liebe* (Long Live Love) with Johannes Heesters and Lizzi Waldmueller; both films would become well known in Germany after the war. Also in the offing was a low-key children's film entitled *Bravo, Kleiner Thomas* (Bravo, Little Thomas) whose cast included a promising young actor named Hardy Krueger.

Berlin, with a population of just over 4,300,000 in 1939, was at that time the greatest industrial and commercial city on the continent of Europe and the sixth largest city in the world. Within its city limits were innumerable prime military targets for, as well as being the capital and administrative center of Germany, it was also hub of the nation's war effort. All three armed services had ministerial buildings in Berlin and in addition there were more than ninety military headquarters, barracks and depots of various sizes scattered throughout the city. Berlin was also an important rail center, with twelve main lines converging on it from all directions; and a well developed system of canals linked it with the Ruhr industrial area in the west and the ports of Hamburg and Stettin.

By the beginning of 1944 the city's vast industrial capacity was devoted almost entirely to war production. In spite of some decentralization more than half the entire German electrical industry was still situated in Berlin, with factories like those of the AEG company in the Hennigsdorf, Moabit and

Oberschoeneweide districts making radio components, insulators and generating equipment; the Telefunken and Lorenz firms at Tempelhof and Zehlendorf respectively, making radio and radar sets; and the Robert Bosch works at Klein Machnow making ignition equipment for vehicles and aircraft. Third in Germany, after Schweinfurt and Bad Cannstatt, Berlin was an important center for the production of ball bearings with the factories of the Norddeutsche Kugellager Fabrik at Lichtenberg and the Vereinigte Kugellager Fabriken at Erkner.

Berlin was also an important center for aircraft production. The Heinkel works at Oranienburg was turning out twenty-six Heinkel 177 four-engined bombers each month; and the Henschel works at Johannisthal was building Henschel 129 attack aircraft and Junkers 88 medium bombers. The Focke-Wulf, Dornier and Flettner companies all had factories in the city making components and sub-assemblies. At the Argus works in the Reinickendorf district engineers were perfecting the cheap but effective pulse-jet engine to power the V-1 flying bomb about to go into mass production. And at Genshagen just to the south of the capital was the Daimler Benz plant, the largest in Germany for the production of aero engines, which alone turned out more than one-fifth of the nation's production.

The capital was also important in the production of military vehicles. The factories of the Auto Union at Halensee and Spandau, and the Alkett works at Spandau, were all mass producing tanks and self-propelled guns while the Maybach factory at Tempelhof built engines to drive them. The Demag works at Staaken, the Buessing works and the Nationale Automobile works at Oberschoeneweide were mass producing trucks and other vehicles for the armed forces.

The demands of the fighting services had, by 1944, stripped German industry of most men of military age. Their places in the factories were taken by hastily-trained German women, volunteer or forced laborers and prisoners of war from the nations occupied by Germany, and concentration camp inmates. For example of the 12,500 strong workforce of the Henschel aircraft company at Johannisthal only about 2,375 were German men employed by the company previously; 4,000 were full-time women workers, 875 were inmates from concentration camps or prisoners of war and the remaining 5,250 were volunteer or forced laborers from the occupied territories. In general prisoners and foreign workers did the unskilled tasks; anyone suspected of sabotage or 'slacking' was dealt with harshly by the police or, in more serious cases, by the *Sicherheitsdienst* – Heinrich Himmler's feared security service.

For those living in Berlin the war was impinging on almost every aspect of daily life. Starting the previous August the Royal Air Force had launched 17 large-scale night attacks on the city which caused widespread damage. Large numbers of pregnant women, mothers with pre-school-age children, school children and old people had been evacuated to safer country areas under a scheme run by the National Socialist Peoples' Welfare Organization. Those whose work was considered essential to the war economy had to stay put and this was enforced by a strict control of ration cards and personal travel documents. During attacks on the city so far, however, casualties had been low and, as a proportion of the whole, relatively little had been destroyed or damaged. The population had had time to get used to the air raids, in so far as human beings can become accustomed to the prospect of sudden death and destruction close at hand.

So far Berlin's geographical position, some 550 miles from the enemy bomber and fighter bases in eastern England, had kept it safe from large-scale air attack by day. Many of the capital's citizens felt this distance, coupled with the powerful flak defenses surrounding the city, would continue to deter the enemy from attempting such an enterprise.

The US 8th Air Force had opened its strategic bombing campaign on German-occupied Europe modestly enough, with an attack by twelve B-17s on railway yards at Rouen in France in July 1942. From then on the force had grown steadily and as it became more confident it was thrown against progressively more ambitious targets. For the remainder of 1942 it confined its attacks to objectives in France and Belgium. Then, in January 1943, came the first large-scale daylight attack on a target in Germany itself when sixty-four B-17s and B-24s attacked Wilhelmshaven on the north coast. In the months that followed raiding forces probed deeper and deeper into Germany. In April they attacked targets near Bremen, in June Huels in the Ruhr area and in July Kassel. Thus far American losses had in general been modest. But in the face of the progressively more ambitious attacks on industrial targets in Germany, mounted by increasingly powerful forces, the Luftwaffe was forced to react. Fighter and flak units were pulled from the eastern front and the Mediterranean to bolster the defenses of the homeland. Events came to a head on 17 August, when 363 B-17s set out for the deepest penetration yet to attack the ball bearing works at Schweinfurt and the Messerschmitt factory at Regensburg. Strengthened by the influx of new units the Luftwaffe reacted vigorously and 60 heavy bombers failed to reach friendly territory after the action. These heavy losses, coupled with bad weather, restricted the 8th Air Force's operations over Germany in September. The first two weeks of October 1943 saw a further burst of activity with attacks on Frankfurt-am-Main, Bremen, Danzig, Gdynia and Muenster. Then, on the 14th, a force of 291 B-17s set out to finish what they had started nearly two months earlier: the destruction of the ball bearing factories at Schweinfurt. Further reinforced by units pulled from the south and the east the Luftwaffe reaction to this second attack was as powerful as that against the first. The US losses were the same: a further 60 heavy bombers destroyed and many more damaged.

The losses incurred during the second attack on Schweinfurt forced an end to the deep penetration attacks by unescorted bomber formations. The heavy bombers, no matter how many guns they carried nor how large or tight their formations, could not prevent German fighters inflicting unacceptable losses. But the bombers' means of salvation lay close at hand: the long range P-38 and P-47 escort fighters which, carrying progressively larger drop tanks, were able to cover bomber formations penetrating deeper and deeper into Germany. And at the end of the year the clean-lined P-51B entered service, with the performance to out-fight the best fighters the Luftwaffe possessed and the range

0   miles   50

PETERBOROUGH

KINGS CLIFFE ●

DEENETHORPE ●   POLEBROOK
                        ●   ● GLATTON

GRAFTON UNDERWOOD ●   MOLESWORTH
                        ●   ● ALCONBURY
        CHELVESTON ●   ● KIMBOLTON

1 BD HQ Brampton Grange □

                    ●   ● THURLEIGH
NORTHAMPTON   PODINGTON   CAMBRIDGE

                    BASSINGBOURN ●
                            DUXFORD

                    STEEPLE MORDEN ●

                                DEBD
                    NUTHAMSTEAD ●

OXFORD

                    HQ VIII Fighter Cmnd.,
                        Bushey Hall

● MOUNT FARM   ■

HQ 8th Air Force,
High Wycombe

LONDON

to cover bombers operating almost anywhere over Germany.

Strengthened by its new-found ability to mount escorted attacks deep into Germany the 8th Air Force entered 1944 with renewed confidence. In spite of bad weather in January the force ended the month with heavy attacks on targets in the Frankfurt-am-Main and Brunswick areas, each with more than 800 bombers. There followed a further period of bad weather then, in the third week of February, bombers struck during the so-called 'Big Week': six days of intensive attacks against German aircraft production centers in western Germany mounted in concert with heavy bombers of the 15th Air Force based in Italy. During 'Big Week' the US Army Air Force put a total of 3,800 heavy bomber sorties over Germany and lost 226 bombers, an acceptable 6 per cent of those committed. For this low loss rate the bomber crews could thank their escorting fighters which time and again broke up German fighter attacks before they could strike home.

By the beginning of March the 8th Air Force felt able to strike at the most difficult and prestigious German target: Berlin itself.

From the Allied air planners' point of view, a large-scale daylight attack on Berlin would serve a three-fold purpose. First, there would be the actual destruction caused to targets and there were plenty of military importance dotted in and around the city. Secondly there would be the blow to the morale of the citizens of Berlin, with the knowledge that even their heavily defended city was no longer safe from daylight attack whenever the Allied leaders willed it. And thirdly there was the expectation that the German fighter force would feel compeled to engage attacks on the capital with everything it could muster and would suffer heavy losses in the process. In the words of the US Official Historians: 'If there was any target for which the German Air Force would fight, surely that target was Berlin.'

The 8th Air Force launched its first attack into the Berlin area on 3 March with the intention of hitting the VKF ball bearing plant at Erkner, the Robert Bosch electrical works at Klein Machnow and the Heinkel aircraft factory at Oranienburg. But on this occasion weather protected the targets far more effectively than could the Luftwaffe: over Germany the bombers encountered dense cloud with tops extending above 28,000 feet in places; formation flying became almost impossible and the mission had to be abandoned. A few bombers attacked Wilhelmshaven or other targets of opportunity on the way out, the others jettisoned their bombs into the sea.

In an attempt to repeat the attack on the next day, 4 March, the raiders encountered similar problems and had to be recalled. One combat wing failed to receive the recall signal however, and thirty-one B-17s of the 95th and 100th Bomb Groups continued to the German capital with part of the fighter escort and bombed through cloud using radar. The attack caused little damage and cost five bombers and 23 escorting fighters, but did show it was possible for a small force to get to Berlin and out again.

The weather on 5 March was unsuitable for a further attempt on Berlin but the forecast for the following day looked much better. Yet again the 8th Air Force prepared itself to attack the German capital.

Since the beginning of 1944 the US 8th Air Force had been under the command of Lieutenant General James Doolittle, 47, with his headquarters at High Wycombe, 20 miles west of London. Doolittle had served in the Air Corps since 1917 and during the years that followed his name had become well known to the American public. Between the wars he had been a famous racing and test pilot and in 1925 he won the Schneider Trophy for his country. When the USA entered the war he held the rank of Lieutenant Colonel and in April 1942 he personally led a small force of twin-engined B-25 bombers off the aircraft carrier *Hornet* for an attack on Tokyo which did much to boost US morale at the time; afterwards Hollywood made a dramatic film of the attack entitled 'Thirty Seconds over Tokyo', in which Spencer Tracy played the role of Doolittle. Just over a year later, in July 1943 when he commanded the US XIIth Bomber Command in North Africa, Doolittle had taken part in the first US air attack on Rome.

When Doolittle had taken over the 8th Air Force it was the largest single combat command in the US Army Air Force and still growing. Indeed, he found the very lavishness of the resources entrusted to him something of an embarrassment after the perennial shortages experienced in North Africa and Italy. As Doolittle wrote to his good friend Army General George Patton: 'Down there [in the Mediterranean] the problem was to make something out of nothing. Up here it requires an equal or greater amount of ingenuity to effectively utilize the almost unlimited resources at our disposal. Down there, when you were not '"under the guns", any modest success was apparently appreciated. Up here, miracles are confidently anticipated. Have been a little low in getting my miracle department organized, but hope for the best.'

Since he had taken part in the first US air attacks on Tokyo and Rome, Doolittle considered it his right to take part in the initial attack on Berlin also. He succeeded in getting permission from his immediate superior in the Air Force, General Carl Spaatz; but when General Eisenhower, the supreme Allied commander in Europe, heard of the idea he firmly squashed it. Doolittle, party to the secrets of the Allied 'Ultra' cypher-cracking successes and also those of the planned invasion of France, knew far too much to be allowed over enemy territory.

Serving under Doolittle and commanding the VIIIth Fighter Command was 51-year-old Major General William Kepner, a First World War infantry officer who had transfered to the Air Corps after the conflict. Kepner remained in the service as a career officer between the wars and became well known as an airship and balloon pilot. In 1938, with the rank of major, he took command of a fighter group. During the years that followed he was appointed to progressively higher posts in the fighter arm, culminating with the VIIIth Fighter Command in September 1943. Although small of stature, Kepner is remembered for his tremendous energy. 'He was a little bantam rooster, a gung-ho! hell-for-leather type,' recalled Captain Jordan Uttal who served on his staff. 'He drove everyone hard. He was the kind of guy who would lose his temper and chew you out, but he was very quick to apologize if he later found that he had been wrong.'

Doolittle's bomber force was split into three divisions. The 1st Bomb Division was commanded by Brigadier General Robert Williams with his headquarters at Brampton Grange near Huntingdon and operated B-17s from bases in Huntingdonshire, Northamptonshire, Cambridgeshire and Bedfordshire. The 2nd Bomb Division was commanded by Brigadier General James Hodges with his headquarters at Old Catton near Norwich and operated B-24s from bases in Norfolk and Suffolk. The 3rd Bomb Division was commanded by Brigadier General Curtis LeMay with his headquarters at Elvedon Hall near Thetford and operated B-17s from bases in Norfolk, Suffolk and Essex.

On the evening of 5 March the combat units of the 8th Air Force possessed the following serviceable aircraft:

Heavy Bombers		Escort Fighters	
B-17s	777	P-38s	130
B-24s	305	P-47s	415
	1082	P-51s	109
			654

When required Doolittle could draw on fighters belonging to the US 9th Air Force in England; and also on long-range fighters of the Royal Air Force. Both these sources would be tapped to provide escorts for the mission on 6 March.

Of the heavy bombers the most numerous type was the Boeing B-17 Flying Fortress, of which there were 777 available on 5 March. This bomber first entered service in 1937 and had undergone considerable modification to render it suitable for action in the European theater, with greatly increased armament and armor. Powered by four Wright Cyclone R-1820 air cooled radial engines which developed 1,200 horse power each for take-off, the latest G version cruised in formation at 180 mph at altitudes up to 28,000 feet; against distant targets such as Berlin it carried a bomb load of 5,000 pounds. The B-17G carried a crew of ten: two pilots, a navigator, a bombardier, a radio operator and five gunners one of whom also served as the flight engineer. For its protection the B-17 carried thirteen .50 caliber machine guns: two each in turrets in the chin, above the cabin, the ball (underneath) and tail positions; and one either side of the nose, either side of the waist and above the radio operator's position. Lieutenant Bryce Evertson, who flew this type with the 91st Bomb Group, was one of many who remembers it with affection: 'It was extremely reliable and no matter how badly it had been shot up I had the feeling that it would always bring me home. It was not much of a challenge to fly, it did not need a lot of close watching. It was very easy to land – just like a great big Piper Cub.'

The other heavy bomber type operated by the 8th Air Force was the Consolidated B-24 Liberator, of which 305 were available on 5 March. A somewhat later design than the B-17, it first entered service in 1941; but like its compatriot it had to be modified to carry a considerably greater armament and armor protection following combat experience over Europe. With a lighter structure than the B-17, the B-24 was a little faster and could carry a greater bomb load somewhat further. Powered by four Pratt and Whitney R-1830 air cooled radial engines which developed 1,200 horse power each for take-off, the latest J version of the B-24 could cruise about 5 mph faster than the B-17. But during the larger attacks this advantage was nullified because it was usual to place B-24s at the tail of the bomber stream and they had to match their speed to the slower B-17s in front. Against a distant target like Berlin the B-24J carried 6,000 pounds of bombs. It carried the same ten-man crew as the B-17 but only ten .50 caliber guns for its protection; the additional three guns in the B-17 were hand-held weapons mounted in relatively ineffective positions either side of the nose and above the radio operator however, and the B-24 lost little for the lack of them. Although the B-24 was a rugged aircraft it was not so good in this respect as the B-17 and was more likely to catch fire. The B-24 was, moreover, a much more difficult aircraft to handle at high altitude particularly in formation. Captain Downey Thomas of the 448th Bomb Group had flown both heavy bomber types: 'The B-24 was a little harder to fly than the B-17. With the B-17 you trimmed it up and it would just about fly itself. But with the B-24 if people moved about you had to keep re-trimming the aircraft. In the B-17 you could fly a really tight formation whereas in the B-24 you had to work hard at it.'

Of the US fighter types the most numerous was the Republic P-47 Thunderbolt, of which there were 415 available to the 8th Air Force on 5 March. The P-47 entered service only at the end of 1942 but had already undergone modifications. The D version, in use by the 8th Air Force, was powered by a Pratt and Whitney R-2800 air cooled radial engine which developed 2,300 horse power for take-off and gave a maximum speed of 426 mph at 30,000 feet. The P-47 was a huge machine for a single-engined fighter and fully loaded without external fuel tanks weighed 14,500 pounds – twice as much as the Me 109 and nearly half as much again as the FW 190, against which it would do battle. With a 108 gallon drop tank under each wing the P-47D had an operational radius of action of 475 miles, allowing 20 minutes' combat at high power settings. By 6 March only a few P-47s had been modified to carry two extra fuel tanks however; most could carry only a single 108 gallon tank under the fuselage, which limited their operational radius of action to 400 miles. The P-47D carried eight .50 caliber machine guns in the wings, an armament which proved extremely effective against enemy fighters. Colonel Hub Zemke, who commanded the 56th Fighter Group which operated Thunderbolts on 6 March, recalled the aircraft as 'A rugged beast with a sound radial engine to pull you along. It was heavy in fire power, enough to chew up the opponent at close range. It accelerated poorly and climbed not much better. But once high cruising speed was attained the P-47 could stand up to the opposition. Strangely, the rate of roll and maneuverability were good at high speeds.' Because of these unusual characteristics Zemke warned his pilots not to attempt turning fights with German single-seaters lower down. 'At altitude, above 20,000 feet, the P-47 was superior to the German fighters. In my book you use your aircraft as advantageously as you can. In the dive, my God, the P-47 could overtake anything. Therefore I made it policy in my group that we used the tactic of "dive and zoom". We stayed at high altitude, dived on the enemy, then zoomed back to high altitude before the next attack. To try to engage 109s and 190s in dogfights below 15,000 feet could be suicidal – that was not playing the game our way.'

The next most numerous fighter type in the 8th Air Force's inventory was the Lockheed P-38 Lightning, of which 130 were available on 5 March. This twin-engined fighter first entered service in 1941. The latest J version was powered by two Allison V-1710 liquid cooled engines each of which developed 1,425 horse power for take-off and had a maximum speed of 414 mph at 25,000 feet. Carrying two 165 gallon drop tanks the P-38 had an operational radius of action of 600 miles. Its armament comprised four .50 caliber machine guns and a 20 mm cannon grouped together in the nose in front of the pilot. During his time in Europe Hub Zemke commanded units operating each of the three fighter types used by the 8th Air Force, so his comments on how they compared are especially relevant. He felt the Lightning was the least effective of the escorts. 'The turbo-superchargers were controlled by an oil regulator and at altitude the oil had a tendency to congeal, which caused serious problems. On two occasions I recall entering combat with enemy single seaters and it became a matter of life and death to get away and survive, though I had started with the advantage. On both occasions the engines either cut out completely or over-revved, when the throttles were cut or advanced.' A further problem with the P-38 was that its airframe was not strong and it had a relatively low maximum diving speed. If German fighters broke off combat by diving steeply the Lightning pilots could not follow. But Zemke did remember the P-38 as having one outstanding feature. 'As a gun platform it was as steady as a shooting stand. With the two engines there was no torque. With a little trim to build up speed in a dive a pilot could ride directly into a target. As to the armament installation I have seen no better: four machine guns and a cannon mounted close together directly in front of the pilot.' Because guns and sight were close together, there was no need for the weapons to converge their fire as with the more usual wing-mounted guns.

The most modern US escort fighter was the North American P-51B Mustang, of which the 8th Air Force had 109 available on 5 March. The B version of the Mustang entered service only at the close of 1943 and married the latest version of the Rolls Royce Merlin engine – license built in the US by Packard as the V-1650 – to the exceptionally clean airframe of the Mustang. The 1,620 horse power gave the fighter a maximum speed of 440 mph at 30,000 feet. Even more important for an escort fighter, the low-drag airframe enabled the P-51 to cruise fast at relatively low power settings with the result that its range was far greater than any other single-engined fighter; with two 75 gallon drop tanks the P-51B had an operational radius of action of 650 miles, sufficient to enable it to escort bombers to Berlin and beyond. The P-51B's armament of four .50 caliber machine guns was the least powerful of those fitted to the US escort fighters but Zemke considered it adequate for engaging enemy fighters: 'At close range – 250 yards or less – there was no doubt what would happen if the trigger was pressed. It was a matter of ducking the flying pieces after that!' Looking back Zemke considers the Merlin-engined P-51 by far the best of the escorts for air-to-air combat especially below 25,000 feet. 'It had a very good radius of action for the type of work we did in Europe. The acceleration from slow cruise to maximum speed was excellent compared with the competition. Its rate of roll was good and it maneuvered easily to a learned hand.' In the dive acceleration was rapid. Visibility in all directions was ample.'

When everything worked properly there is no doubt the P-51B was a superb fighter and master of anything it met in the air on equal terms. But in March 1944 the P-51B was new to the service and there was a considerable shortage of spare parts. 'We were forced to scrounge, steal, improvise, and often cannibalize grounded planes for parts,' remembered Lieutenant Bernard Ginsberg who served as an engineering officer with the 354th Fighter Group. The Merlin engine as such was not new but the Packard-built version was and it still suffered several teething troubles. Among the problems pilots had to face were rough running engines, fouling of spark plugs, coolant leaks, magneto failures, high oil temperatures and failures of high altitude blowers and electrical systems. Propellers would shed oil which ended up as a fine opaque film on the windscreens; drop tanks would fail to feed at high altitude. And if the Mustang did keep going long enough for its pilot to get into a firing position on an enemy, there was always the risk that ammunition belts would jam if guns were fired during a tight turn. On 6 March nearly a third of the P-51Bs which took off would be forced to return early with various types of unserviceability. The new fighter held great promise for the future but at the beginning of March 1944 its chronic unreliability almost canceled out its superlative performance.

The US daylight bombing tactics had been conceived around the idea of the 'Combat Box', a formation of heavy bombers with sufficient combined fire power to ward off attacks from enemy fighters. During the latter part of 1943 the boxes had suffered heavily from German fighters attacking *en masse* and it had become necessary to provide escort fighters. But the escorts could not be present in strength everywhere along the bomber stream, so if German fighters did break through to the bombers the latter were still expected to defend themselves.

The combat box formation took many forms during the course of the war and was the subject of continual change in the search for improvement. Typically, in March 1944, a box formation comprised 21 heavy bombers in three-aircraft Vees divided into three squadrons: the lead squadron with 6 aircraft, the low squadron with 6 and the high squadron with 9. The high and the low squadrons flew on opposite sides of the lead squadron, so the assembled box formation took the form of a letter 'V' pointing in the direction of flight but tilted at 45 degrees.

The spacing of bombers in the box formation depended upon several conflicting requirements. The bombers needed to be close together to concentrate their defensive fire power, give a tight bombing pattern on the ground and prevent the enemy fighter or flak defenses picking off single aircraft. But they should not be so close that the formation became unwieldy, aircraft got in each other's way during the bomb run or ran into each other's slipstreams. And it was important that no more than one bomber could be damaged by the explosion of an enemy rocket or shell no matter how fortuitously placed. A spacing of between one and two wingspans – 100 to 200 feet – separating each of the three aircraft in a Vee formation was judged to give the best compromise between these requirements.

The disposition of combat boxes within the bomber stream varied greatly
from bomb division to bomb division. In the 1st Bomb Division there were three
combat boxes to each combat wing and the combat wings flew in twos in line
abreast, with succeeding pairs of wings following behind at 12-mile intervals. In
the 2nd Bomb Division there were three combat boxes to each combat wing and
wings flew in line astern. In the 3rd Bomb Division there were four combat
boxes to each combat wing. But each wing was divided into an A and a B
formation, each with a lead and a low box, with the B formation flying in
echelon on the A formation. The succeeding combat wings followed each other
in line astern.

When fully assembled, the bomber stream for a large attack could be more
than 90 miles long. Because they cruised somewhat faster than bombers and
had to zig-zag to maintain station on them, individual fighter groups could not
cover bombers for much more than 30 minutes at a time before fuel began to
run low and they had to break away. As a result only a small proportion of the
available escort fighters would be in position to cover bombers at any one time.
On 6 March only rarely would there be more than 150 escorts in position; if
these were distributed evenly along the length of the bomber stream there
would be an average of only three fighters for every two miles of airspace. Such a
split force would obviously have been ineffectual and easily overwhelmed by
the enemy; so it was usual to position about a third of the fighters near the head
of the bomber stream – that part most vulnerable to head-on attack – and
distribute the remaining fighters in 8-aircraft units along the length of the
stream. It was inevitable, therefore, that from time to time some combat wings
would have no fighters covering them.

The escort fighters and the bombers' own guns could do much to ward off
attacks from German fighters. But neither could do anything to lessen the effect
of the flak encountered at all important targets, though routes were carefully
chosen to reduce this danger to a minimum. In the target area the simplest way
to avoid predicted flak would have been for bombers to make continuous
changes to heading and altitude while being engaged. But it was difficult for
heavily laden bombers to do this and remain in formation and impossible to do
it and carry out an accurate bombing run. The bombers' main safeguard
against flak was altitude; the higher the bombers flew, the less accurate the fire
became and the safer they were from this hazard. If cloud was present German
gunners had to use their Wuerzburg radar to aim the guns and these radars
could be jammed. A few American heavy bombers were fitted with the 'Carpet'
jamming transmitter which radiated interference on wavelengths used by the
Wuerzburg. And all bombers carried 'Chaff', bundles of aluminium foil dropped
in the flak zones to produce spurious echoes on Wuerzburg radar screens.

Under practice conditions a good bombardier could usually put down his
bombs within about 300 yards of the aiming point from 20,000 feet, using the
Norden bombsight. Under operational conditions, however, numerous factors
came into play which greatly increased aiming errors. To get good results with
the Norden the bombardier needed to make an undisturbed straight and level
bomb run lasting three minutes (about nine miles) and be able to observe the
target through his sighting telescope during that time. During operational

attacks poor visibility or haze would often conceal targets, as would smoke and dust after attacks from previous formations. And powerful flak defenses encountered during the bomb run could also add greatly to bombing errors. Under operational conditions bomb aiming errors could be anything up to five times as great as those on practice ranges, for visual bombing.

If they arrived to find their target obscured by cloud American bombers could attack distant targets such as Berlin only by using their H2X or H2S radar. These sets were fitted to pathfinder B-17s and B-24s operated by the 482nd Bomb Group, one of which led almost every combat bomb wing formation. Radar bombing was considerably less accurate than visual bombing however, and a bomb pattern within a mile of the aiming point was considered good. Because of this radar bombing was unsuitable against individual factory complexes and was usually used to make what amounted to area bombing attacks on city targets.

During the bomb run only the lead and deputy lead aircraft in each formation carried out aimed runs. The pilots in other aircraft simply concentrated on maintaining a tight formation and their bombardiers released when they saw the leader's bombs and smoke markers going down. If the lead aircraft was shot down during the bomb run following aircraft continued with the deputy leader and dropped their bombs when he did.

Of the senior commanders in the Reich air defense organization the man with the greatest influence on how German fighters fought their defensive battle was 31-year-old Generalmajor Adolf Galland, since the end of 1941 the Luftwaffe General of Fighters. By 1944 Galland had amassed a vast experience in air fighting. He had fought in Spain, France and during the Battle of Britain and been credited with 94 aerial victories. From his headquarters at Kladow near Berlin Galland was directly responsible to Reichsmarschall Hermann Goering, commander in chief of the Luftwaffe, for general direction of the fighter force. He and his staff were responsible for formulation and development of fighting tactics to keep pace with the changing war situation, training requirements for new fighter pilots, selection of new Gruppe and Geschwader commanders, advising on equipment and modification of new and current fighter types in production, as well as numerous matters of lesser importance. Galland and his staff played no part in the control of fighters during individual air actions but otherwise his personal influence pervaded almost every aspect of German fighter operations. His contact with front-line fighter units was close and continuous, so much so that on one occasion Goering commented 'If someone drops a pin anywhere in the fighter force, Galland will hear of it!'

So far as Galland was concerned the greatest problem in March 1944 was that the Reich air defense fighter units were not receiving a large enough share of the available resources. 'Not a high enough priority had been given to fighter production, the training of fighter pilots or to air defense in general,' he explained to one of the authors. 'At this time Hitler's thinking was still on the offensive; he paid much more attention to an attack by 50 of our bombers on England, than one by 500 enemy bombers on Germany. And of the fighter types which were built we lost many to other arms of the Luftwaffe. For example ground attack units received large numbers of Focke-Wulf 190s and reconnaissance units received both FW 190s and Messerschmitt 109s. The fighter force did not receive the best pilots from training schools and there were never enough of them anyway.'

Adolf Galland's complaint is borne out by the German records: in February 1944 the Luftwaffe accepted from manufacturers a total of 310 FW 190s and 715 Me 109s (of all versions, including ground attack and reconnaissance aircraft). At the beginning of March the single-engined fighter units on all fronts possessed about 1,200 serviceable fighters of which just over 600 or about half belonged to units engaged in the defense of Germany itself. At this time losses of single-engined fighter aircraft in the Luftwaffe, destroyed or damaged from all causes and on all fronts, were running at about 1,000 per month. Even allowing for repaired aircraft put back into service it is clear that production of new FW 190s and Me 109s was doing little more than cover attrition, with hardly anything to spare to expand Reich air defense units to keep pace with the massive expansion of the US Army Air Forces in England.

Although outranked by others in the Reich air defense hierarchy, Adolf Galland's proven experience in air fighting and his close contact with Goering meant he had a greater degree of *de facto* control over the fighter force than anyone else. Air Fleet Reich, the organization responsible for all fighter and flak units situated in Holland and Germany, came under the command of 53-year-old Generaloberst Hans-Juergen Stumpff with his headquarters at Wannsee near Berlin. During the First World War Stumpff had served with some distinction as an infantry officer. In 1933 he transferred to the Luftwaffe and qualified as a pilot, but Stumpff's bent was towards administration and he had little contact with front-line units. Of him Adolf Galland later commented: 'He did not have much influence on events. He delegated responsibility to the divisional commanders, who had experience in modern air fighting. He did not like to interfere or do anything for which he might later be blamed.' Luftwaffe fighter pilots questioned about Stumpff remember him only as a man whose name they heard but whom they never saw. Some recalled the wartime catch-phrase *Die Spitze der Luftflotte Reich ist stumpf* – 'the sharp-end of Air Fleet Reich is blunt' (a word-play on the commander's name which, spelled with one 'f', means 'blunt').

The Ist Fighter Corps, commanded by 42-year-old Generalmajor Joseph Schmid with his headquarters at Zeist near Utrecht in Holland, was responsible for the operational control of fighters based in the Air Fleet Reich area. Like Stumpff, however, Schmid had come from the army and had little expertise in air fighting; his previous post had been that of commander of the Hermann Goering Panzer Division during the closing stages of the fighting in Tunisia.

The fighter units in the Ist Fighter Corps area were divided between four fighter divisions, each of which was commanded by a previously operational pilot who had considerable experience in air fighting. Fighter Division 1 was commanded by Oberst Guenther Luetzow with his headquarters at Doeberitz near Berlin and controlled units based in northeastern Germany. Fighter Division 2, commanded by Generalmajor Max Ibel with his headquarters at Stade near Hamburg controlled units in the central-northern German sector.

Fighter Division 3, was commanded by Generalmajor Walter Grabmann with his headquarters at Deelen near Arnhem in Holland and controlled units based in northwestern Germany, Holland and eastern Belgium. Fighter Division 7 was commanded by Generalmajor Joachim-Friedrich Huth with his head-quarters at Schleissheim near Munich and controlled units based in southern Germany and Austria. In addition there was Fighter Division 4, commanded by Oberst Karl Viek with his headquarters at Metz in France and which controlled units based in eastern France and western Belgium; strictly speaking this division was outside Air Fleet Reich but Schmid could call on it for reinforcements if necessary.

On 6 March the numbers of serviceable aircraft available to Fighter Divisions 1, 2, 3, 4 and 7 were as follows:

	Fighter Divisions					
	1	**2**	**3**	**4**	**7**	**Total**
Single-engined day fighters (Me 109 and FW 190)	78	128	54	116	182	558
Twin-engined day fighters (Me 110 and Me 410)	21	5	—	—	66	92
Single-engined night fighters (Me 109 and FW 190)	41	—	17	—	30	88
Twin-engined night fighters (Me 110, Ju 88, Do 217, He 219)	74	67	46	32	41	260
Miscellaneous	8	15	3	—	—	26
Totals	**222**	**215**	**120**	**148**	**319**	**1024**

For a more-detailed breakdown of the strength of the German fighter force, by units and bases, see Appendix C.

At first sight the number of aircraft available for the defense of the Reich, 1,024, might seem perfectly adequate for the task of beating off an attack by 700 American heavy bombers with an escort at any one time of about 150 fighters. But this total figure belied the weakness of the Luftwaffe. Of the total, 251, or nearly a quarter, were twin-engined night fighters liable to suffer heavy losses if they attempted to engage escorted bomber formations by day. A further 88 fighters, those from the single-engined night fighter units, were for the most part flown by men with little or no day fighting experience. Thirty-one of the single-engined fighters were operated by the eight so-called Industrial Fighter Units; the fighters were brand new machines straight off the production lines flown into action in threes or fours usually by works test pilots from factory airfields. Fifteen single-engined fighters came from the Fighter School Operational Units and were flown by instructors; but these, in many cases, lacked operational fighting experience. The 26 'miscellaneous' aircraft belonged to trials or airborne tracking units which would not normally engage the enemy directly or in strength. Subtracting these from the original total of 1,024 aircraft we find that little over half – 512 single-engined and 92 twin-engined fighters – belonged to regular operational day fighter units. Moreover the very size of the

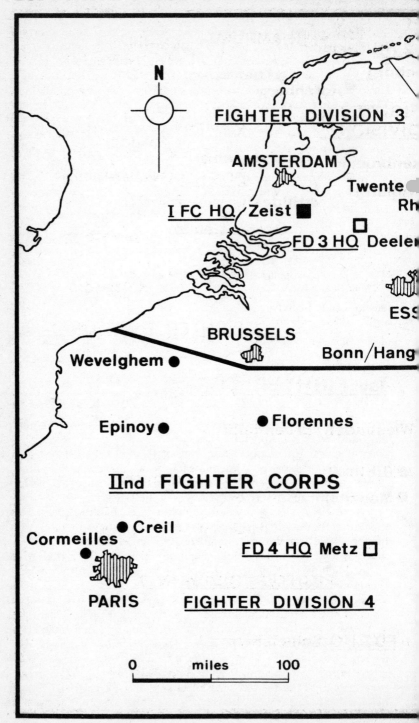

FIGHTER DIVISION 3

AMSTERDAM

Twente

Rh

I FC HQ Zeist ■

FD 3 HQ Deeler

ESS

BRUSSELS

Bonn/Hang

Wevelghem ●

Florennes ●

Epinoy ●

IInd FIGHTER CORPS

Creil ●
Cormeilles
FD 4 HQ Metz □

PARIS   FIGHTER DIVISION 4

0   miles   100

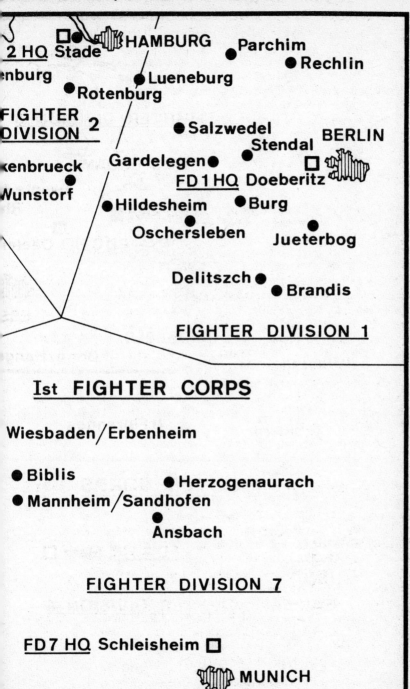

2 HQ Stade HAMBURG •Parchim
  •Rechlin
nburg •Lueneburg
  •Rotenburg

FIGHTER
DIVISION 2 •Salzwedel BERLIN
  Stendal
kenbrueck Gardelegen• •
  FD 1 HQ Doeberitz
Wunstorf •Hildesheim •Burg
  Oschersleben• •Jueterbog

  Delitszch• •
  •Brandis

FIGHTER DIVISION 1

Ist FIGHTER CORPS

Wiesbaden/Erbenheim

•Biblis •Herzogenaurach
•Mannheim/Sandhofen
  •Ansbach

FIGHTER DIVISION 7

FD 7 HQ Schleisheim □

  MUNICH

area to be protected by the five fighter divisions was such that if there was an attack on northern Germany relatively few fighters deployed in the south or west could be moved into position to meet it. To meet an attack on Berlin, for example, the regular day-fighting units based in Holland and northern Germany possessed a mere 236 single-engined and 26 twin-engined fighters; in other words, the force could expect to be outnumbered three-to-one by an 8th Air Force attack coming from England. This inferiority could be redressed by pulling in units from the south and west; by sending the western units into action twice, during the approach and the withdrawal of the raiders; and, most effective of all, by concentrating a large proportion of the defending force against a small part of the bomber stream.

Of the fighters available for the defense of the Reich the most effective was the Focke-Wulf 190, of which there were about 185 available on 6 March. Powered by a BMW 801 air cooled radial engine which developed 1,700 horse power for take-off, the latest A-8 version had a maximum speed of 408 mph at about 20,000 feet and took just over ten minutes to climb to this altitude. This version carried a built-in armament of four 20 mm cannon and two 13 mm heavy machine guns, powerful enough to knock down the American heavy bombers if the pilot could get in an accurate burst; but there was sufficient ammunition for only 15 seconds' firing. 'It was a nice stable aircraft and an excellent firing platform,' recalled Hauptmann Anton Hackl who flew this type with Fighter Geschwader 1*. 'The big air-cooled radial engine was tremendously rugged and would keep going even with one or two cylinders shot away. With the engine and the toughened glass windscreen in front of him the pilot was well protected from enemy fire from ahead.' Most German pilots felt that in the FW 190 they had a better fighter than either the P-38 or the P-47; the P-51 was, as yet, a relatively unknown quantity.

The most numerous German fighter type was the Messerschmitt 109, of which there were about 465 available for the defense of Germany on 6 March. This type had first gone into service in 1937 and by 1944 it was at the end of its development life. Powered by a Daimler Benz 605 liquid-cooled engine developing 1,475 horse power for take-off, the latest G-6 version had a maximum speed of 386 mph at 22,000 feet and took just over six minutes to climb to 19,000 feet. These figures relate to the lightly armed version of this fighter, however, fitted with a single 20 mm cannon firing through the propeller hub and two 13 mm machine guns; this armament was adequate for fighter-versus-fighter combat but quite insufficient against the tough American heavy bombers. The majority of Me 109s in the Reich air defense units therefore carried a heavier armament and as a result performance suffered. The most common addition was a 20 mm cannon in a blister under each wing, giving a total armament of three of these weapons and the two 13 mm machine guns. In other aircraft the 20 mm cannon firing through the propeller hub was replaced by a 30 mm weapon. The lighter-armed version of the Me 109 was considered

*The strengths of fighter Geschwader varied considerably at this stage of the war. The nominal strength was three or four Gruppen each of 68 aircraft but no Gruppe operating on 6 March possessed anything like this number.

the best of the German fighters at high altitude; this equipped four Gruppen designated as 'top-cover' units, to protect the heavier armed fighters from the American escorts. 'In my view by 1944 the Me 109 was no longer suitable as a weapon against enemy heavy bombers,' felt Hauptmann Rudolf Sinner who flew the type with Fighter Geschwader 54. 'With its liquid-cooled engine it was too vulnerable to enemy fire. Even with the two additional 20 mm cannon it had insufficient fire power to engage enemy heavy bombers and these cannon reduced performance to such an extent that the Me 109 became too vulnerable to enemy fighters.'

Yet if pilots flying the more heavily armed versions of the Me 109 felt vulnerable to attack from American escorts, this feeling of helplessness was as nothing compared with that of crews flying the German twin-engined fighters. The latter, the so-called 'destroyers', were intended to be the mainstay of the defense against heavy bombers attacking by day. These aircraft had twice as much ammunition; most carried a battery of four huge 21 cm ($8\frac{1}{4}$ inch) air-to-air rockets launched from tubes mounted under the wings. The destroyers were thus well equipped to engage in long running battles of attrition with enemy bomber formations – provided the American escort fighters did not intervene. The most numerous destroyer type early in 1944 was the Messerschmitt 110, of which there were 75 available for the defense of the Reich on 6 March. Like the Me 109, however, this type had been in service since before the war and was now at the end of its development life. Powered by two Daimler Benz 605 engines each developing 1,475 horse power for take-off, the latest G-2 version had a maximum speed of just over 300 mph at 20,000 feet carrying a full armament load. The forward firing armament comprised two 30 mm cannon and four 20 mm cannon, usually supplemented by a battery of four 21 cm rockets. For rear defense against fighter attack the radio operator was provided with two rifle-caliber machine guns. Had there been no escort fighters to contend with the aging Me 110 could still have performed usefully as a bomber-destroyer. But by the beginning of 1944 its day had passed. 'It was not much use at this time. It was far too slow and it could not climb or dive fast enough to avoid the American escorts,' explained Major Hans Kogler who commanded IIIrd Gruppe of Destroyer Geschwader 26. When they were caught by American escorts the destroyer units often suffered terrible losses. For Kogler's Gruppe this had happened just two weeks earlier, on February 20: that afternoon its formation of thirteen Me 110s had been 'bounced' out of the sun by P-47s of the 56th Fighter Group which shot down eleven, killing 8 pilots and 9 radio operators; shortly afterwards, as if to twist the knife in the wound, other American fighters strafed Kogler's base at Wunstorf and damaged a further nine aircraft. On March 6 the Gruppe had still not recovered from this mauling.

The type now replacing the Me 110 in the destroyer units was the Messerschmitt 410, a more modern twin-engined aircraft also used in the bombing and reconnaissance roles. Seventeen were available for the defense of the Reich on March 6. Powered by two Daimler Benz 603 engines each developing 1,750 horse power for take-off, it had a maximum speed of about 350 mph at 22,000 feet. It carried a similar forward-firing armament to the

Me 110, plus a considerably more effective rearward-firing armament of two heavy machine guns in remotely controlled barbettes. 'Though it was much better than the Me 110, the Me 410 was still not good enough', felt Oberleutnant Fritz Stehle who commanded IInd Gruppe of Destroyer Geschwader 26. 'It was too heavy and not maneuverable enough. And carrying full armament its overtaking speed on a bomber formation was so low that it took a long time to get into a firing position.' If Me 410s were caught by enemy escorts they were in almost as difficult a position as the Me 110s. 'If your Me 410 was attacked by a Mustang you could only pray. And hope your gunner shot well!' Stehle continued. 'My Viennese gunner, Feldwebel Alois Slaby, was very experienced and knew exactly when the enemy fighter was about to open fire. He would say "Not yet, not yet – NOW!" and I would chop the throttles and the 410 would decelerate rapidly; if we were lucky the enemy fighter would go screaming past. Or sometimes I would put the 410 into a skid with the wings level and the enemy rounds would flash past the wing tip. We knew if we could buy a little time that often meant survival: once American escorts had dropped their tanks they could not fight long near Berlin, before they had to break off and head for home. But the 410 was useless as a dogfighter, it couldn't turn or do anything like that. We felt rather as if we had been entered for the Kentucky Derby on a carthorse!'

By far the worst off in any daylight battle, however, were the German twin-engined night fighter units if they were ordered up. Not only were the lumbering Me 110s, Dornier 217s, Junkers 88s and Heinkel 219s slowed by the drag of their large radar aerials and flame dampers, but their crews had neither experience nor training in day fighting. By night the crews went into action singly and closed to within 200 yards before opening fire on their usually unsuspecting victims; any attempt to adopt similar tactics by day against a formation of heavy bombers usually resulted in a rough handling. Following the loss of several highly trained crews in this way, the Luftwaffe High Command decreed that twin-engined night fighters were to be employed only sparingly by day and the more successful crews were specifically forbidden from this hazardous work. The best the night fighter crews could hope was to find damaged American bombers straggling singly and pick these off.

The German fighters were directed into action from the huge concrete bunkers which served as headquarters for each of the five fighter Divisions involved in the defense of the Reich. These carefully camouflaged bunkers, 200 feet long, 100 feet wide and 60 feet high, were protected by roofs of reinforced concrete 12 feet thick and walls 10 feet thick; air tight doors and an air conditioning system protected the occupants from possible gas attack. These bunkers served as clearing houses for the mass of information coming in on movements of hostile and friendly aircraft from the radar chain, from ground observers, from spotter aircraft and from the fighter crews themselves. The inner core of the building comprised a large operations room, along one side of which was a huge vertical screen on which was painted a gridded map of the divisional area; plots on the movements of friendly and hostile aircraft were projected on this screen by women auxiliaries using special narrow-beam flashlights fitted on moveable mountings. In front of the screen sat the divisional operations officer, his fighter controllers and liaison officers, in contact with the airfields by telephone and aircraft airborne by radio. Adolf Galland later described what it was like inside these 'battle opera houses':

> On entering one was immediately infected by the nervous atmosphere reigning there. The artificial light made faces appear even more haggard than they really were. Bad air, cigarette smoke, the hum of ventilators, the ticking of the teletypes and the subdued murmur of countless telephone operators gave one a headache. The magic center of attraction in this room was a huge frosted-glass panel on which were projected the position, altitude, strength and course of the enemy as well as of our own formations. The whole was reminiscent of a huge aquarium lit up, with a multitude of water-fleas scuttling madly behind the glass walls. Each single dot and each change to be seen here was the result of reports and observations from radar sets, aircraft-spotters, listening posts, reconnaissance and contact planes, or from units in action. They all merged together by telephone or wireless in this center to be received, sorted and within a few minutes transposed into transmittable messages. What was represented here on a giant map was a picture of the air situation in the sector of a fighter division, with about one minute's delay.*

The tactics employed by German fighter units stemmed from the most recent Combat Instructions issued by Generalmajor Galland's headquarters. By March 1944 the strength of the American escort forces, and their ability to cover bombers all the way to and from targets deep in Germany, had led to a profound change in defensive tactics. Previously individual Gruppen of about twenty fighters had taken-off, assembled and gone into action against the bombers as and when they could. If escorts were present, however, these piecemeal attacks were easily broken up; as a result German fighter losses began to increase alarmingly while successes against the bombers fell. In the Atlantic the German navy had learned the best way to strike at an escorted convoy was to concentrate U-boats into a 'Wolf Pack' then launch a massed attack. Now these same 'Wolf Pack' tactics were to be used against American bombers over Germany. 'To achieve success against escorted formations we had to attack with the greatest possible number of fighters, concentrated in time and in space. Only in this way could we achieve local air superiority', Galland explained.

Under the new tactical plan, two or more Gruppen were to form into attack formations (*Gefechtsverbaende*) which the divisional fighter controllers would direct into the enemy bomber formations. To make such tactics work the controllers needed accurate and up-to-date information on the position, altitude, heading and composition of the enemy bomber stream. As well as the network of ground radar stations and observer posts, Air Fleet Reich made frequent use of shadowing aircraft. These machines, single Ju 88s, Me 110s, Me 210s or FW 190s, would link up with the enemy formation then, keeping a respectful distance usually far below, maintain a running commentary on the bombers' movements. Contrary to what some other accounts have suggested, the Luftwaffe *never* used captured B-17s or B-24s to shadow enemy formations. Quite apart from the fact that there was nothing in this role a captured heavy bomber could have done any better than the standard German fighter types normally used, there would have been a continuous risk to the captured

*From *The First and Last* by Adolf Galland. Henry Holt & Co, New York; Methuen & Co. London

bombers themselves. 'The use of captured aircraft in action against the enemy bomber formations would have been of absolutely no value,' stressed Adolf Galland. 'In spite of their German markings you could be sure our younger pilots would have shot them down first in any engagement! A B-17 is a B-17 and in action nobody would have looked at the markings before he shot at it!'

By this stage of the war the most successful German fighter units always tried to carry out attacks on heavy bomber formations from the head-on position. 'The head-on attack was the only way to knock down the bombers,' thought Hauptmann Anton Hackl who flew an FW 190 with Fighter Geschwader 11 and was one of the leading German tacticians. 'If one came in from the rear there was a long period, closing from 1,000 meters to our firing range of 400 meters, when the bombers were firing at us but we could not fire at them. This was a very dangerous time and we lost a lot of aircraft trying to attack that way.' Because they carried ammunition for only 15 seconds' firing German fighter pilots had strict orders not to open up at long range. And once they were inside the bomber formation and had completed their attacks, German pilots had the problem of extricating themselves from the lethal mesh of defensive fire. 'An alternative was to attack the bombers from above in a dive; for that we needed to start from a position at least 1,000 meters higher and 500 meters in front of the bombers,' Hackl continued. 'Then we could dive with plenty of speed and the bomber made a nice fat target. But the problem with this type of attack was that it took time to set up and if we were caught in the climb by enemy escorts things could get difficult. So at this time I always led my Gruppe into the attack from head-on.'

The head-on attack by a large formation required precise control from the ground and, since the German fighters closed with the bombers at about 500 mph or 200 yards per second, there was time for only a brief half-second burst at about 500 yards before the fighter pilot had to pull up to avoid ramming his victim. Against these disadvantages, however, were the over-whelming advantages for German fighter pilots that they were in range of the defensive fire for only three seconds before they themselves could open fire and as they flashed through the bomber formation the crossing speed was so great that gunners had great difficulty following them. A further advantage of the head-on attack was that the bombers' armor was mainly positioned to give protection from rear attacks, so from the front less hits were needed to knock them down. Compared with an average of twenty hits with 20 mm rounds required to knock down a bomber in an attack from the rear, four or five were sufficient from the front; from the rear an average of 3 hits with 30 mm rounds were needed, whereas from the front a single hit anywhere on the nose was enough. 'One accurate half-second burst from head-on and a kill was guaranteed. Guaranteed!' asserted Anton Hackl.

For those attacking with rockets, however, the head-on attack allowed little prospect of success. The 80 pound warhead could cause damage to bombers out to 30 yards from the point of detonation. But at this time the Germans had no effective proximity fuse so the air-to-air rockets were detonated by simple time fuses after a pre-set time of flight, typically 3¾ seconds (equivalent to a firing range of 800 yards for rear attacks or 1,475 yards for head-on attacks). It was left to the fighter pilots to judge these distances, which had to be accurate to within 60 yards if there was to be any chance of inflicting damage on the target aircraft. But such was the closing speed during head-on attacks the pilot was in firing range for only $\frac{1}{4}$ of a second – small wonder the rockets almost invariably exploded harmlessly either in front of or behind their intended victims. German fighter pilots regarded the rockets only as 'frighteners', weapons which would hopefully cause bombers to open formation sufficiently to make easier follow-up attacks with cannon. If the rockets ever scored a kill it was regarded as a bonus.

With enemy bombers now causing fearful destruction to the German homeland, Adolf Galland was willing to push almost any weapon or tactical scheme he thought had a reasonable chance of knocking them down. Many people came to Galland with proposals and suggestions, including Major Hans-Guenther von Kornatzki who asked to be allowed to lead a special unit of volunteer pilots who would ram the American bombers. 'I did not think it a good idea,' commented Galland. 'To get into position to ram, pilots had first to break through the screen of escorts and then close with the bombers. But if they could get that close, a short burst with ordinary cannon would be lethal anyway and the fighter pilot would have a much greater chance of escaping with his life.' From these discussions the idea evolved of employing volunteers to fly especially heavily armored FW 190s in the close-infighting or *Sturm* role. In addition to the normal steel armor around the seat and the toughened glass windshield in front of the pilot, the *Sturm* version had additional armor down the sides of the cockpit and extra toughened glass panels along the sides of the canopy. Thus protected pilots could close from the rear to within 200 yards of the bomber to deliver their lethal burst. On March 6 Kornatzki's unit, *Sturm* Staffel 1, had seven modified FW 190s ready for action at Salzwedel north of Magdeburg.

One further major problem facing the Luftwaffe, after $4\frac{1}{2}$ years of war, was that its pilot training schools could no longer turn out adequately trained pilots as fast as they were being lost in action. As a result quality had to be sacrificed to make up the necessary numbers. By the beginning of 1944 new pilots were being sent into action with about 160 hours flying time, half that given to their American and British counterparts. 'Our older pilots were very good,' explained Anton Hackl, 'but the new ones coming from the training schools could do little more than take-off and land the aircraft; they could not fly well enough to do much in action. I had my younger pilots fly with the more experienced ones and told them to stay close to their leaders. Of course if the leader was shot down, the inexperienced pilot was almost helpless.'

The fighters were the main element of the German defense against the daylight bombing attacks. But as the increasing numbers of American escort fighters made their operations more difficult, the anti-aircraft gun defenses assumed a progressively greater importance. At this stage the flak defenses of the Reich comprised 1,656 heavy batteries with 6,220 guns of 88 mm or larger; and 782 light flak batteries with a total of 14,083 smaller guns.

Berlin itself, and the area immediately around it, came under the aegis of Generalmajor Max Schaller's 1st Flak Division. On March 6 this controlled 78

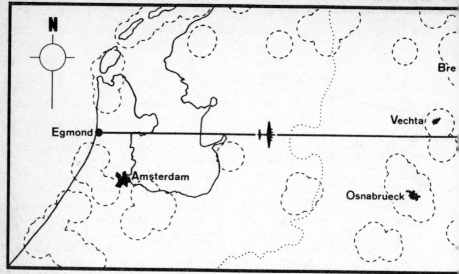

As was usually the case, the bombers were routed to avoid flak zones wherever possible, without have to make too many turns on the way to the target. Apart from the target area, the planned route crossed only one flak zone, the moderately defended area round Vechta. The raiding force was to cross the Dutch coast at Egmond and fly due east to Celle, then east southeast to the Initial Points each 18 miles down-wind of the targets at Erkner, Klein Machnow and Genshagen. At the Initial Points the bombers were to turn into wind for their bomb runs. After attacking, the bombers were to leave the Berlin flak zone as quickly as possible, then reassemble with the other bomb divisions northwest of the city for the return flight.

heavy batteries with a total of 414 guns of calibers 88 mm, 105 mm and 128 mm. In addition there were 14 light flak batteries with 331 smaller weapons. The division had its headquarters in the Charlottenburg district near the center of the capital.

The heaviest guns, the 128 mm, and those belonging to mobile units, were manned by all-regular Luftwaffe units. The remainder of the flak units covering Berlin, the great majority, were manned by small cadres of regular Luftwaffe men in command positions with large numbers of non-regular personnel to complete their complement.

The demands of the war had led to a steady drain of able-bodied men away from the static home defense units. In their place came a hodge-podge collection of old men and boys: *Wehrmaenner*, factory workers assigned to man the guns when enemy bombers approached; *Luftwaffenhelfern*, 15- and 16-year-old schoolboys who left their lessons to man the guns; and slightly older youths of the *Reichs Arbeits Dienst*, the labor service, into which all young men were recruited after leaving school. There were of course problems with the younger

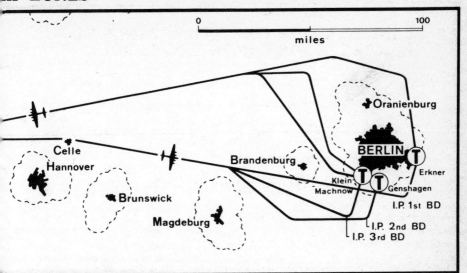

boys. Luftwaffenhelfer Goetz Bergander recalled 'I couldn't find a helmet which would fit me properly, since I'd just turned 16 and was still too small and too thin to get a good fit. In addition my throat microphone was too large, with the result that I had to pad it with a handkerchief so its diaphram pressed against my throat properly.'

On the other hand the various tasks around the guns could be learned parrot-fashion and, after countless practice drills, the boys felt they could do what was expected of them. 'The regular soldiers did their best to give us a good training,' affirmed 16-year-old Luftwaffenhelfer Gottfried Gottschalk of Light Flak Abteilung 722 defending the Siemensstadt district. 'At the end of it we went for a practice shoot on a firing range, shooting at a canvas target towed behind an aircraft, and achieved good results. So we were confident of our ability as gunners.' Seventeen-year-old Oberhelfer Hans Ring served with Heavy Flak Abteilung 437 in the Spandau district and recalled the ambivalent position in which the boys found themselves; his battery, typical of those in and around Berlin, was manned by 90 schoolboys, 36 regular Luftwaffe men mainly in command positions and had 20 Russian prisoners to perform menial cleaning and laboring tasks. 'We were in an odd position, sometimes treated as soldiers and sometimes as schoolboys. We were not allowed to see adults' films – and, goodness knows, German adults' films at that time were harmless enough! We were expected to shoot down enemy planes with our 105 mm guns but we were not considered old enough to carry rifles when we went to round up enemy aircrew who came down by parachute.'

The American bomber crews feared the German flak more than the fighters, even though the latter caused by far the greater proportion of losses. As Lieutenant Thurman Spiva of the 446th Bomb Group explained: 'There was so

PLANNED ORDER OF COMBAT WINGS IN
BOMBER STREAM, ROUTE TO TARGET

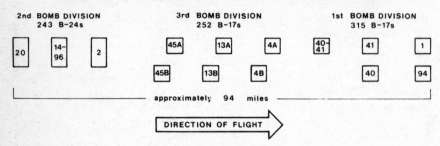

The 1st Bomb Division was to head the attack, with 315 B-17s. The 1st Combat Wing was to lead, with the 94th flying abreast and to the left of it. Twelve miles behind the 1st and 94th came the 41st and 40th Combat Wings; and 12 miles behind the 41st came the Composite 40th-41st Combat Wing Formation. Twelve miles behind the 1st Bomb Division came 252 B-17s of the 3rd Bomb Division. The 4th Combat Wing, A Formation, was to lead with B Formations echeloned to the left of it. Twelve miles behind came the 13th Combat Wing similarly disposed, 12 miles behind that the 45th Combat Wing. Twelve miles behind the 3rd Bomb Division came the 243 B-24s of the 2nd Division. The 2nd Combat Wing was to lead, 6 miles behind came the Composite 14th-96th Wing, 6 miles behind them 20th Combat Wing. When fully assembled the bomber stream would be about 94 miles long.

little one could do to combat flak. Outside of minor evasive action and the dropping of chaff to foul up their radar, there was nothing you could do. You just had to sit there and let them shoot at you. With fighter attacks you could at least fight back and have a definite effect on the enemy fighter's actions. All the briefings in the world to the effect that flak accounted for very few of our losses while fighter action accounted for many times more, made little difference how you felt when you had to penetrate a flak area like they had around Berlin.'

It was the weather that had caused the failure of the first two US daylight attacks on Berlin, on March 3 and 4. By mid-day on the 5th, however, it was clear matters were about to improve. An area of high pressure building up over Ireland was expected to intensify and drift eastwards over England during the next 24 hours. With a further area of high pressure to the east of Moscow this promised a ridge of high pressure and associated better weather extending across northern Europe. Now, at last, there was a good chance of reasonably clear skies all the way from the US bases in East Anglia to the German capital. To the south of the ridge of high pressure a warm front was advancing from the southeast bringing a blanket of cloud with snow in places; so if the 8th Air Force was to visit Germany at all the next day, it would have to go for a target in the north.

Armed with the forecast of improved weather Doolittle's staff officers laid plans for yet another attack on Berlin. Yet again this was to be a 'maximum effort' involving almost all 8th Air Force operational fighter and bomber units. In addition, 9th Air Force and Royal Air Force fighters were to be called in to support the mission.

The initial plan called for the bombers to go for the same three targets that were to have been hit during the earlier attacks. The 1st Bomb Division with 315 B-17s was to hit the ball bearing works at Erkner on the eastern side of Berlin. The 2nd Bomb Division with 243 B-24s was to hit the Heinkel aircraft works at Oranienburg on the northern side of the city. And the 3rd Bomb Division with 252 B-17s was to hit the electrical equipment works at Klein Machnow on the southwestern side of Berlin. If cloud forced any formation to resort to radar bombing their secondary target was to be the Friedrichstrasse railway station – a euphemism for the center of Berlin.

As the weather picture became clearer, however, it was seen that the wind at the target would be from the north northeast; and since for accuracy bomb runs had to be made into wind, to attack Oranienburg the 2nd Bomb Division would have had to fly across western Berlin and through some of the heaviest flak defenses. So on the evening of the 5th Oranienburg was deleted from the target list. Instead the 2nd Bomb Division was to hit the Daimler Benz aero engine plant at Genshagen to the south of Berlin.

Although the weather over northern Europe on the 6th was likely to be better than on previous days it still imposed some constraints on the attackers' freedom of action. Poor visibility at bases in East Anglia was expected to prevent the escorts taking off before 10 am; and after 5 pm visibility at the bases was expected to deteriorate sharply. That meant the raiding force would have to go to Berlin by the most direct route possible, with only slight deviations to keep the bombers out of the heavier flak concentrations. For the main part of the route, to the large town of Celle three-quarters of the way to the target, the raiders were to follow the 52° 37' line of latitude; this would keep them clear of all flak zones apart from one moderate concentration around Vechta. The B-17s of the 1st Bomb Division were to lead the attack, followed by those of the 3rd Division and with the B-24s of the 2nd Bomb Division in the rear. When fully assembled the planned formation of 810 bombers was to occupy a volume of airspace about 94 miles long, a mile wide and half a mile deep.

After it passed Celle the bomber stream was to head east southeast to a point just north of Magdeburg. There the three bomb divisions would split up, as each made its way independently to its Initial Point and there turned into its bomb run. After boming, the 1st Bomb Division was to continue northwards, the 2nd and 3rd Bomb Divisions were to turn sharply westwards, to get out of the Berlin flak zone as rapidly as possible. After they had picked their way past flak concentrations around Brandenburg the 2nd and 3rd Bomb Divisions were to link up with the 1st Division to the northwest of Berlin, then the force would regain the route it had taken going in and return along that. During the return flight the divisions were to fly in line abreast with the 1st Bomb Division in the north, the 3rd in the middle and the 2nd in the south. The bombers would thus form a huge mass about 20 miles wide and 30 miles long which would be much easier to escort than the lengthy bomber stream that had come in.

The weather forecasters expected aircraft above 23,000 feet to leave

THE ESCORT PLAN

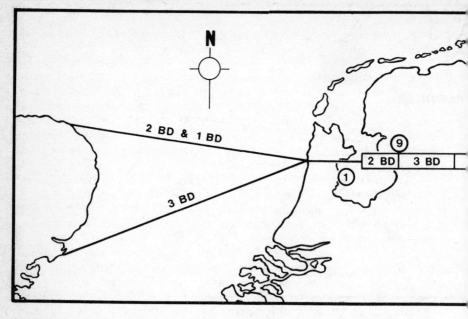

The plan for escorting the bombers on 6 March, using a total of nearly 800 P-38s, P-47s and P-51s. The 94-mile long bomber stream, to be flown during the route to the target, is drawn to scale and shows the order of the three bomb divisions. During the return flight the bomb divisions were to fly in line abreast. In each case the fighters flew with the bombers approximately 100 miles along the route.

1. Two groups of P-47s were to join the bombers at this point and escort the 1st and 3rd Divisions.
2. Two groups of P-47s were to join the bombers at this point and escort the 1st and 2nd Bomb Divisions.
3. Two and a half groups of P-47s were to join the bombers at this point, one group escorting the 1st Bomb Division, one escorting the 3rd and a half group escorting the 2nd Bomb Division.
4. Three groups of P-51s were to join the bombers at this point, one escorting each bomb division.
5. Three groups of P-38s were to join the bombers in this area, one escorting each bomb division.
6. Three squadrons of Royal Air Force P-51 Mustangs were to join the bombers at this point.
7. Two and a half groups of P-47s were to join the bombers at this point.
8. Three groups of P-47s, one flying its second mission of the day, were to join the bombers at this point.
9. Two groups of P-47s, both flying their second mission of the day, were to join the bombers at this point.

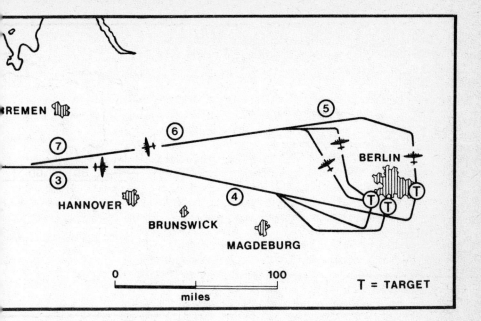

condensation trails; these would make it more difficult for bombers to hold
formation and easier for German fighters to find them. To avoid this nuisance
bomber formation leaders were ordered to stay below 21,000 feet.

Eleven groups of P-47s, three of P-38s and three of P-51s plus three squadrons
of Royal Air Force Mustangs, a total of nearly 800 fighters, were to provide
cover for the attack. Relays of P-47s were to cover the bombers on their
outbound and homebound routes as far east as Brunswick. As it entered the
target area each bomb division would be escorted by a group of P-51s and as it
left the target area these would be replaced by a group of P-38s. Three fighter
groups, with a total of 140 P-47s, were each to fly two sorties in support of the
mission; the first to cover the bombers during the initial part of the route in, the
second during the latter part of their route out.

All in all it was an attack plan that lacked any great subtlety or tactical
elegance. But it was sound, based on considerable experience from previous
attacks and, above all, it was workable.

Early on the evening of 5 March the basic plan for the next day's operation,
Mission 250, was complete and just before 6.56 pm the teletype machine at
High Wycombe began clattering out initial operation orders to the VIIIth
Fighter Command headquarters, the three bomb division headquarters, the
combat wings and groups and other interested agencies. At the receiving end a
clanging bell drew the operators' attention to the importance of the signal being
tapped out. This initial signal served as the cue for ground crews to begin the
massive task of preparing the aircraft for the mission. Like some giant clockwork

spring the 8th Air Force was being wound up for action.

As darkness fell scores of thousands of men were hard at work in the dimmed and carefully shielded lighting around the aircraft, preparing for the 'maximum effort' demanded by their commander. Those aircraft which were serviceable were filled with fuel, more than 2,500 gallons into each heavy bomber; in the case of the fighters the external tanks were lifted into place, then they were refuelled with 740 gallons for each P-38, 478 or 586 gallons for each P-47 and 419 gallons for each P-51.

As each bomber completed its refuelling armament teams moved in to load the bombs: ten 500-pound high explosive or incendiary bombs, or forty-two 100-pound incendiaries, per B-17; twelve 500-pounders or fifty-two 100-pound incendiaries per B-24. Each group lead and deputy lead aircraft was loaded with one or two smoke marker bombs in place of part of its bombload. The radar-equipped pathfinder B-17s and B-24s of the 482nd Bomb Group were each loaded with two smoke markers, six red flares with which to mark the Initial Points for the bomb runs and four 500-pound bombs.

The 500-pounders were winched into place in the bomb bays, the 100 pound incendiaries were simply lifted on their shackles by a couple of men. One of those involved was Private Bill Norko, who took part in loading the 384th Bomb Group's B-17s at Grafton Underwood: 'It was hard work but we were in our prime, we were strong. We would lift by hand any bomb weighing less than 500 pounds'. A few B-17s and B-24s were converted into what was derisively known as 'Bullshit Bombers' and loaded with boxes of leaflets instead of bombs; the men who flew them uniformly hated the idea of risking their lives to deliver such a harmless load on the enemy.

After the bombers had been loaded with fuel and bombs there came the more intricate task of re-fitting the guns, which had been removed from the aircraft for cleaning after the previous mission. Then the armament teams had to fill the ammunition containers in each aircraft. 'The ammunition came in 500-round wooden boxes, which we had to transfer to the containers in the aircraft. The ammunition belts were laid in the boxes layer upon layer and we would check it as we put it in. With a bit of practice one could feel if there was anything wrong with the belt even in the half light,' Norko remembered.

For the aircraft already serviceable, or nearly serviceable, the task of preparation was relatively simple. But if there was a maximum effort, as in this case, previously damaged aircraft had to be repaired hurriedly. 'Usually we would receive the order the night before if there was to be a maximum effort. If my squadron had been unfortunate and badly hit, there might be only five serviceable airplanes. So when the serviceable planes had been prepared and gassed up I would take the men off those and they would work to ready the ones that had been hit,' explained Captain Fritz Nowosad, an engineering officer with the 384th Bomb Group. 'That's when we would start taking bits off our worst aircraft, swapping parts with the other squadrons to get as many good aircraft as possible. And the engineering officers at the other squadrons would be doing the same thing.'

As the field order for the mission arrived at each subordinate headquarters the signals staff acknowledged receipt, then it was torn off the teletype machine and passed to the duty intelligence officer who fumbled through the five-foot long continuous length of paper to learn how it affected his particular unit. During the remainder of the night and the small hours of the morning the teletype machines would rarely fall silent for there was a steady stream of amendments and clarifications to the original signal. The routes to and from the target were plotted on the large wall map in the briefing room at each base and the required approach and target maps were pulled from the secret filing cabinets and set out ready to be passed to the aircrewmen.

Soon after 3 am orderlies began rousing the bomber crewmen who were to take part in the mission. Sleepy men blinked themselves awake, crawled out of their beds and began dressing, pulling on the warm underwear and electrically heated suits necessary for the long flight at high altitude. Over the top they donned light outer garments; there was still more than four hours to go before take-off.

When dressed the men made their way to breakfast, then to the base operations buildings where the briefing rooms were situated. It was now about 5 am. Noisily men filed into the room, checking names against lists held by the guards at the entrance. Some, still sleepy, spoke in murmurs; others, already beginning to feel strain over what the day might bring, remained silent; yet others reacted to their nervousness differently and were openly boisterous. At the far end of each room, hidden by a curtain, was the map showing the route for the day and, most important of all, the target. Where today? At the back of each room was a blackboard with an outline map of the airfield painted on giving positions of the aircraft on the ground. Other boards showed the aircraft numbers and crews assigned to them. After a glance at the boards the men took their seats and the chatter continued.

The mood changed the instant the military policeman at the door called everyone to attention. The hubbub ceased as each man struggled to the standing position briefly then sat down when the group commander, usually a colonel, took his seat. At each base the feelings of the men were similar as the briefing officer pulled back the curtain to reveal the map bearing the route to and from the target:

> There was a roar of consternation as the briefing officer slowly opened the curtain from left to right and the red tape marking the route went on and on and on, finally to the big red mass on the map which was Berlin.
>
> Captain Harry Crosby, 100th Bomb Group, Thorpe Abbots

> The intelligence officer pulled back the curtain over the wall map and there was the route to the target marked out in wool. 'Men', he said pointing with his stick, 'today you will bomb Berlin.' I don't know about any men being there in the room, I do know there were a lot of frightened boys!
>
> Sergeant Ed Leighty, 447th Bomb Group, Rattlesden

> 'Yes, by damn,' said our group commander, 'we're going back to Berlin and this time we're going to do it right. And I'm going to be right up there in the first plane, because the 91st Bomb Group is going to show the way. We're going to lead the 1st Combat Wing of the 1st Air Division of the 8th Air Force. We're going to hit that ball-bearing works in Erkner, which is 16 miles southeast of Berlin, and we're going to

destroy it just like we did the ball-bearing works at Schweinfurt.' This was not a highly motivational remark because it had been nip and tuck for a while which would be wiped out first – the 91st or Schweinfurt. However our leader recovered quickly by adding that we were invited to shoot down any and all ball-bearingless Luftwaffe fighters that might come near us.

Lieutenant Les Rentmeester, 91st Bomb Group, Bassingbourn

At each base the briefing officer waited a few moments for the chatter to die down, then went on to describe the target to be attacked by the unit, the approach to it and the turning points along the route to and from the target. Next it was the turn of the operations officer who described the manner in which the force was to assemble, the targets of other bomb divisions, the points where successive groups of escorting fighters would rendezvous with the bombers and other pertinent information. After that came the briefing by the Intelligence officer who outlined the defenses that could be expected. Some went into great detail, others felt that was unnecessary. Captain Sam Arauz, who delivered this part of the briefing to the 384th Bomb Group at Grafton Underwood, explained 'On the Berlin mission I told them: "Remember we are talking about the German capital, they are going to defend it to the hilt with everything they've got, fighters and flak." The men understood that, there was no need to go further.' At Framlingham, home of the 390th Bomb Group, Lieutenant Billy-Joe Holt heard the Intelligence officer give more than his usual number of humorous remarks about the German defenses: 'Don't worry, two FW 190 pilots are sick, one Me 109 pilot broke his glasses and can't fly and four of the 1,700 A.A. guns around Berlin are out of commission for parts!'

After the Intelligence officer had his say it was the turn of the weather officer. For take-off crews could expect some haze, with 3 to 6 tenths strato-cumulus cloud base 4,000 feet and tops at 7,000 feet. Visibility would be 1,000 to 1,500 yards at the surface, 5 to 10 miles above cloud. The surface wind was 5 mph from the northeast. Bomb group commanders were warned of condensation trails above 23,000 feet and the need to keep the high aircraft in their formations below this altitude. Over Berlin itself crews could expect between 4 and 6 tenths cumulus cloud between 2,000 and 3,000 feet, with a few streaks of high cirrus above 25,000 feet. The weather at the bases on return would be similar to that during the take-off.

Next one of the briefing officers gave a time check and each man glanced down to synchronize his watch. Then the group commander rounded off with some remarks of his own and emphasized the need to hit the target hard. 'We don't want to have to go back to that one!' was a phrase often used.

Following the main briefing the crews left the room and went to the more-detailed briefings for each of the aircrew specialties: for the pilots and copilots, the navigators, the bombardiers, the radio operators and the gunners.

Having received their specialist briefings those who wished slipped away to the small room set aside where they could ask for God's protection for the day's undertaking:

Almighty and everlasting Father, we humbly beseech thee to protect those of us who will be flying today. We submit ourselves into your hands and trust you to give us victory over the dark forces we oppose. May the terrible destruction we bring about, bring a rapid end to the madness of this war and may we find peace with you, our Maker, and may that peace become a reality for the torn world we live in. May we fly in the knowledge that not even a sparrow falls without your being aware of it and may we give our lives to you for your service. In your name we pray, amen.

Les Rentmeester was one who leaned heavily on this form of spiritual encouragement: 'Figuring that I needed all the help I could get I invariably received Holy Communion and the Last Rites of the Catholic Church before going on a mission. Bill Behrend my copilot and some other members of the crew seemed to take comfort in the fact that I checked in with the Lord before each mission.'

The next call was to the mens' locker rooms to pick up the large hold-alls containing the heavy fleece-lined outer flying suits, helmets, oxygen masks and parachutes. Then the men boarded the trucks waiting outside in the darkness, one ten-man crew in each; when the full crew was aboard the vehicles set out in ones and twos. It was now shortly after 6.45 am.

On arrival at their aircraft's dispersal the crew piled out of their truck and carried their hold-alls and other gear to the dimly lit bomber. Each aircraft had a little 'putt-putt' generator beside it providing electricity until the engines were started; the entire airfield seemed to reverberate with noise from these small engines. Quietly each aircrew set about a thorough check of the machine on which the men's lives were to depend for the next nine hours, each man responsible for checking a small part of the whole. 'I was deadly serious in checking every detail of our plane and equipment,' stressed Lieutenant Lowell Watts of the 388th Bomb Group at Knettishall, about to set out on the 25th and last mission of his combat tour. There would be a celebration when he returned. 'I told Harry Allert, our Crew Chief, to expect a first class buzz job over his tent when we got back.'

Then came one last briefing from the captain of each bomber in front of the aircraft. This was particularly important for those crewmen assigned to fill places in strange crews, for until now there may have been no opportunity to meet the men with whom they were to go into action. At Framlingham Lieutenant John Flottorp of the 390th Bomb Group went through his usual procedure 'I gathered everyone around me for my crew briefing and to get acquainted. I covered how I wanted things done – interphone discipline, fire control, emergency procedures etc. And I sought any intelligence the newcomers might have pertaining to pubs, local girls and such important information as the rest of us might have missed.'

This final ritual over the men boarded their aircraft and made ready to go to war. Now they pulled on heavy leather flying suits and jackets and clipped parachute harnesses into place. Close at hand in each position was a protective flak jacket and steel helmet. Navigators spread out charts and equipment on their dimly lit tables; gunners fingered guns and ammunition belts to check all was as it should be.

The first streaks of light were showing above the eastern horizon at 7.15 am as the B-17s of the 447th Bomb Group at Rattlesden, scheduled to be the first to take-off of the entire mission, began starting their engines. After a short period of warming up the aircraft began to taxi out of their dispersal points in prearranged order. With the squeal of brakes, bomber followed bomber around the perimeter track. The lead bomber, with Lieutenant Bryce Smith at the controls, moved on to Runway 06, lined up, then lurched to a halt. One after another the following B-17s came to a halt just off the runway.

As each bomber reached its place in the line its pilots ran through the engine run-up checks. With brakes locked firmly, each engine was run-up at 1,500 rpm and the generators checked. The turbo-superchargers were switched in and out, then the propeller controls were moved through the various rpm settings to get the controlling oil circulating through the system. Each engine was run at high manifold pressure to check each of the two magnetoes in turn, then for a short burst at maximum power. After a final check that the turbo-super-chargers were correctly set for take-off the pilot pulled back his throttles to idle and ran through the rest of his pre-take-off checks.

There were still a few minutes before take-off and now, in the first light of day, the bombers sat waiting with engines grumbling. Men glanced nervously at watches as the final seconds deliberately ticked off. At 7.45 am, right on time, a green flare climbed slowly from the squat control tower at Rattlesden: Mission 250 was on.

CHAPTER 2

ARRAYING FOR BATTLE

7.45 am to Noon

Some of us must die; cross yourselves and march forward.
Major General Rosecrans to his men,
before the battle at Murfreesboro, 1862

Bryce Smith eased forward the throttles of his four Wright Cyclone engines until they were roaring at 37 in manifold pressure and 2,500 revolutions per minute, then released the brakes. Shuddering under the 4,800 horse power the bomber trundled down the dark asphalt runway slowly gathering speed. Forty seconds later, after a ground run of just over one thousand yards, the Fortress reached 110 mph and the lift from the 1,420 square feet of wing equalled the thirty-one ton weight of the fully laden aircraft. Smith eased back on the wheel and slowly the bomber lifted into the air. Copilot Lieutenant J. Noyd pressed his toes against the brake pedals to stop the spinning wheels then flicked the switch to retract them. With a whirr of electric motors, the gear folded into its housings. Still with full power the aircraft continued to gain speed until it reached 140 mph, then Noyd throttled back to 2,300 rpm for the climb away.

As the first B-17 climbed away from Rattlesden, the next lined up and began its take-off run. Sixty seconds later followed a third, sixty seconds after that a fourth. As the fifth B-17 started its take-off run at Rattlesden others began taking off from other units: the lead aircraft of the 92nd Bomb Group at Podington, the 390th at Framlingham and the 452nd at Deopham Green. Within minutes the leading aircraft of the remaining twenty-four bomb groups assigned to the mission began their take-off runs also. At scores of remote villages and towns throughout Norfolk, Suffolk and Essex, Cambridgeshire, Huntingdonshire, Bedfordshire and Northamptonshire, the breakfasting inhabitants harkened to the now-accustomed rumble of hundreds of heavy bombers taking off and gathering into formation.

Apart from Wendling and Horsham St Faith, in Norfolk, where fog patches reduced visibility to below 600 yards in places, the weather at the bombers' bases was almost the same everywhere with slightly better visibility but more cloud than forecast: visibility 1 to 2 miles in haze at ground level, with a light breeze from the northeast; almost complete cloud cover between 3,000 and 6,000 feet with some patches of higher cloud between 8,000 and 15,000 feet.

At the controls of his B-24 Lieutenant Hubert Cripe of the 453rd Bomb Group ran through his pre-take-off checks at Old Buckenham:

> Set 20 degrees of flap, high rpm, manifold pressure set, hydraulic pressure OK. . . . Then our turn came and we taxied to the far side of the runway to avoid the propwash of the B-24 in front. A green light from the tower: we were clear to go. Holding the aircraft on the brakes I ran it up to maximum power. Then off came the brakes and the agonizingly slow take-off roll began. Sweat, baby, sweat. With wide-open throttles the Pratt and Whitneys bellowed out their song of 4,800 horses. Cool Hand Luke, the engineer, calmly called out the slowly increasing airspeed: '60 – 65 – 70 – 80 – 90 – 95 – 100'. Holy Smokey I can already see the end of the runway! Come on, baby! Keep that nose down and get all the speed you can. At 110 mph I eased back on the wheel and the heavy plane lightened and we became airborne.'. . . 112 – 115 – 118 – 120 . . .' With such a terrific load we can scarcely climb. 'Gear up!' I screamed. 'Gear up!' came Russ the copilot's reassuring answer and the gear swung outward and upward into the wings. Russ reset the manifold pressure and rpm and pulled in the flaps. At 150 mph we started to climb.

The only serious mishap during the take off was at Wendling, where a B-24 of the 392nd Bomb Group ran into a mist patch just off the end of the runway, failed to gain altitude, struck a tree and burst into flames. All ten crewmen lost their lives. In B-24 'Jaw-ja Girl', in the line two behind the crashed aircraft, Lieutenant James Muldoon saw the flash and orange glow suddenly appear in front of him. There was a green light from the control tower and with a roar the next B-24 began its take-off run. Then it was Muldoon's turn. 'Visibility was poor, we could see only the glow of the fire. Nothing was said over the radio but everyone knew what had happened. The big sweat was that the bombs might detonate as we passed over the crash site. There was no choice but to take off and try to swerve around the burning wreck.' Muldoon pushed forward his throttles and accelerated the heavily laden bomber to flying speed, lifted it off the ground and eased it to one side of the orange glow, then leveled out and began his climb.

To assemble in formation the aircraft climbed away from their airfields individually at set rates and designated headings after take-off. Once at briefed altitude over cloud and orbiting above their assigned radio beacons, the bombers assembled into combat box and wing formations. From the take-off of the first bomber, until a wing was formed up at 10,000 feet and ready to move away, took just over an hour.

Even before the first attacking formations had formed up, the raiders came within the gaze of the German radar early warning system. At about 8.50 am, more than an hour before the vanguard of the 1st Bomb Division was due to leave the coast of England, powerful Mammut and Wassermann radars on high ground near Calais picked up the first echoes from a concentration of enemy aircraft near Ipswich: almost certainly B-17s of the 447th Bomb Group from Rattlesden now assembling in that area. The report was immediately passed by landline to the headquarters of the fighter and flak units in Germany and the western occupied territories: enemy aircraft gathering in map square Heinrich Caesar. Soon these initial plots were supplemented by many others, as more and more bombers popped above the radar horizon.

With these clear pointers that yet another big American attack was in the offing, fighter units of Air Fleet 3 in France and Belgium, and Air Fleet Reich in Holland and Germany, were ordered to Readiness 30 Minutes. In practice this higher readiness state meant little: unless weather prevented flying the pilots of each Gruppe assembled at the operations building at their airfield early each morning; and outside every serviceable fighter had already been fully fuelled, armed and warmed up ready for action.

At their headquarters at Zeist, near Utrecht in Holland, the fighter controllers of Fighter Corps I began laying their dispositions to meet the threatened attack. From the forecast weather it seemed unlikely the enemy target was in southern Germany: over large stretches there was continual cloud cover, with snow in some places. But over northern Germany there was relatively little cloud, and the enemy would certainly know this; this might even be another attempt to strike at Berlin, following the failure of the attack two days earlier.

In accordance with the latest tactical directives issued by General Adolf Galland's headquarters, once the enemy bombers started to come in Fighter Divisions 2 and 3 based in Holland and northwestern Germany were to assemble their day fighter units into a large attack formation to go into action soon after the bombers crossed into western Germany. Fighter Division 1, covering northeastern Germany including Berlin, was to wait on the ground until the situation became clearer; if, as seemed likely, the target was somewhere in the divisional area, its single-engined fighters and destroyers were to assemble into a large attack formation over Magdeburg and go into action from there. Fighter Division 7, covering southern Germany and Austria, was to send two Gruppen of destroyers to bolster the defenses in the north; these lumbering twin-engined fighters would have to get airborne soon after the bombers crossed the coast of Europe, for their cruising speed was little higher than that of the bombers they were expected to engage. Once it was clear the enemy target was not in their area, the fighter units of Air Fleet 3 in France and Belgium were to re-deploy to bases in western Germany and go into action against the bombers on their way out. This overall plan was passed by landline to the headquarters of the fighter divisions concerned, where staff officers worked out the tactical details before passing the necessary orders to the Gruppe commanders.

At Rotenburg near Bremen Hauptmann Rolf Hermichen, commanding Ist Gruppe of Fighter Geschwader 11 with FW 190s, was informed he was to lead the attack formation of Fighter Division 2 with four complete Gruppen. Only the previous day the division had mounted a full-scale fighter assembly exercise over Lake Steinhuder near Hanover. Now the lessons learned were to be used: the four Gruppen, with about 80 fighters, were to assemble in exactly the same place and then the divisional fighter controller would direct them into the incoming stream of bombers.

At Twente in eastern Holland Major Karl Schnoor, commanding Ist Gruppe of Fighter Geschwader 1 with FW 190s, was told that after take-off his unit was to link up with the IInd Gruppe over Rheine near Osnabrueck, then receive further orders.

At Wunstorf near Hanover Major Hans Kogler, commanding the IIIrd Gruppe of Destroyer Geschwader 26 with Me 110s, was informed that he was to lead the Fighter Division 1 attack formation. After the order to scramble he was to link up with other units over Magdeburg at 10,000 feet: the two Gruppen of Me 110s from Fighter Division 7 in the south; one Gruppe of Me 410s; three Gruppen of Me 109s of Fighter Geschwader 3 to help the destroyers punch through the screen of escort fighters; and any other fighters the division could scrape together. Altogether there would be over a hundred single-engined fighters and destroyers in this, the largest attack formation yet sent into action by the Luftwaffe.

Once he had his orders from division, each Gruppe commander held a short briefing to put his pilots in the picture. Nowhere can this event have been more moving than at Kogler's Gruppe, whose Me 110s had suffered so heavily from the American escort fighters during the previous weeks. The single-engined fighters would cover the destroyers until they reached the bombers; after that all German fighters were to engage the bombers. The destroyers would have to fend for themselves and it was then the losses usually occurred. Now the Gruppe had available only nine patched-up Me 110s ready for action. With morale as low as it was, Kogler was loath to order men into the air and asked for volunteers. Nobody moved. Then he appealed to his men, 'You can't let me fly alone against the enemy bombers . . .' One by one the hands went up until he had the nine crews he needed. It was a poignant scene, for each of those who volunteered knew that if it came to a fight with the escorts his chances of surviving the day were slim.

Their briefings complete, the pilots resumed their seats in the crew rooms. Men read books, chatted, wrote letters, played cards – anything to take their minds off the battle likely soon to begin. For the time being it was a case of waiting, waiting for the enemy to come to them.

Still under the watchful eye of the German radars the heavy bombers continued to gather over East Anglia. Altogether 814 B-17s and B-24s had taken off for the attack, of which one had crashed immediately after take-off. After the formations were complete 38 bombers returned to their bases; they had taken off as spares to replace others which might have become unserviceable. Now they were not needed and their crews managed to conceal the disappointment at not being able to take part in the mission.

At 9.15 am the 1st Combat Wing, comprising 58 B-17s of the 91st and 381st Bomb Groups and led by two pathfinder aircraft of the 482nd Bomb Group, began moving away from its assembly point over Bassingbourn near Royston. During the minutes that followed the other combat wings of the 1st Bomb Division, the 40th, 41st, 94th and the Composite 40th-41st, completed their assembly also and began moving toward the divisional assembly line between Kings Lynn and Cromer. The only major hitch occurred as the Composite Wing neared Kings Lynn: the leader of the 384th Bomb Group flying in the high position, finding himself being crowded out by another wing approaching the same point, pulled his group to the left just as the wing leader turned right to ·

cut a corner and make his correct time at the departure point. Within half a minute the two parts of the wing were two miles apart and diverging rapidly; in spite of efforts to regain their place in formation the 18 B-17s of the 384th were unable to do so, and eventually had to abandon the mission and return to Grafton Underwood. The Composite Wing of the 1st Bomb Division, less one third of its strength but still with 36 aircraft, continued on without them.

At 10.01 am, one minute behind schedule, the vanguard of the 1st Bomb Division left the coast at Cromer at 14,000 feet heading east. At 10.12, right on time, the lead bombers of the 3rd Division set out from Orfordness and, aiming at the same point on the Dutch Coast, slowly converging on the division ahead. Finally at 10.28, one minute late, the lead B-24s of the 2nd Bomb Division began leaving Cromer following the route of the 1st Division. Mission 250 was now on its way, the B-17s and B-24s rumbling purposefully towards their targets at 170 mph, just under three miles per minute and climbing slowly to attack altitude. As they left friendly territory many bomber crewmen felt their throats begin to dry as tension increased. Hubert Cripe's feelings were typical: 'As the shores of England fell behind I felt like a little kid having his security blanket taken away. How I wished I could call it all off and go home to Mom's fried chicken and gravy. But no, this was war. The cold North Sea crept below us as we continued climbing.'

As the last B-24s left Cromer at 10.38, the greater part of the fighter escort was already airborne and heading after the bombers: seven Groups of P-47s with 307 aircraft and three groups of P-51s with 118 aircraft. To conserve fuel the fighters cruised at speeds around 260 mph which gave them an overtaking speed of 80-90 mph on the bombers. At this rate it would take the P-51s just over two hours to catch up with the leading B-17s and effect a rendezvous just short of Berlin itself.

The departure of the leading wings from the Norfolk coast had been observed at the German early warning stations and the phrase most hated by Luftwaffe fighter pilots was broadcast over the reporting network: 'Enemy concentrations in map squares Dora-Dora and Dora-Emil, moving east.' This was the signal for fighter units in France, Belgium, Holland and Germany to be brought to Readiness 15 Minutes. The pilots left their comfortable crew rooms at the operations buildings and walked to the more spartan Staffel huts situated close to the aircraft dispersals. Still the German fighter controllers had only a vague idea of where the blow was aimed but, from the strength of the radar echoes from the incoming formations, it was clear General Doolittle was using almost all his aircraft. The Luftwaffe would have to put up everything it could to contest the incursion.

By 10.40 am the leading bombers were two-thirds of the way across the North Sea heading for the Dutch coast and the first German fighter units were brought to *Sitzbereitschaft* – cockpit readiness. The pilots slipped on life jackets, climbed into their waiting aircraft, buckled on and tightened parachute and seat harnesses and pulled on flying helmets. 'For me the minutes between being ordered to Cockpit Readiness and receiving the order to take-off were the most terrible of all,' felt Leutnant Hans Iffland, an Me 109 pilot with Fighter

Geschwader 3. 'After the order came to get airborne one was too busy to think about one's possible fate; but waiting to go, with nothing to do but think about what might happen, that was the worst time. My own greatest fear was that I might be seriously wounded with permanent injuries. Death was of course a fear but that would have been an end. But the thought of being a cripple for the rest of my life, that held the greatest terror of all for me.'

In the pathfinder B-17 at the very head of the bomber stream Colonel Ross Milton, deputy commander of the 91st Bomb Group and airborne commander of the 1st Air Division, found the sight of box after box of bombers coming up behind very impressive indeed. 'I looked back and I remember seeing one Hell of a lot of airplanes following me.' Others were similarly impressed. Lieutenant Roy Menning, piloting a B-17 of the 94th Bomb Group in the middle of the stream about 40 miles behind Milton: 'I could see the bomber stream in front of me and behind as far as the eye could see, like an endless river. I felt the Luftwaffe just did not have enough fighters to attack us all and any German people looking up at us would feel their war was lost, when they could see so many enemy aircraft in the sky over their homeland.'

Once over the sea the bombers' gunners loosed off short bursts to test their weapons. It was a necessary move, though not without hazard. One B-17 of the 385th Bomb Group had a cartridge case from an aircraft above smash through its nose plexiglas and injure the bombardier. The crew was forced to abandon the mission and turn back. Over the North Sea 44 other bombers dropped out of formation for less dramatic reasons, mainly technical failures.

While crossing the North Sea the bombers encountered headwinds slightly stronger than forecast and the vanguard reached the Dutch coast 8 minutes late, at 10.52. As the head of the bomber stream moved inland Major John Murphy led the first wave of escorts, 53 P-47s of the 359th Fighter Group, reassuringly into place to cover them.

At this stage the only significant problem was that the 13th Combat Wing, in the middle of the bomber stream, had become separated from the 4th Combat Wing in front. The gap between the two wings was about 20 miles instead of the planned 12 miles and normally this would not have been serious. On this occasion however, in combination with another departure from plan, it was to prove the first ingredient in a recipe for disaster for the 13th.

The second ingredient was that Colonel Milton's pathfinder B-17, at the head of the bomber stream, suffered a radar failure. Normally this would not have been serious either, but on this occasion the navigator failed to correct sufficiently for the 45 mph wind blowing from the northeast and the lead aircraft moved inland on a track 10 degrees south of that planned. The succeeding combat wings followed. The deviation south of the planned track was not rapid – only one mile every two minutes – but it remained unnoticed and gradually it became significant. Even so, had all of the combat wings followed the leader off track, the relatively minor error in navigation would scarcely have warranted mention in any history book. But as it crossed the Dutch coast some 17 minutes behind the lead aircraft, the 13th Combat Wing – which had become separated from the one in front – took almost exactly the planned track for the target. A 'step' now began to develop in the middle of the bomber stream which grew larger and more pronounced with each minute that passed. And within less than an hour that 'step' was going to have terrible consequences for the 13th Combat Wing.

Unaware of the trouble brewing Lieutenant John Flottorp, piloting a B-17 of the 390th Bomb Group which was part of the 13th Combat Wing, watched the Dutch coast slide underneath his aircraft. 'It was all eyeballs on "maximum scan" as we approached the coast. A few isolated flak bursts well off to the side greeted us. Routine crew oxygen checks were all we had over the interphone for quite some time and the tension of waiting for something to happen began to mount.'

At 10.55, three minutes after the vanguard of the attacking force crossed the Dutch coast, the first German fighter units were ordered into the air. At Twente in eastern Holland the pilots of Ist Gruppe of Fighter Geschwader 1, already at cockpit readiness in their Focke-Wulfs, saw a green flare rise from the operations building and heard the loudspeakers around the airfield barking the order: 'Alarmstart! Alarmstart! Alarmstart!' First one, then another, then several powerful BMW engines burst into life. The Gruppe commander, Major Karl Schnoor, pushed open the throttle and his fighter began to accelerate across the grass followed closely by the other three aircraft of the Staff unit. As Schnoor reached the center of the airfield on his take-off run, the 1st Staffel began its take-off run at right angles to his across the airfield; when they were at the center of the airfield the 2nd Staffel followed, at right angles to them; then the 3rd Staffel followed in the same way. Immediately after take-off Schnoor curved left and flew a circuit of the airfield; the other three Staffeln slotted into position behind him. Then, the sixteen FW 190s turned northeast and climbed to rendezvous with the IInd Gruppe. This well-practiced drill enabled a fighter Gruppe to take-off and assemble within two minutes of the scramble order.

Soon this scene was being repeated at airfields across the north German plain: that of Fighter Geschwader 1 at Rheine, those of Fighter Geschwader 11 at Rotenburg, Wunstorf and Oldenburg and that of IIIrd Gruppe of Fighter Geschwader 54 at Lueneburg, as the single-engined Messerschmitts and Focke-Wulfs roared into the air. And at Ansbach, deep in Frankonia more than three hundred miles to the southeast of the incoming bombers, 24 twin-engined Me 110s of Ist and IInd Gruppen of Destroyer Geschwader 76 took off each laden with four large air-to-air rockets; their orders were to head for Magdeburg 190 miles to the north and, unless orders were received to the contrary, join Hans Kogler's attack formation which would by then be assembling there.

From bases in France and Belgium 35 Me 109s and 36 FW 190s belonging to Fighter Geschwader 2 and 26 were ordered to scramble and patrol over Reims, in case the raiding force unexpectedly swung southwards.

At 11.30 Luftwaffe ground observation posts reported the leading enemy formations passing over the border into Germany. The bomber stream, now fully assembled and slightly elongated, was about 100 miles long and extended all the way across Holland with the rearguard, the B-24s of the 20th Bomb Wing, just approaching the coast. Covering the bombers at this time were 150 P-47s zig-zagging in fours and eights to maintain station on their slower charges.

By now the divergence of the leading bomber wings from the planned track had grown markedly, with the vanguard already 18 miles off track and the gap still widening. One immediate effect of this departure from the planned route was that B-17s of the 1st Bomb Division ran over the flak zones at Zwolle and Enschede and came under uncomfortably accurate fire which caused damage to several aircraft. One of the Fortresses, piloted by Lieutenant Wallace Upson of the 92nd Bomb Group, had a salvo of shells burst nearby and became the first bomber to fall to enemy action that day. The right waist gunner, Sergeant Neal Persons on his first mission, heard an explosion seemingly in the bomb bay: 'The left waist gunner poked me in the back and I turned around and looked out, and the whole left side of the plane was on fire. Then Maurice Hargrove, the top turret gunner, came dashing back along the fuselage to the door, pulled the jettison handle and out he went. In fact if the door hadn't opened he would have broken his neck, because he was diving out at the same time as he pulled the handle!' One by one the crewmen jumped from the aircraft. Persons fell clear and found himself falling on his back and unable to judge altitude, so to be on the safe side he pulled the ripcord. 'The chute opened, it jerked me upright and almost broke my back. Then I could judge the altitude, I must have been about 14,000 feet up. Below me I could see a couple of parachutes.' The descent seemed to take for ever. After a few minutes the bomber stream receded into the distance and Persons felt very lonely. Then he saw a twin-engined aricraft coming straight towards him. 'I recognized it as a Junkers 88 and it was coming right at me. I had heard of people being shot up on their parachutes and I thought "My God! They don't really do that, do they?" But still he kept coming straight at me. Then, at about 500 yards, he broke off and flew a wide circle around me. And the pilot waved. Boy, that was almost as good as seeing the Statue of Liberty! I waved back at him, I almost broke my arm waving I was so happy!' Persons finally landed in a small wood, hid his parachute and made his way away from the scene.

Meanwhile the 13th Combat Wing, at the head of the second half of the bomber stream, continued eastwards almost exactly on the planned route and oblivious to what was in store for it.

As the bombers thundered deeper into hostile territory German fighters began assembling over Lake Steinhuder in readiness to meet them. Under the direction of the controller of the 2nd Fighter Division at Stade, Hauptmann Rolf Hermichen led the Stab and 1st Gruppe of Fighter Geschwader 11 with four Me 109s and 13 FW 190s, down from the north. As he neared the lake other Gruppen from the same Geschwader joined him: Hauptmann Anton Hackl's IIIrd Gruppe with 18 FW 190s; and Major Guenther Specht's IInd Gruppe with 15 Me 109s which, ordered to provide top cover, moved into a position 3,000 feet above and up-sun of the others. Then Hauptmann Rudolf Sinner led his Gruppe, IIIrd of Fighter Geschwader 54 with 20 Me 109s, into position between Hermichen's and Hackl's Gruppen. Shortly afterwards the two Gruppen from Fighter Geschwader 1 tagged on to the end of the force: Major Karl Schnoor's Ist Gruppe with 16 FW 190s and Major Heinz Baer's IInd Gruppe with 21 more. The assembled formation of 107 Messerschmitts and Focke-Wulfs was not large by American standards but for many German pilots it was by far the largest they had ever been part of. 'We seldom flew on operations with more than 20 Messerschmitts,' explained Feldwebel Friedrich Ungar, who flew with Sinner's Gruppe.

At 11.40 Hermichen was ordered to lead his formation out from Lake Steinhuder northwest then, a few minutes later, he was directed on to due west. The 13th Combat Wing was still more than 120 miles beyond the range of Hermichen's guns but the fate of many of its members was already sealed: the two forces were now on a collision course and closing at a combined speed of about 500 mph.

By 11.55 the vanguard of the bomber stream had passed east of Osnabrueck and was about 20 miles south of the planned route. By now the heading error had been noticed and was being corrected for, and the lead wing had taken up a slightly more northerly heading which would bring it back on the planned route. Covering this first half of the bomber stream were 60 P-47s belonging to the 56th and 78th Fighter Groups. Meanwhile the 13th Combat Wing, leading the second half of the bomber stream, had just crossed the German-Dutch border and was flying the planned route. Eight Thunderbolts of the 56th Fighter Group, which should have been with the leading bomb division, had tacked on the 13th Combat Wing. Further back were 31 P-47s of the 353rd Fighter Group, and covering the B-24s at the rear of the bomber stream were 34 more Thunderbolts of the 56th Fighter Group. Altogether there was a total of 133 escort fighters in the vicinity of the bomber formations, rather more fighters than Hermichen had in his force. But nearly half of the American fighters were in position near the head of the bomber stream, considered the most likely to suffer head-on attack from German fighters. Only eight escorts were in any position to block such an attack on the 13th Combat Wing.

There is no evidence that the German fighter controllers at Stade had made any deliberate attempt to exploit the 'step' in the American bomber stream. Indeed, the southwards drift by the head of the bomber stream had been so gradual that it may well have escaped notice at the fighter headquarters. The route planned for the bombers, which would take them clear of the flak zones, had been used before when attacking targets in northern Germany and it was assumed it was being used on this occasion too. Because of the high closing speeds involved, setting up a head-on attack was difficult enough without attempting to pick out a bomber formation which might temporarily lack an escort. It was far more important for defending fighters to get into a bomber formation fast and in force, hit hard, then get out before the escorts could mount an effective counter-attack.

Following the instructions of his ground controller as he flew westwards, Rolf Hermichen squinted through the blur of blades in front of him for the first glimpse of the enemy bombers he knew had to be there. But so far he could see nothing against the clear blue sky above the cloud patches. Obviously the

THE OPPOSING FORCES AT 11.55 am

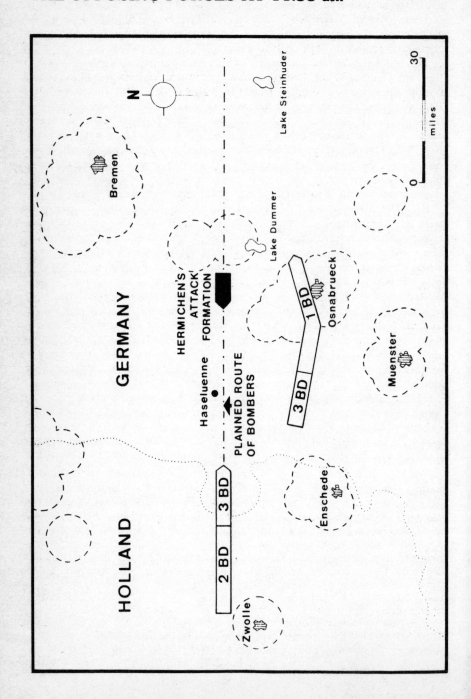

bombers were not leaving condensation trails, that made it much more difficult to see them at long range.

Then, suddenly, Hermichen caught sight of the enemy bombers looking like a cluster of stationary gnats on the western horizon. The time was 11.58 and the enemy aircraft were right on his nose.

The bombers the German leader was now preparing to attack belonged to the 13th Combat Wing. Led by a single pathfinder B-17 of the 482nd Bomb Group, the formation comprised a further 80 B-17s of the 95th, 100th and 390th Bomb Groups. The German fighters were far smaller than the American heavy bombers so it would be some time before the crews on board the latter perceived their peril. So far the mission had been quiet, as Lieutenant Bob Shoens piloting B-17 'Our Gal Sal' of the 100th Bomb Group afterwards remembered: 'It was one of those days when you could see for miles. Western Europe lay before us like a map. Even though the thermometer was well below zero at our altitude, the sun was warm. It was so comfortable it began to look too good . . .'

Rolf Hermichen ran a practiced eye around his cockpit to check his guns were set to fire and everything was ready for combat. Next he selected one of the clusters of specks near the middle of the enemy formation as the target for his Gruppe and eased down the nose of his Focke-Wulf to bring it into his gunsight. Rudolf Sinner, leading the Gruppe immediately behind Hermichen's, could now see which part of the enemy formation his leader was making for and selected one of the higher bomber squadrons for his attack.

It was 11.59 and the American bombers, now about 8 miles in front of the German fighters, were still no more than sharply defined dots in the distance. So far there was no sign of escort fighters but Hermichen had no doubt they were there somewhere. Despite the 500 mph closing speed of the two formations, more than 8 miles per minute, the bombers were growing in size only very slowly.

Thirty seconds later, at range 4 miles, Hermichen noticed the dots in front of him had begun to sprout wings. He selected one of the dots as his own victim.

Now at last Bob Shoens suddenly noticed the enemy formations lined up to attack: 'There appeared ahead of us what looked like a swarm of bees, fighters several miles off but coming at us, dozens of them. It became obvious in a few

Approximate positions of the opposing forces at 11.55 am. Due to an equipment failure the leading American bomber had taken the front half of the bomber stream slightly south of the planned route and into the flak zones around Zwolle, Enschede and Osnabrueck. The error had been noticed, however, and the leader had altered heading to the north to bring him back on the planned route. Escorting these bombers were 60 P-47s of the 56th and 78th Fighter Groups. The rear part othe 3rd Bomb Division, led by the 13th Combat Wing, had become separated from the front half of the bomber stream and with the 2nd Bomb Division was flying the correct route. Escorting the 13th Wing were eight P-47s of the 56th Fighter Group and covering the 2nd Bomb Division were a further 31 P-47s of the 353rd Fighter Group. Rolf Hermichen's attack formation, comprising a total of 107 Me 109s and FW 190s, had left its assembly point over Lake Steinhuder and was heading due west on a collision course with the 13th Combat Wing.

seconds that we were their target. They came straight at us.' Sergeant Van Pinner of the 100th Bomb Group, celebrating his 23rd birthday in the top turret of B-17 'Ronnie R', also watched the German fighters coming in. 'We could see we had a good fight coming. But there was no time to think about it, I was too busy getting my sight on them and preparing to open fire. At a time like that you just do what you are trained to do and do it automatically.'

Also at this time Lieutenant Bob Johnson, flying P-47 'Lucky' at the head of a flight from the 56th Fighter Group just to the north of Shoens and Pinner, caught sight of the enemy: 'I noticed a large box of planes coming at us at the same level. There were about 40 or 50 to a box and I saw 2 boxes at our level and one box at 27,000 or 28,000 feet. I called in to watch them, then that they were FW 190s. There were only eight of us . . .' Bravely Johnson swung his small force south to engage the attackers but from the start it was clear they were too few and too far out of position to ward off the initial blow.

Twenty-four seconds later, at range one mile, the wings of the bomber framed in Hermichen's gunsight began to thicken into engines. Now the German pilot devoted his entire attention to holding his victim in the center of his glowing graticule, for he knew that during the final part of the attack events would follow each other with bewildering rapidity.

Three seconds later, with the distance between the rapidly closing formations down to about 1,000 yards, Sergeant Glen Hudson manning the nose turret of Shoens's B-17 began firing short bursts at the approaching fighters. Sergeant Willie Eresman in the top turret joined in, as did Van Pinner and the gunners on board the other threatened bombers.

Rolf Hermichen gave a final shouted radio call to his Gruppe: *'Hinein!'* – Get in!. Then he tensed every muscle as he prepared to open fire on the bomber steadily growing in his gunsight. Two seconds later the distance had closed to 600 yards and the graticule was exactly over his victim. Half a second later, at 500 yards, Hermichen's right hand squeezed the firing trigger of his four cannon and two heavy machine guns.

CHAPTER 3

CLASH OVER HASELUENNE

Noon to 12.25 pm

*When things are going badly in battle the best tonic is to take one's
mind off one's own troubles by considering what a rotten time one's
opponent must be having.*
Field Marshal Sir Archibald Wavell

Rolf Hermichen had got there first with the most. His huge formation of
Messerschmitts and Focke-Wulfs charged headlong into the B-17s of the 13th
Combat Wing over Haseluenne, a small town just inside Germany 12 miles
northeast of Lingen. There was time for only a brief half-second burst before he
had to ease back on the stick and skim close over the top of his victim.
Hermichen saw his rounds burst on the B-17 he had chosen as target just before
it flashed past. So did Oberfeldwebel Hermann Reinthaler in one of the
Me 109s to the right of the leader. So did Feldwebel Heinz Hanke in an FW 190
following close behind and his wing man saw the bomber start to catch fire and
swing out of formation.

In the B-17s the gunners loosed off burst after burst at the Messerschmitts and
Focke-Wulfs streaming past. One of those hotly engaged was Van Pinner:
'There were fighters everywhere. They seemed to come past in fours. I would
engage the first three but then the fourth would be on to me before I could get
my guns on him. I knew our aircraft was being hit real bad – we lost the ball
turret gunner early in the fight . . .' A few hundred yards to the left of Pinner,
Lieutenant August Briding in the nose of 'Berlin First' of the 95th Bomb Group
was also letting fly at the enemy: 'The fighters came in one lot after another,
there were hardly any gaps in the attacks. With the other gunners I was firing
the whole time at them. The ball turret gunner, Sergeant Andrew Brown,
complained that the belt links and spent cases from my chin turret were raining
past his turret so thickly he could not get his sights on any of the enemy fighters.
He was our youngest crew member and he said he wanted a chance to strike at
them too!' In the radio room of the same bomber Sergeant Edgar Jurist opened
up with his single gun whenever he saw a fighter flash over the B-17: 'There was
a continual babble over the interphone from the nose gunner and the top
gunner, telling us how the fighters were coming in. People were getting very
excited, one could tell from their voices.'

HEAD-ON ATTACK ON A B-17

1

2

3

4

5

6

Hard on the heels of Hermichen's Gruppe came the Me 109s of Rudolf Sinner's. Sinner himself picked a B-17 in a squadron slightly higher than the one Hermichen had hit and saw his rounds strike the nose and starboard wing before he had to break away. Feldwebel Friedrich Ungar, behind Sinner in the main Gruppe formation, saw his rounds strike the left inboard engine of a B-17 and observed pieces flying off. 'There was no time for jubilation. The next thing I was inside the enemy formation trying to get through without ramming anyone. Nobody fired at me then, they were too concerned about hitting each other,' Ungar later wrote. 'When we emerged behind the formation things got really hot; we had the tail gunners of some thirty bombers letting fly at us with everything they had. Together with part of our Gruppe I pulled sharply to the left and high, out to one side. Glancing back I saw the Fortress I had hit tip up and go down to the right, smoking strongly.'

Close behind Sinner's Messerschmitts came the Gruppen of Anton Hackl, Karl Schnoor then Heinz Baer, all with Focke-Wulfs. From the cockpit of his B-17 Bob Shoens watched the seemingly unending procession of enemy fighters stream past: 'They came straight at us and in an instant they went through us.' Several gunners claimed German fighters during these attacks. One was Lieutenant J. Fisher, manning the front guns of a B-17 of the 95th Bomb Group as Focke-Wulfs attacked his formation: 'On the first four that came in I got the second enemy aircraft in my sight and kept firing all the way in. The enemy aircraft went straight under the nose of our aircraft, its engine smoking.' What Fisher and many others did not know was that, because of the low quality fuel issued to Luftwaffe units at this time, German fighter engines often trailed smoke when running at full power. Many were mistakenly claimed destroyed for this reason.

In the top turret of B-17 'Our Mark' of the 100th, flying immediately to the left of the leader of the Low Group, B Formation, Sergeant George Madden engaged each wave of fighters in turn. Then, a little behind the final wave, came a single FW 190 making straight for the lead bomber, 'Nelson King' piloted by Lieutenant Jack Swartout. Madden fired a short burst into the German fighter as it came past then glanced down to check his guns. When he next looked up almost the entire fin and rudder of 'Nelson King' had gone: the Focke-Wulf had

Hold this diagram a comfortable arm's length (about 2 feet) from your eyes to see the apparent size of the B-17 at the various ranges. During a head-on attack the closing speed of the two aircraft was about 500 mph, or more than 200 yards per second.
1. Range 800 yards. At this distance the bomber had to be centered in the fighter's gunsight graticule if it was to be hit.
2. One second later, range 600 yards, the fighter about to open fire.
3. Half a second later, range 500 yards, the fighter commenced firing.
4. Half a second later, range 400 yards, the fighter ceased firing.
5. Half a second later, range 300 yards, the fighter began to move out of the path of the bomber.
6. Half a second later, range 200 yards. If the fighter was not out of the bomber's path by this time, a collision was almost inevitable.

collided with or rammed its victim and carried away almost the entire assembly. 'There was just a spar holding on what was left of the rudder which was swinging from side to side, I don't know how it stayed on. We could no longer fly formation on him so our pilot eased up to tack on the high group.'

Following the German fighters came the eight P-47s of the 56th Fighter Group led by Bob Johnson, trying vainly to divert at least part of the powerful onslaught. But as the Messerschmitts, Focke-Wulfs and P-47s flashed through their formations the B-17 gunners blasted away at everything single-engined. Later survivors from the 100th Bomb Group would report:

> There is conclusive evidence that enemy aircraft are doing everything possible to cause our gunners to mistake them for our escort. Both FW 190s and Me 109s passed within 50 feet of some of our aircraft and were seen to be camouflaged exactly like P-47s. They also imitated the maneuvers of the escort fighters. They staged mock dogfights and flew with our formations several minutes before attacking. On several occasions they played around ahead of our formation, circling several times before peeling away and diving in for an attack. It is not believed many of our gunners were fooled by these maneuvers. . . .

But the aircraft 'camouflaged exactly like P-47s' which 'imitated the maneuvers of escort fighters' were Johnson's Thunderbolts; none was hit by the 'friendly' bombers' fire.

From start to finish the initial German attack on the 13th Combat Wing took less than a minute. But before its end mortally wounded Fortresses had begun to lurch drunkenly and spectacularly out of formation. Lieutenant John Harrison, piloting B-17 'The Savage' of the 100th Bomb Group, saw the formation start to dissolve around him: 'The engine of one Fort burst into flames and soon the entire ship was afire. Another was burning from waist to tail. It seemed both the pilot and copilot of yet another ship had been killed. It started towards us out of control. I moved the squadron over. Still it came. Again we moved. This time the stricken Fortress stalled, went up on its tail, then slid down.'

The B-17 that had moved so threateningly on 'The Savage' was Captain David Miner's aircraft. In the nose the bombardier, Lieutenant Earl Richardson, had seen the German fighters attacking from in front: 'That first FW 190, I am sure, must have hit the pilot's compartment and killed Captain Miner and the copilot. They never said a word on the intercom and the noise was terrific.' As the bomber tumbled out of the sky the speed built up rapidly, then the tail broke away. The force of the airflow in the dive pushed in the plexiglas nose and the unfortunate navigator was thrown out before he could clip on his parachute. Richardson was knocked unconscious but came to shortly afterwards: 'God gives one time to gather one's wits, everything slows down. I found my parachute, clipped it on one side and dived out of the nose where the plexiglas had been'. Richardson pulled his ripcord and the parachute popped open. At the rear of the bomber one of the waist gunners, Sergeant Sam Pry, leapt from the rear exit to find himself falling with the plunging Fortress and engulfed in flames trailing from the blazing right inboard engine. Though badly burned he was able to open his parachute and descended without further injury. A twenty-eight ton B-17 initially moving at three miles per minute had considerable momentum and even though it had catastrophic structural

Hitler shaking hands with Luftwaffe fighter ace Major Anton Hackl, following the award of the Knight's
[Cross] with Oakleaves for his missions in defense of the Reich. Hackl was credited with the destruction of two
[aircraft] on 6 March 1944. (Hackl.)

The German senior commanders, during the action on 6 March 1944. **Top left:** Generaloberst Hans-Juer Stumpff, the commader of Air Fleet Reich, controlled all fighter and flak units defending Germany in March 1944. **Top right:** Adolf Galland, who held the rank of Generalmajor in March 1944, was responsib the formulation and development of the tactics employed by the fighter units. **Below:** Generalmajor Josep Schmid (seated, center) commanded 1st Fighter Corps responsible for the operational control of fighter u based in the Air Fleet Reich area. (Ring, Sachs.)

German single-engined fighter types. **Above:** Messerschmitt 109Gs of IIIrd Gruppe of Fighter Geschwader
Below: a Focke-Wulf 190A of 1st Gruppe of Fighter Geschwader 1. (Schroer, Demuth)

The German twin-engined bomber-destroyers. **Left:** Messerschmitt 110Gs of 1st Gruppe of Destroyer Geschwader 76. **Center:** a Messerschmitt 410 of IInd Gruppe of Destroyer Geschwader 26. Both types carry four launching tubes for 21 cm rockets under the outer wing sections. **Bottom:** loading a rocket into its launching tube. (Schob, Stehle, Bundesarchiv.)

American senior commanders ~~~ng the action on 6 March 1944. ~~~ht:~~ Lieutenant General James ~~~little (right), commander of the ~~~ Air Force. With him is Major ~~~eral Orvil Anderson, Deputy ~~~mmanding General for ~~~rations (center) and Brigadier ~~~eral Charles Banfill, Director of ~~~lligence (left). **Below:** Major ~~~eral William Kepner (left), ~~~mmander of the VIIIth Fighter ~~~mmand. To the right is ~~~tenant Bob Johnson of the ~~~ Fighter Group who, leading ~~~t P-47s, tried unsuccessfully to ~~~ect the massive German attack ~~~ation engaging the 13th ~~~nbat Wing over Haseluenne on ~~~arch 1944. (USAF.)

escorts that made possible the attack on Berlin. **Left:** P-51B Mustangs of the 354th Fighter Group, one of 9th Air Force units which took part in the mission. **Above:** P-38J Lightnings of the 364th Fighter Group. **Below:** P-47D Thunderbolt of the 56th Fighter Group. (USAF.)

The two heavy bomber types used during the 6 March mission. **Above:** B-17G Fortresses of the 381st Bomb Group. **Below:** a B-24J Liberator of the 445th Bomb Group. (USAF, Miller.)

otos taken at Rattlesden, home of the 447th Bomb Group, early on the morning of 6th March 1944. This
t's B-17s were the first to take off for the attack on Berlin. **Above:** crews at the briefing at about 5 am;
geant Ed Leighty, one of the witnesses, is third from the left in the front row. **Below:** about to set out by
ck for their aircraft at 6.45 am; Leighty is in the truck, on the left. All the Group's bombers returned after the
ssion. (Leighty.)

Above: view from above as B-17s of the 388th Bomb Group, forming the Low Box of the 45th Combat Wing A Formation, assemble on top of cloud over Wisbech at 9.45 am on the morning of 6 March. When complete the formation would comprise 11 aircraft; five would not return from the mission. **Below:** B-17s of the 94th Bomb Group climbing to attack altitude as they cross the North Sea, at about 10.20 am on 6 March. (USAF)

…otos taken from B-17s of the 94th Bomb Group, over enemy territory on the way to the target on 6 March …44. **Above:** one of the Group's aircraft, flying as part of the 4th Combat Wing B Formation. In the background …n be seen the A Formation, which led the 3rd Bomb Division during the mission. **Below:** view from the rear …he Group formation, showing the aircraft in front. (USAF, Menning.)

: the German early warning 'Wassermann' radar at Bergen in Holland, almost directly under the point where
bomber stream crossed the coast on its way to Berlin on 6 March.
ve: aerial view of the German fighter control bunker at Deelen in Holland, from which the operations of
ter Division 3 were controlled. **Below:** artist's view of the inside of a German fighter control bunker during
ction. On the far right is the translucent screen used as a situation map, on which were projected from the
lights to show the positions of hostile and friendly aircraft. The fighter controllers sat at the desks in the center.

Left: Hauptmann Rolf Hermichen the commander of Ist Gruppe of Fighter Geschwader 11, led the German attack formation which struck at the 13th Combat Wing over Haseluenne. During the action that followed he was credited with the destruction of two B-17s and P-47.

Below: the Me 109 piloted by Feldwebel Friedrich Ungar of Fighter Geschwader 54 (inset) crash landed near Homfeld after being hit by Lieutenant Barney Casteel in a P-47 of the 56th Fighter Group. (Bundesarchiv, Ungar.)

...nel 'Hub' Zemke led the P-47s of the 56th Fighter Group during the ...on on 6 March. During one of the initial combats he shot down the ...190 piloted by Leutnant Wolfgang Kretchmer (inset); the German pilot ... able to bail out of his blazing fighter only seconds before it plunged ...the ground. (USAF, Kretchmer.)

Above: Oberleutnant Heinz Kn⸢e⸣
of IInd Gruppe of Fighter
Geschwader 11 seated on his
Messerschmitt 109. Knoke was
action twice on 6 March, and w
shot up on the ground at Wuns
by a strafing Mustang. During t⸢he⸣
initial action, east of Haseluenn⸢e⸣
he was credited with a B-17
destroyed. By coincidence his ⸢wife⸣
Lilo and daughter Ingrid, **left**, w
photographed watching the bat⸢tle⸣
high above from beside their
guesthouse at Pogenhagen nea⸢r⸣
Wunstorf. (Knoke.)

damage would continue forward a long way before it struck the ground four miles below. The wreckage of Miner's bomber came to earth just outside the small town of Quakenbrueck, 20 miles to the east of Haseluenne. Six of the ten crew descended, more slowly, by parachute.

Lieutenant William Terry's B-17 'Terry and the Pirates' also fell away in a diving spiral and suffered a similar fate to Miner's aircraft. Again the tail section broke away and the plexiglas nose caved in. Navigator Lieutenant Robert Schremser managed to struggle out of the hole and parachute to safety; behind him the copilot and bombardier, fighting to open the front escape hatch, went down with the aircraft. The tail gunner went down trapped in his compartment as did one of the waist gunners who became entangled in loose control cables which flayed around after the tail had broken away. But ball turret gunner Sergeant James Bain, in the most difficult position of all to escape, succeeded in extricating himself from his turret and jumped from the open rear fuselage. The wings and fuselage of the bomber fell near Quakenbrueck and the bomb load exploded. The tail section fluttered to earth some distance away. There were only three survivors.

Lieutenant George Brannan's bomber was hit during the attack and Sergeant Robyn Fulton in the ball turret suffered wounds to his right arm and leg, and his intercom was shot out. He lowered his guns to the vertical position and opened the hatch at the back of the turret, then painfully eased himself up into the fuselage. As he emerged he was horrified to see both right engines burning fiercely. 'I looked forwards toward the bomb bay and a great stream of gasoline was pouring out of the right wing. It was quite evident it would only be a matter of seconds before the plane blew up. I put on my parachute then tried to release the waist hatch but it would not go. So I took a hard dive at the hatch and out I went, hatch and all! A few seconds later the ship exploded.' Eight of the crew managed to jump to safety.

Less fortunate were the crew of Lieutenant Zeb Kendall's B-17, which left the formation at about this time and disappeared without trace. It probably blew up before anyone could jump clear, there were no survivors.

Three of the crew managed to bail out of Lieutenant Merril Rish's B-17 before it blew up; and afterwards the navigator, top turret gunner and a waist gunner were lucky to be thrown clear by the explosion and to parachute to earth. Wreckage cascaded down over a wide area just outside Quakenbrueck.

Piloting B-17 'Half and Half' Lieutenant John Lautenschlager saw his position was hopeless as the fire began to take hold in the fuselage behind him. He gave the order to abandon the bomber then climbed out of his seat and, standing in the catwalk, held the aircraft straight to give his crew time to jump. Then he made his way to the nose escape hatch where he found his top turret gunner seemingly stuck in the exit. Lautenschlager pushed the man clear then dived after him. The blazing bomber continued eastwards in a shallow descent.

From his vantage point with the 45th Combat Wing, following the 13th, Lowell Watts observed the wild and frenzied scene in front of him: 'About two or three miles ahead of us was the 13th Combat Wing. Little dots that were German fighters were diving into the formations and attacking. Out of one high squadron a B-17 slowly climbed away from the formation, the entire wing a mass of flame. I looked again a second later. There was a flash – then nothing but little specks drifting, tumbling down. Seconds later another bomber tipped up on a wing, rolled over and dived straight for the ground. Little white puffs of parachutes began to float beneath us, then fall behind.'

Altogether ten B-17s went down as a result of the initial onslaught by the German fighters, nine from the 100th Bomb Group and one from the 390th. Their wrecks fell all around Quakenbrueck.

Although most of his B-17's fin and rudder had been smashed away when the FW 190 collided with it and he had been forced to leave the protection of the formation, Jack Swartout managed to hold his aircraft under control and continued determinedly eastwards. Two other B-17s of the 100th Bomb Group, knocked out of the formation at the same time, were forced to abandon the mission.

Lieutenant Mark Cope's B-17 'Superstitious Aloysius' had its left outboard engine knocked out and was forced to leave the formation. Almost immediately it came under further attack from German fighters and two gunners were severely wounded. Cope jettisoned the bombs and took the aircraft in a high speed descent for the safety of clouds below. Then he set course westward, alone.

Lieutenant Sam Barrick's aircraft, 'Barrick's Bag', had two engines knocked out and it too was forced to drop clear of the formation. The crew jettisoned the bombs and decided to head for the nearest non-German territory, Denmark, and put the B-17 down there.

High above the mêlée the 15 Me 109s of Guenther Specht's Gruppe, providing top cover for the attackers, now shed their drop tanks as they prepared to go into action. To the bomber crews even this innocuous move by enemy fighters appeared to have sinister overtones. Afterwards crews of the 13th Combat Wing reported: 'In the Dummer Lake area single-engined enemy aircraft were observed to drop aerial bombs which passed through the formation tumbling end over end, each leaving a grey non-persistent trail of smoke. None was seen to explode . . .'

Next it was the turn of the German fighters to suffer losses as Johnson's eight 56th Fighter Group Thunderbolts caught up with the attackers emerging from the bomber formation. Feldwebel Franz Steiner and his comrade Heinz Neuendorf, flying FW 190s with Hermichen's Gruppe, suddenly and unexpectedly came under attack from the escorts. Afterwards Major James Stewart, piloting one of the P-47s, reported: 'I took my wing man in front of the bombers and tacked on to the last of the FW 190s making these attacks. I saw 4 blazing bombers as I passed under them less than 1,000 feet. About this time I lined up good on the rear FW 190 and saw a lot of hits on the wings and fuselage. The enemy aircraft rolled over and dived vertically into cloud which was at about 3,000 feet.' Steiner looked around for Neundorf but he was nowhere to be seen. Then his own Focke-Wulf came under attack. Stewart's account continued: 'I finally closed up to within 400 yards of him and hit him first on the right wing, then on the fuselage and finally on the cockpit. His canopy blew off and he rolled over to the right and dived vertically down through the clouds.' Stewart's rounds had shattered Steiner's engine and instrument panel, the Focke-Wulf no longer responded to the stick and the German pilot could control it in its earthwards plunge only by using trim. Then the cabin began to fill with smoke and Steiner knew the time had come to part company with his fighter. He jettisoned the canopy then struggled out of the cockpit against the howling slipstream. As he fell clear his right leg struck the tail a glancing blow which dislocated the knee. Safely clear Steiner pulled the ripcord and with a reassuring 'thwack' the canopy opened.

As he emerged from the rear of the bomber formation after attacking with Sinner's Gruppe, Friedrich Ungar also found himself in trouble with P-47s. He became separated from his comrades and came under attack by Captain Walker Mahurin, another member of Johnson's force. Afterwards the American pilot reported: 'After considerable maneuvering in order to cut both altitude and speed I was in a position to attack one of these enemy aircraft, a single Me 109. As I came down on him he saw me. After one turn to the left he headed down for the clouds. I found myself closing on his tail. I fired several bursts, none of which hit him. He finally disappeared into the clouds.'

When he thought he had shaken off the enemy Ungar pulled out of his dive at about 6,000 feet. But unfortunately he emerged from cloud right in front of Mahurin's wingman, Lieutenant Barney Casteel, who takes up the story: 'The Me 109 pulled up in front of me. I gave him a couple of short bursts and saw several hits on the fuselage. I then had to rejoin Captain Mahurin when he came out of cloud.' Inside the Messerschmitt there had been a loud bang and Ungar's left foot received a stunning blow. The German pilot gave a despairing glance behind expecting to see his enemy coming in for the kill. Instead he saw a lone fighter pull out of its dive and curve away to the right. Ungar wondered why his assailant should have broken off the attack just when he had the Messerschmitt cold, but he was grateful the American pilot did. He looked down and saw the rubber sole of his flying boot torn and blood from his foot running over the floor of the cockpit. Worried he might faint at any moment from loss of blood Ungar selected a suitable field and took his Messerschmitt down for a belly landing. He set the fighter down and as it skidded over the ground it spun through a semi-circle ending up going backwards. Then, suddenly, everything was still.

The sight of the blazing bombers going down, and their frantic radio calls for assistance, drew in escort fighters from all directions. Colonel Hub Zemke, commander of the 56th Fighter Group, brought his eight Thunderbolts from the southeast where they had been covering the severed front-half of the bomber stream, and arrived at the 13th Combat Wing shortly after the initial attack ended. The only German fighter immediately visible was Oberleutnant Wolfgang Kretschmer's FW 190 which had become separated from Heinz Baer's Gruppe. Covered by the other P-47s Zemke promptly shot down the lone Focke-Wulf.

P-47s of the 78th Fighter Group also moved in to protect the bombers but they immediately became embroiled with the Me 109s of Guenther Specht's Gruppe providing top cover. Oberleutnant Heinz Knoke, leading one of the Messerschmitt Staffeln, wheeled with the German fighters as they moved to block the enemy approach: 'Specht had seen the incoming enemy fighters and took our Gruppe in a descending turn to the left to head them off. The

Thunderbolts came in below us, 12 or 14 of them. We dived on four of the P-47s but they saw us and reacted in the usual way, splitting into two pairs which turned in opposite directions. Those in front of me turned to the left but I knew the others would be curving to the right to come around behind me.' Feldwebel Hans-Gerd Wennekers, leading a pair of Messerschmitts covering Knoke's tail, moved to engage these Thunderbolts and radioed a brief warning to his leader: '*Achtung!* Indians [enemy fighters] behind you!' Knoke replied with a curt '*Danke!*' and, holding his turn as he tried to get into position to fire at the P-47 in front, glanced back in an attempt to see the enemy fighter behind. But the latter was nowhere to be seen; almost certainly it was in the most dangerous position of all behind his tail. Knoke broke off the chase and pulled into a steep climbing turn, then glanced back and caught sight of the Thunderbolt beneath him with a Messerschmitt close behind. Wennekers loosed off an accurate burst and the escort fell away trailing smoke. The American pilot, Flight Officer Edward Downey of the 78th Fighter Group, went down with his aircraft. Triumphantly Wennekers informed his leader 'I've got him!' '*Dankeschoen!*', replied Knoke.

The dogfight now became general with Messerschmitts and Thunderbolts curving tightly trying to get into firing positions or to avoid enemy fighters endeavouring to do so. Wennekers fired a brief burst at a second P-47 which flashed across his nose, then pulled hard left to get on yet another of the American fighters. The P-47 Wennekers had fired at second, piloted by 1st Lieutenant Walter Tonkin of the same squadron as Downey, swung around vengefully on to Wennekers's tail however. Glancing rearwards the German pilot noticed Tonkin behind about 800 yards away but felt so long as he was in the turn the range was too great for accurate shooting; he kept up the chase, keeping a wary eye on his own pursuer. Afterwards Tonkin reported: 'We were bounced by Me 109s who were diving at extreme angles. One of them fastened on Lockyear White 2's tail. I followed from 23,000 feet at 350 mph and fired several short bursts at a range of 700 yards to shake the enemy aircraft off the Number 2's tail. Shortly afterwards the enemy aircraft broke off.'

Tonkin's despairing attempt to force the Messerschmitt off his comrade's tail was more successful than he could have hoped. He saw hits but claimed the enemy fighter only as 'damaged'. In fact Wennekers's aircraft had been badly hit. One round went clean through the German pilot's left forearm, knocking it off the throttle and spattering the cockpit with blood. Knowing he could not land the aircraft without being able to operate his throttle and fearing he might pass out for lack of blood at any moment, Wennekers jettisoned the canopy and undid his seat straps. He then thrust the stick hard away from him and popped cleanly out of the cockpit, like a cork out of a champagne bottle. Deep in shock and feeling no pain, Wennekers clutched his bleeding left arm and curled into a ball as he tumbled earthwards. On the way down he passed disconcertingly close to one of the bomber formations thundering noisily eastwards. After a lengthy free-fall to the warmer air Wennekers opened his parachute.

After he had shot down Wolfgang Kretschmer's Focke-Wulf, Hub Zemke led his P-47s to attack a Messerschmitt and it too went down on fire. The escorts then reformed and were climbing back to altitude when a lone Me 109 was seen some distance away, seemingly circling aimlessly. As Zemke led his flight in to attack, however, the Messerschmitt went into a steep dive: 'Very shortly thereafter this enemy aircraft broke into violent flame and went tumbling in a vicious spin towards the earth. No rounds of ammunition had been expended by my Flight and there had been absolutely no one in the vicinity of this aircraft to cause him to burn. He was almost totally consumed by the flame before he struck the ground.' Almost certainly this 'mystery victim' was Hans-Gerd Wennekers's badly damaged Messerschmitt, from which he had jumped. The German pilot had delayed opening his parachute and so was not seen by Zemke or his pilots.

In an air battle such as this events follow each other rapidly. Everything described in the narrative of the action so far, from the time Rolf Hermichen first led his attack formation into the 13th Combat Wing, had taken place within about three minutes: between noon and 12.04 pm on that fateful Monday. So far the air battle had claimed ten B-17s and a P-47 on the American side, and three FW 190s and two Me 109s on the German side. Some 50 Americans and two Germans were descending silently by parachute and would continue to do so for several more minutes: a man on a parachute falls at about 1,000 feet per minute and several survivors had opened their parachutes above 15,000 feet.

It was 12.04 pm and, following their initial massed attack, the German fighters split into smaller units to re-attack the depleted formations of the 13th Combat Wing. Some fighters moved in to make new attacks on the formations from behind; others went down to finish off bombers which had suffered damage and been forced to leave the protection of their formations; but the majority of those German units which maintained cohesion swung around on an easterly heading and rapidly overhauled the bombers as they moved into position for further head-on attacks.

One German pilot now preparing to attack from head-on was Heinz Knoke who, following his inconclusive brush with the Thunderbolts, had decided to go for the bombers. With his wingman Unteroffizier Franz Zambelli close behind he moved out until he was about 8 miles in front of the bomber formation. Then he pulled his Messerschmitt through a semi-circle and lined up for the attack: 'I picked out one of the black specks in front and lined it up in my reflector sight. There was no movement of the bomber – I was approaching from exactly head-on. Slowly at first, but then very rapidly, he grew in my sight. At a range of about 500 meters I opened fire.' Knoke's Messerschmitt trembled as his cannon spewed 30 mm explosive rounds through the propeller hub, then small flashes appeared around the bomber's nose; slowly the B-17 sagged away from the formation.

The second German head-on attack on the 13th Combat Wing was not so concentrated as the first but it too claimed several victims. One of the first to go down was B-17 'Berlin First' of the 95th Bomb Group. Edgar Jurist in the radio compartment glanced out his window and saw the skin of the right wing peel back and part of the cowling of the right outboard engine fly off as the cannon shells burst. 'Pieces of debris flew back towards the tail of the aircraft. The attack was over in an instant. Then I had the impression we were losing height, falling away from the formation. As we were falling we came under attack again and this time we took 20 mm hits on the right side of the ship, a series of jagged holes appeared along the right side of the radio room. Tom Barksdale gave the order to bail out over the interphone. "We're going down. We're going down. Bail out! Bail! Bail!" ' In the nose of the B-17 bombardier August Briding made his way to the open escape hatch. The navigator seemed to be hesitating beside the opening so Briding 'assisted' him out, then followed. Jurist clipped on his parachute and made his way to the door at the rear of the aircraft. 'The ball turret gunner, Andrew Brown, could not get his turret into the vertical position to get out. He was trapped. But Charles Hatton, one of the waist gunners, began using the hand crank to wind the ball turret into the vertical position so Brown could escape. There seemed nothing I could do so I made my way to the exit.' As Jurist jumped he heard the roar of the bombers' engines and the 'Took – took – took' of gunfire quickly recede. Then everything went quiet. 'I found it exhilarating rather than frightening with no real sense of falling. It all seemed unreal. I could not believe this was happening to me and my crew.' After a long fall Jurist finally pulled his ripcord. 'Immediately after my chute opened there was an Me 109 coming past me. He must have seen nothing, then suddenly the blossoming of a chute to one side of him within 100 feet. I couldn't believe my eyes and neither could he! He just looked at me in astonishment, and continued on his way.'

August Briding also made a long drop before he pulled his ripcord. After his parachute opened he looked up and saw nine other white canopies: all the crew had escaped from the bomber, which crashed near the small village of Barnstorf.

To the left of where Jurist and Briding's aircraft had been in the 95th Bomb Group formation, Lieutenant Tom Keasbey's B-17 was also hit. In the nose bombardier Lieutenant 'Hoss' Bowling had been busily engaging the German fighters coming from ahead when the navigator tapped him on the shoulder and pointed to the blazing left outboard engine. 'Nothing was heard on the intercom but I assumed the time had come to abandon the aircraft. I slipped off my flak suit, clipped on my chest parachute, unclipped my oxygen mask and went out of the front hatch after the navigator. I must have then passed out for lack of oxygen because the next thing I knew I was falling through space. I immediately pulled the ripcord and my chute opened. I saw our ship go down and hit the ground.' Bowling's aircraft crashed 8 miles south of Bremen after all of the crew had bailed out safely.

After checking there were no escorts near, Rudolf Sinner pulled his Messerschmitt in pursuit of a Fortress which had been knocked out of the formation. But before he could get close he saw the crew abandoning it. The bomber was already done for. Then he spotted another B-17 which appeared to be in a similar predicament and moved to engage it. Sinner closed rapidly but before he reached firing range for his weapons the American gunners were scoring hits on the Messerschmitt. The fighter suffered damage and Sinner's left thigh was cut by flying splinters. In spite of the pain he closed in to short range and opened up with cannon and machine guns at the bomber. His explosive rounds were bursting around the tail when the Messerschmitt's guns stopped firing. Sinner squeezed the trigger again but nothing happened. He knew he had plenty of ammunition: almost certainly enemy rounds had damaged the electrical firing circuits. As the fighter rapidly overhauled the Fortress, Sinner banked steeply to the left and curved underneath it. Then, suddenly, the Messerschmitt shuddered under the impact of hits from its intended victim. Immediately afterwards there was a further, far heavier, blow against Sinner's left thigh: a .50 caliber round had gone right through it from top to bottom almost parallel to the bone. At the same time the engine burst into flames and the Messerschmitt fell spinning out of control. Sinner released his canopy and undid his straps but because of the wound to his leg he found it almost impossible to stand in the cockpit against the 'G' forces induced by the spin. And when he finally managed it the powerful slipstream got hold of his arms and whisked them against the sides of the fuselage, pinning him helplessly against his back armor half in and half out of the blazing fighter. For what seemed an eternity but was probably closer to ten seconds Sinner was unable to move against the hurricane blast of ice-cold air. Then, with no action on his part, he was mercifully free and tumbling clear of the aircraft. After a lengthy drop he opened his parachute.

Not far from where Sinner had engaged the B-17, Oberfeldwebel Hermann Reinthaler pulled his Messerschmitt in behind to finish off another: 'Ronnie R' of the 100th Bomb Group, which had already been hit and forced out of the formation. Reinthaler fired a long burst into the bomber and saw it start to go down. Manning the top turret Van Pinner heard the bail-out order with a certain annoyance: 'I was so busy concentrating on my gun sight there was little time to notice what was going on around me. Even though our aircraft was going down I didn't want to get out – there were still some good targets for me to shoot at. I had been enjoying the fight up till then, I was having a ball!' Sergeant Bob Ray in the radio compartment viewed the world around him with somewhat less enjoyment. Reinthaler's rounds had started a fire there which soon reached the rack containing recognition flares; the scene was like a firework display that had got out of control: 'There were reds and greens shooting off, hurtling down the fuselage and bouncing off the walls.' Because of the fire Ray's only escape route was through the bomb bay where the bombs were still in place in the racks. 'The bomb doors were shut but they were supposed to swing open if a pressure greater than 100 pounds was exerted on them. I jumped off the catwalk on to the bomb doors but they just stayed closed, firm as a rock. Then as I was trying to climb back on the catwalk somebody salvoed the bombs and the next thing I knew they were falling and I was going down after them!' Van Pinner followed Ray through the bomb bay clutching his parachute pack under his arm, then calmly clipped it on the harness as he was falling through space: 'I was amazed to see the amount of debris, bits of aircraft and falling men on parachutes all around me. I remember seeing one man falling with his parachute streamed out behind him like a ribbon; he was looking up at it and there was a trail of smoke coming from it. It had burned . . .'

Reinthaler sat off to one side and watched the American crewmen bail out of 'Ronnie R'; all jumped safely apart from the ball turret gunner who had been killed during an earlier attack. The B-17 went down steeply and smashed into a small wood just west of Bassum. Reinthaler circled the crash to note its position so he could claim the kill later then, his fuel beginning to run low, he turned northeast for his base at Rotenburg.

As he rolled out on the new heading Reinthaler noticed three fighters, which he took to be FW 190s, coming towards him. Moments later he realized his error: they were P-47s. Reinthaler slammed open his throttle to get maximum speed but with the advantage of altitude the American fighters overhauled him easily. Leading the escorts was Lieutenant Robert Wise of the 78th Fighter Group, who afterwards reported that during his dive after the Messerschmitt he passed a B-17 breaking up in the air and several parachutes. Then 'I shot two or three bursts of two seconds each at the 109 with about $1\frac{1}{2}$ to $1\frac{3}{4}$ rings deflection at 600 yards. No hits were observed. I closed to 300 yards and with three one-second bursts I saw hits around the fuselage. By the time he reached the deck I had to pull up over him.' By this time Wise was alone; he had outdistanced his companions who broke off the chase. Wise pulled his fighter into a sweeping turn to the left and in doing so lost sight of his victim, which appeared only to be damaged; 36 years would pass before he would learn of the effect of the attack.

In fact Wise's rounds had caused fearful damage to both the Messerschmitt and its pilot. Hermann Reinthaler is a big man, more than six feet tall and powerfully built; now his very size proved a terrible disadvantage, for his frame overlapped the back armor plate of the Me 109. One of Wise's rounds slammed into the German pilot's left elbow, carrying away the joint and leaving his forearm hanging from a few strips of flesh. Reinthaler felt no pain and it seemed he was no more than an interested spectator to the horrifying scene. Thinking with great clarity despite the shock of his wounds, he saw flames licking back from his engine and realized he had to get out of the fighter. He hauled the nose of the Messerschmitt into a vertical climb, converting airspeed into precious altitude. Then he grasped the useless left forearm, placed it across his lap and released the canopy. By now the Messerschmitt was standing on its tail almost stalled. Reinthaler released his straps and kicked himself away from the blazing fighter. As he fell backwards and clear, the tail flashed past his head.

Although now out of the Messerschmitt Reinthaler still faced ghastly problems. He was perilously close to the ground and his initial grab failed to find the D-shaped ripcord handle in its accustomed place on the left of his stomach; he glanced down and saw that part of the harness had been ripped to pieces by enemy bullets, the ripcord itself swinging freely in the airflow. It did not help that the remains of his left forearm, now attached only by the tendons, flailed around above his head in grotesque imitation of a helicopter rotor. With a desperate lunge Reinthaler grabbed the handle and pulled it. In the next instant, before the canopy had time to open properly, his fall was checked by a large oak tree which luckily happened to be in the way and whose branches caught the silken folds. The pilot was snatched to a halt, bouncing up and down like a yo-yo hanging from his rigging lines. He came to rest six feet off the ground. Reinthaler released his straps and fell to earth, where a sharp pain announced he had been wounded in the left foot also. Collapsed in a bleeding heap on the ground the pilot was still fully conscious; such is the fickleness of shock he felt no pain from his shattered left arm, while the relatively minor wound to his foot gave agony.

After hitting a B-17 in his initial head-on attack, Officer Cadet Feldwebel Emil Demuth hit a second during a further head-on firing pass in his FW 190 and his wingman saw it leave the formation. Moving back to rejoin the fray he caught sight of a lone B-17 far below the others heading westwards. A straggler! That would make an easy victim for his wingman, an inexperienced young officer whose bravery had been called to question a few days earlier. As Demuth led the officer into a firing position, however, the pair were observed by P-47s of the 56th Fighter Group led by Lieutenant Joe Icard: 'In the vicinity of Dummer Lake I spotted two FW 190s at about 8,000 feet flying in close formation. Attacking from dead astern, I closed to about 250 yards then opened fire. There was a heavy concentration of strikes all over the fuselage and the Jerry immediately burst into flames.'

The 'Jerry' Icard had hit was Emil Demuth who, in guiding his inexperienced companion into a firing position, had allowed his search for enemy fighters to lapse for a few disastrous moments. The first thing he knew of the attack was when his Focke-Wulf shuddered under the impact of hits, oil sprayed over his windshield and the cockpit started to fill with smoke. Demuth pulled around sharply to the left and was horrified to see five P-47s curving in to attack. Before he could do anything to extricate himself from this embarrassing position the Focke-Wulf was hit again and this time the engine burst into flames. Demuth jettisoned his canopy and felt a searing pain as the flames swept over his head, burning all flesh not protected by his flying jacket, goggles, oxygen mask and helmet. He undid his straps, kicked the stick forward and the fighter fell away leaving Demuth falling clear. After a long fall he opened his parachute only to find that those terrible flames were still with him: looking down, he saw his pants on fire. Struggling like a madman, suspended from his parachute harness in space, he reached down and beat out the flames with his gloved hands.

While the 13th Combat Wing was being cut to pieces by the German fighters, the front half of the bomber stream wandered through further flak zones as it endeavored to get back on the correct route. One bomber hit at this time was Bryce Smith's aircraft, the 447th Bomb Group B-17 which had been the first of all to take off for the mission. The supercharger of the left inboard engine was wrecked and shell splinters punctured two tanks causing fuel to run into the wing and stream out of the trailing edge. Smith abandoned the mission and turned for home.

Another aircraft hit by flak was that piloted by Lieutenant Ben Fourmy of the 91st Bomb Group. His B-17 had a salvo of shells burst close alongside which knocked out an engine on each side. Fourmy ordered the bombs jettisoned and dived away from the formation, turning westwards for home as he did so. By hugging the ground Fourmy hoped it would still be possible to get back to England. But the move would bring only a temporary respite.

With the American bombers passing over his airfield at Quakenbrueck, Oberleutnant Hermann Greiner of Night Fighter Geschwader 1 was worried in case it might come under attack at any moment. So he considered it prudent to order the Messerschmitt 110s of his night fighter training unit to get airborne and keep out of the area until the danger had passed. Greiner himself had just taken off and was climbing through 600 feet when he was astonished to see a B-17 about 300 feet higher than he was flying west across his nose: 'I was probably even more surprised than the B-17 crew!' Leaving flaps and landing gear down Greiner curved left to bring his sight to bear, opened fire and saw his rounds bursting on the bomber. At the end of the firing pass Greiner found himself in trouble; when he had first seen the enemy his Messerschmitt had bare flying speed and in pulling around to attack he had taken the night fighter perilously close to a stall. Now he had to leave the bomber, ease his wings level retract the flaps and gear and let his speed build up, before he could do anything else.

The bomber Greiner had attacked was Ben Fourmy's B-17, which had blundered across Quakenbrueck airfield on its way to England at low altitude. In the copilot's seat Lieutenant Herbert Markle caught a brief glimpse of Greiner's Messerschmitt, then the latter's accurate burst knocked out one of the two good engines and started an uncontrollable fire in the fuselage. Lacking power, Fourmy searched for a suitable field in which to crash-land. At about this time the B-17 came under fire from 20 mm automatic guns of Light Flak Abteilung 844 and Home Guard Flak Batterie 95-IX; such was the confusion on board the Fortress, however, this attack went unnoticed.

By the time Greiner had his Messerschmitt in fighting trim the B-17 had disappeared. Fearing there might be escorting Thunderbolts in the area he hastened back to Quakenbrueck and landed.

Ben Fourmy put the B-17 on the ground at Loxton to the southwest of Quakenbrueck. When the blazing bomber came to rest the surviving crew members scrambled out though for Herbert Markle this was no easy task: 'In the panic to get out I forgot to take off my flak jacket. As I tried to push my way out of the cockpit side window I got stuck and I couldn't get in or out! All around me the plane was ablaze and I thought it was going to explode at any moment. After a tremendous struggle I managed to get back into the cabin, threw off my flak jacket, then I did get out.' Two of the crew had been killed by enemy fire or in the crash; the other eight ran clear of the burning aircraft and soon afterwards were rounded up by German troops.

Quite apart from the bombers forced out of formation by enemy action, there were those forced to abort the mission over enemy territory by technical troubles. B-24 'Balls of Fire' piloted by Lieutenant Neal Serkland of the 445th Bomb Group was well east of Quakenbrueck when it suffered a complete electrical failure to the left inboard engine. The engine lost power and Serkland was unable to feather the propeller. The bomber fell back from the formation and its crew was forced to jettison the bombs and turn back. Then an even more serious problem arose. The tremendous strain, as the windmilling propeller turned the failed engine, caused the propeller shaft to snap. The propeller, now spinning freely, started to move forwards away from the engine until Serkland could see it some 6 inches adrift from its normal position. Afraid the propeller might come away and smash into the side of the aircraft, the pilot throttled back and was relieved to see the propeller move back into its proper position. But to hold it there Serkland had to reduce speed to 130 mph. By now he was down to 12,000 feet, alone, heading west across Germany. Suddenly the bomber came under uncomfortably accurate fire from a heavy flak battery. One round scored a direct hit on the bomber but fortunately was fused to explode somewhat higher; it passed clean through the wing between the two left engines leaving a jagged hole about a foot across.

There was little time to give thanks for the narrow escape when the lone B-24 came under attack from German fighters. 'They just came in from behind, stayed there and shot us up. The bomb bay caught fire and I gave the order to abandon,' Serkland later recounted. As the pilot struggled to prevent the aircraft going into a steep dive the loose propeller finally did come away. 'It smashed through the side of the cabin and knocked me to the floor. The blade must have hit my leg flat or it would have taken the leg off; it certainly hit me hard,' Serkland later explained. 'Then the aircraft blew up. One moment I was on the floor of the cabin after being hit by the propeller, the next thing I knew I was on my back falling through space – with the entire nose section of the B-24 coming down directly above me!' After what seemed an age the nose section drifted to one side and Serkland was able to open his parachute. Three of the bomber's crew were killed or mortally wounded during the action. The tail gunner had had his left leg nearly shot off during one of the fighter attacks; he succeeded in bailing out of the bomber but on reaching the ground his parachute caught in a tree and he bled to death before he could be reached. The bombardier also bailed out and opened his parachute but the canopy was set on fire by burning debris from the aircraft and the unfortunate man fell to his death. The remains of the B-24 came to earth scattered over a wide area to the northeast of Fürstenau.

It was Van Pinner's 23rd birthday and he was not happy. After parachuting from his B-17 he landed in a plowed field, but even before he touched down an excited crowd of German civilians was advancing on him menacingly. Pinner quickly shed his parachute then drew his pistol to hold them at bay: 'One old man had a long scythe, he looked just like Old Father Time. I'm sure he would have sliced me up for washers if he hadn't seen the pistol. Some of the others started to throw rocks at me but the pistol stopped them from doing what I should have done in their place.' Shortly afterwards a pair of German soldiers arrived on a motor cycle. They quickly dismounted and, while one dropped to one knee and leveled his rifle at Pinner, the other advanced on the American and held out his hand for the pistol. Only too pleased to have them take him prisoner, Pinner carefully handed over the weapon. Deprived of their prize the civilians·shook fists and hurled insults at the captured *Terrorflieger*.

Bob Ray, the radio operator in Pinner's crew, came down in an open patch of ground surrounded by woodland. And nearby Charles Allen, one of the waist gunners, also landed. Ray had just hidden his parachute in a snow-covered ditch when: 'Charles Allen came running into the clearing and shouted "The Germans are right behind me!" Sure enough, there were two or three soldiers. They pointed their guns at us and I started grabbing air. One of them asked "*Pistole?*" I just pointed down to my holster. I didn't want to give him any excuse to shoot me, I just let him get it.' Disarmed, the two airmen were escorted to the soldiers' Volkswagen 'jeep'.

Hermann Reinthaler, who had shot down Pinner's, Ray's and Allen's B-17 and then himself been shot down by Robert Wise in his Thunderbolt, lay on the ground after he released himself from the parachute harness suspended from the trees. His left arm, almost severed at the elbow, was bleeding profusely. Then he caught sight of three women in tall white hats running towards him, nuns who worked as nurses at the nearby maternity hospital. One was binding his arm when a new Mercedes car came bumping across the grass and stopped beside the cluster of people. 'Get in!' the driver shouted. Still deep in shock Reinthaler replied 'I can't. You'll get blood all over your seats!' 'Never mind. Get in!' the man ordered and Reinthaler, not really wishing to argue, complied. The car bounced slowly over the grass to the nearby road then, as it accelerated away, it passed the remains of Reinthaler's Messerschmitt. The aircraft had bored its way deep into the ground and only the tail could be seen. Shortly afterwards the wounded pilot was off-loaded at the maternity hospital at Bassum. He was wheeled straight into the operating room where the resident doctor gave him an anesthetic and began working on the shattered arm.

A few miles away Ed Jurist landed in a potato field, stunned, after bailing out of his B-17. He released his parachute and the wind carried it away. Then he looked up and all around he saw parachutes, twenty or thirty of them, hanging in the sky like white flower petals. He watched, fascinated, as they descended out of sight. Then he noticed eight or nine German civilians, some with hunting rifles, advancing on him excitedly. 'At first their leader thought I was German; then the truth dawned and he pointed his rifle at me. I didn't put my hands up – I was still too stunned. They took me to a farmhouse where the farmer, his wife and young daughter were having lunch. I was offered a chair and sat down and watched them eat.'

After bailing out of his Messerschmitt, Hans-Gerd Wennekers ended up caught in a tree, dangling from his rigging lines about twelve feet off the ground. The bullet wound to his left forearm was bleeding so he wound his scarf around it to staunch the flow. The first on the scene was a farm laborer who ran to get help. Shortly afterwards three German soldiers arrived and one pointed his rifle at the pilot. 'Put that gun away *Arschloecher*!' Wennekers swore at him. The soldier, no doubt feeling only a German would employ such a low form of abuse, lowered his rifle. One of the soldiers commandeered a ladder and a horse and cart and after getting Wennekers down the men took him to the hospital at Quakenbrueck.

Ralph Bowling came to earth after bailing out of his B-17 to find his right ankle broken; almost certainly he had struck some part of the bomber immediately after leaving the escape hatch. As he landed two young German boys and a man with a gun were waiting for him. Bowling released his parachute and the party advanced on him: 'The Germans could see I had injured my ankle ar,d they helped me to the nearby farm house. The family were having lunch and they offered me some but I was still in shock and not very interested. They were friendly but spoke only German, so I could not talk to them,' Bowling was given a chair and while he waited two others from his bomber were brought in.

After crash landing his Messerschmitt, following the brush with P-47s, Friedrich Ungar was too shaken to climb out of the aircraft. He just opened the canopy and sat in the cockpit examining his wounds. An explosive .50 caliber round had struck the left of the fuselage and made a large hole, sending splinters into his left arm, thigh and foot. The worst injuries were to his foot and he noticed a splinter almost an inch long embedded in his shin bone. Though he was losing quite a lot of blood Ungar felt no pain. After waiting some minutes the German pilot fired three red flares from his signal pistol to summon attention. A few minutes later he heard voices and shouted in their direction 'Come here and help me, I'm wounded!' A farmer and laborer arrived on the scene, helped Ungar out of his aircraft and carried him to the farm house some distance away. 'There,' Ungar later wrote, 'the Eickhoff family spared no effort to make me comfortable. The bed in the guest room was freshly made and I had to get in. The farmer's daughter, Dora, brought me a bottle of schnapps. She said I was to take a swig whenever I felt pain. Whenever I felt anything I did and the pain immediately went away!' Farmer Eickhoff telephoned for an ambulance but there were so many calls for them that afternoon that Friedrich Ungar would have to remain some hours in his not-unpleasant surroundings.

Earl Richardson landed by parachute only about a hundred yards from the blazing wreckage of the B-17 he had so recently abandoned. After shedding his harness he ran to a nearby ditch where he took off his flying suit and distinctive leather flying jacket. On the horizon about a mile away he could make out a wooded area and decided to make for it and hide till nightfall. But he had got only a few yards when he heard a shouted order to halt and, looking around, found himself being covered by two German soldiers with rifles.

Rob Fulton ended up dangling from a tree on his parachute, his feet just off the ground. But because of wounds to his right arm he could not release the harness. The first to reach him were a farmer and his small son. 'I do not know how I could have understood the conversation because I do not speak German. But it was as clear as if he had spoken in English. He wanted to know if I was carrying a gun and I told him "No". He then pulled out a big knife and could tell from the look of horror on my face I thought he was going to butcher me. But he hit himself on the chest and said "Good German!" Then he used the knife to cut away the shrouds of the parachute to free me.' Fulton dropped to the ground unable to walk and was picked up soon afterwards by Luftwaffe personnel who drove him to the nearby airfield at Quakenbrueck.

By 12.25 pm the battle was starting to peter out, as those German fighters with ammunition remaining began to run short of fuel and were forced to land. The defending pilots put down their aircraft at the nearest convenient airfield, with the result that there was considerable fragmentation of units. The IInd Gruppe of Fighter Geschwader 1 based at Rheine, for example, had sent off 21 FW 190s that morning; of the 18 which survived the action only two returned to Rheine, the remaining 16 landed in ones and twos at nine other airfields spread across the north German plain.

Oberleutnant Heinz Knoke of IInd Gruppe of Fighter Geschwader 11

ANATOMY OF A DISASTER

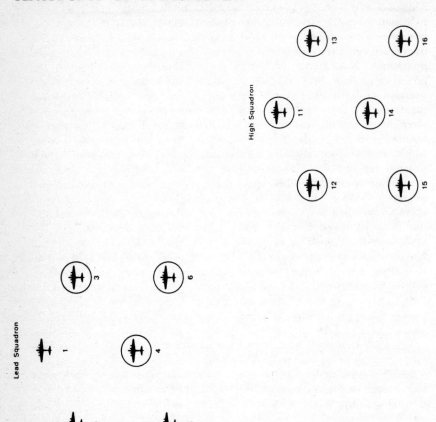

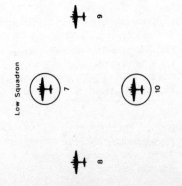

returned to his base at Wunstorf and flew low overhead, rocking the wings of his Messerschmitt to tell everyone he had scored a kill. Then he pulled around for a tight pattern, pushed the button to extend the gear, checked both green lights had lit to show the wheels were locked down then lined up for a landing. 'At that moment a red flare rose in front of me and I heard an excited voice in my earphones: "Your right wheel is not down!" I checked my panel and the two green lights were still showing. Obviously something was very wrong! I overshot and tried to retract the gear, but the green lights remained on indicating the gear was down and locked.' Knoke made a wide circuit and set the fighter down on the grass as gently as he could. 'At first everything seemed normal, then as I lost speed the right wing slowly dropped and the Messerschmitt skidded off in a wide circle to the right. Only the wing tip suffered damage before the aircraft came to rest.' Knoke pulled himself out of the cockpit to see the ambulance and fire truck speeding towards him. Their services would not be required. Then he examined the landing gear for some explanation for the odd indications he had seen in his cockpit. One glance told him the lights had not lied, the right leg was indeed locked down. But enemy bullets had severed the leg about one-third of the way down. The rest of the leg and the wheel had gone, only the stump remained. The enemy rounds had also torn away the hydraulic lines to the leg; this had prevented Knoke from retracting his gear for a belly landing.

Seen from above is the Low Box of the 13th Combat Wing, B Formation, the unit hardest hit by German fighters which began attacking over Haseluenne at noon. Twenty B-17s of the 100th Bomb Group had taken off for the mission and assembled into the Box, but four had turned back before or soon after reaching enemy territory. The positions of the aircraft, with pilot's names, are shown at the time the German fighters attacked; bombers which failed to return are ringed.

1. Swartout, near Haseluenne rammed by or collided with an FW 190 which knocked away the top of the fin and rudder. Seriously damaged, the bomber continued the mission.
2. Helmick, flew mission.
3. Handorf, survived the initial fighter attacks and reached Berlin, shot down on the return flight.
4. Brannan, shot down during the Haseluenne action.
5. Shoens, flew mission.
6. Rish, shot down during the Haseluenne action.
7. Montgomery, shot down during the Haseluenne action.
8. Ferbasche, flew mission.
9. Lacy, flew mission.
10. Koper, shot down during the Haseluenne action.
11. Miner, shot down during the Haseluenne action.
12. Kendall, aircraft and crew missing without trace, probably shot down during the Haseluenne action.
13. Barton, shot down during the Haseluenne action.
14. Radke, shot down during the Haseluenne action.
15. Terry, shot down during the Haseluennea action.
16. Barrick, seriously damaged during the Haseluenne action, landed in Sweden.

On his two surviving engines Lieutenant Sam Barrick of the 100th Bomb Group managed to get his B-17, 'Barrick's Bag', as far as Denmark. After a slow descent he was able to hold the crippled aircraft level at about 1,500 feet. Suddenly, however, the crewmen were horrified to see a large airfield passing beneath them with numerous black-crossed aircraft sitting in the dispersal points. Top turret gunner James Brady felt his throat dry as he gazed on the scene: 'Somebody in our plane remarked "Now our goose is cooked!" If I had had any toilet paper I could certainly have used it then! But for some reason they ignored us, there was not even any flak.' Considering everything the B-17 was holding up remarkably well. Barrick resolved to try and make it to neutral Sweden.

From start to finish the battle had lasted about 25 minutes and extended some 75 miles eastwards from Haseluenne. Altogether twenty bombers had been shot down; one more had suffered damage and was on its way to Sweden and other damaged bombers were making their way back to England. Three escorting P-47s had also been shot down. For its part the Luftwaffe lost about twelve Messerschmitts and Focke-Wulfs during the action.

The defenders had concentrated their attentions against the 13th Combat Bomb Wing, and in particular against the B Formation which suffered a fearful mauling. By the end of the action the Low Group had ceased to exist as a fighting unit. Originally it comprised sixteen B-17s of the 100th Bomb Group, after five had aborted the mission early. Now nothing remained of the High Squadron, there were only three bombers of the Lead Squadron and two from the Low Squadron continuing the mission; after the shock of seeing comrades going down all around them the survivors moved out to join other formations. The Lead Group of the B Formation had lost three bombers, all from the 100th Bomb Group. The A Formation of the 13th Wing had also suffered heavily, though not so severely as its companion: during the action the Low Group, again, had suffered the heavier losses and there the 95th Bomb Group lost six B-17s; the Lead Group, drawn from the 390th Bomb Group, lost only one. Although one bomber wing had suffered a terrible battering, the other ten had been untouched by the savage German attack and now continued eastward in stately procession.

Thus far the laurels for the action had gone to the Luftwaffe. Less than half its fighters had yet been committed and they had inflicted severe blows on two bomb groups. An even stronger attack formation, comprising single-engined and twin-engined fighters of the Luftwaffe 1st and 7th Fighter Divisions, was already assembled and being directed into position to intercept the bombers thundering eastwards. Behind these were the powerful flak defenses covering the target. And on their return flight the bombers would have to run the gauntlet of fighters now refuelling and re-arming at airfields in northwestern Germany, being made ready for their second mission of the day. The raiders had passed only the first of four great hurdles.

CHAPTER 4
THE DESTROYERS STRIKE

12.25 to 1.04 pm

You could not be successful in such an action without a large loss.
We must make up our minds to affairs of this kind sometimes, or
give up the game.

The Duke of Wellington

Even while the attack formation of the Luftwaffe 2nd and 3rd Fighter Divisions was opening its battle with the American bomber formations over Haseluenne, the attack formation from the 1st and 7th Fighter Divisions was starting to assemble over Magdeburg to the west of Berlin in readiness for the next great battle. Leading this formation was Major Hans Kogler of the IIIrd Gruppe of Destroyer Geschwader 26, with seven Me 110 twin-engined fighters. 'There were clear skies over Magdeburg and from 3,000 meters we could see the city clearly,' Kogler later recalled. 'Had there been cloud the flak people would have fired colored smoke shells to mark the assembly point for us, but on this occasion there was no need. I led my Gruppe in a sweeping left turn and one by one the other destroyer and fighter Gruppen slotted in behind.'

Immediately behind Kogler's unit came ten Messerschmitt 410 destroyers of the IInd Gruppe led by Oberleutnant Friedrich Stehle, each with four 21 cm rockets under its wings. Behind them came twenty-four Me 110s of Ist and IInd Gruppen of Destroyer Geschwader 76, also carrying rockets and led by Hauptmann Hermann Kaminski, which had come up from Ansbach in Frankonia 190 miles to the south.

Following the twin-engined destroyers came 55 Messerschmitt 109s from the Ist, IInd and IVth Gruppen of Fighter Geschwader 3. 'Our orders were to cover the destroyers so they could get through the enemy escorts and reach the bombers,' explained Leutnant Hans Iffland of the IVth Gruppe. 'But once they were through to the bombers they had to look after themselves, for then the single-engined fighters' orders were to attack the bombers also.' Tagged on the end of the formation were the remaining fighter units, of varying effectiveness against daylight raiding forces, which the Luftwaffe had been able to scrape together for the action: seven FW 190s of Sturmstaffel 1, especially heavily armored for short range fire-fights with the American bombers; eight Me 109s of the single-engined night fighter unit Fighter Geschwader 302; and a couple of

THE OPPOSING FORCES AT 12.40 pm

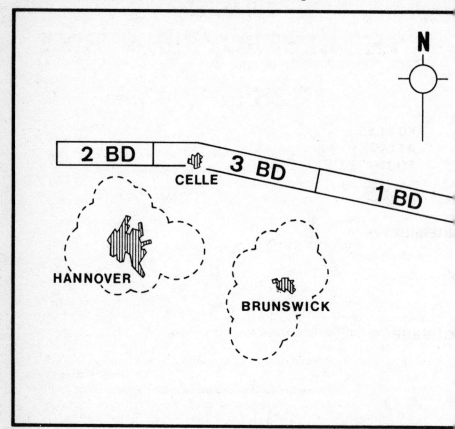

Approximate positions of the opposing forces at 12.40 pm. The two parts of the bomber stream had rejoined and the raiding force was back on the planned route and passing the turning point at Celle. The 4th and 354th Fighter Groups, with a total of 59 P-51s, were escorting the 1st and 3rd Bomb Divisions respectively. By this time the bomber stream was about 20 minutes late along its planned route. The 33 P-51s of the 357th Fighter Group, which were to have escorted the 2nd Bomb Division through the target area, arrived at their rendezvous point on time and were about to join the escort of the 1st Bomb Division. It was a fortunate error for the latter unit, which was now under imminent fighter attack from the enemy. Hans Kogler's attack formation, comprising 72 single-engined Me 109s and FW 190s and 41 twin-engined Me 110s and Me 410s, had been directed into a position west of Berlin to block the direct route to the capital. But with the American swing towards the south of Berlin, Kogler found that his force was too far to the north. He was now moving down to engage.

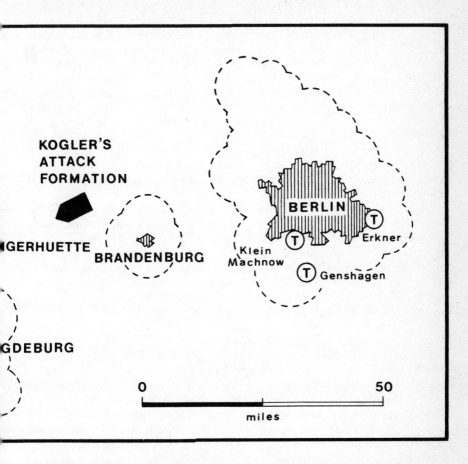

**KOGLER'S
ATTACK
FORMATION**

GERHUETTE
BRANDENBURG

BERLIN

Klein
Machnow

(T) Erkner

(T) Genshagen

GDEBURG

0   50

miles

Me 109s from the works airfield at Delitzsch near Leipzig. There were,
therefore, 72 single-engined and 41 twin-engined fighters airborne and
assembling over Magdeburg to engage the raiders. In addition fifteen Me 110
night fighters of Night Fighter Geschwader 5 had been scrambled from bases in
the Berlin area, and two more from the Luftwaffe Test Establishment at
Rechlin; these lumbering machines, fitted with radar and the other parapher-
nalia for night fighting, were suitable only to pick off straggling bombers and
were separate from the main attack formation. Five FW 190s of the 1st Fighter
Division's special airborne tracking unit had taken off from Parchim some time
earlier and made contact with the bombers; now they were passing a running
commentary on the composition, altitude, speed and heading of the bomber
stream to the divisional headquarters bunker at Doeberitz just outside Berlin.

   Shortly before 12.30 pm Hans Kogler received instructions from the ground
controller to leave the Magdeburg assembly point and lead his formation
northeast to block the path of the incoming bombers. He did not have far to go.

A few minutes later he caught sight of the enemy bomber stream. 'They looked like a swarm of little black dots, barely visible at first,' he later recounted. Kogler's powerful attack formation was assembled and in position; everything seemed set for a second hammer blow against the American bombers.

Hans Kogler had made contact with the head of the bomber stream, the 1st and 94th Combat Wings flying side by side and consisting of 112 Fortresses drawn from the 91st, 351st, 381st, 401st and 457th Bomb Groups. A few minutes earlier there had been a short hiatus in the escort as the bombers passed beyond the operating radius of the P-47. But at about the time the German formation leader caught sight of the bombers, twenty-five P-51s of the 4th Fighter Group moved into covering positions around the vanguard of the 1st Bomb Division. Shortly afterwards 34 P-51s of the 354th Fighter Group caught up with the 3rd Bomb Division.

Then the American fighter pilots sighted the German attack formation in front of them. Lieutenant Nick 'Cowboy' Megura of the 4th Fighter Group afterwards reported: 'We rendezvoused south of Berlin and positioned ourselves on the lead box. Twelve-plus smoke trails were seen coming from 12 o'clock and high, 30 miles ahead. "Upper" positioned the Group up-sun, below condensation height, and waited. The trails finally positioned themselves at 9 o'clock to the bombers and started to close.' 'Upper' was fighter ace Lieutenant Colonel Don Blakeslee, commander of the 4th, leading his unit. The 'smoke trails' Megura had seen were condensation trails from Me 109s of Ist Gruppe of Fighter Geschwader 3, providing top cover for Kogler's attack formation.

By now Kogler was finding the planned head-on attack on the bombers was going to be more difficult than he had thought. The fighter controller at Doeberitz had expected the American bomber stream to continue straight towards Berlin and had not appreciated the significance of the slight turn away to take the bombers to their Initial Points south of the capital. As a result the German formation had been positioned too far north for it to attack from exactly in front. As the range closed Kogler found it impossible to get into position for a true head-on attack, and had to lead his force in from one side.

Kogler ordered the Me 110s in his Gruppe to close into line abreast formation for the attack, '*Vorkommen, aufschliessen, aufschliessen!*' – close up! It was important to attack in tight formation so the bombers' gunners could not concentrate their fire on individual Messerschmitts. Kogler scanned the sky for the expected escort fighters but saw none: Blakeslee's order to his Group to position up-sun below trails height had paid off. Then the German pilot concentrated his attention on the bomber he had selected as victim, slowly growing in his sight.

In the nick of time, as the German attack formation was closing in, the US escort received a powerful reinforcement in the shape of 33 P-51s of the 357th Fighter Group. Major Thomas Hayes, leading these Mustangs, afterwards commented: 'There was a three-way rendezvous. We made our rendezvous with the bombers, just at the time the German fighters made their rendezvous with us!' Flight Officer Tom McKinney flying behind Hayes saw the huge gaggle of German fighters ahead and suddenly felt a long way from home: 'I thought that they would put up all they had, and the best they had, to stop that run to Berlin. We were in deeper than we'd ever been before and the odds seemed stacked against us. I thought "Well, I'll never get back to England!" '

Lieutenant Clyde Mason, piloting B-17 'Hell and High Water' of the 91st Bomb Group, watched the German fighters with considerable alarm. 'They seemed to be in groups of 30 or 40. It looked like they were throwing the entire Luftwaffe at us!' Captain Ed Curry, bombardier on B-17 'Breezin' Home' of the 401st, felt especially vulnerable at the sight of the enemy in front of him. 'Sitting in the nose of the B-17 one felt terribly exposed. The nearest thing to it is that dream where you are walking down the road with no clothes on; that was what it felt like when the battle began. You knew the glass around you wasn't worth ten cents for protection, the smallest round or fragment would go clean through it.

At 1,000 yards from the bombers Hans Kogler opened fire and saw his tracers streaking out in front. The B-17 he had selected belonged to the High Group of the 1st Combat Wing, a composite formation drawn from the 91st and 381st Bomb Groups. Sergeant W. Kaltenbach of the 91st, top turret gunner of the B-17 flying to the left of the leader, afterwards reported engaging Kogler's Gruppe: 'Several Me 110s were coming in from 9.30 to 10 o'clock high. I singled out the closest one and opened fire. He was 600 yards away when I started. His left engine started smoking . . .' At 250 yards Kogler saw his rounds stitching into the Fortress then broke off the attack and eased up his nose to pass close over the top of the bomber. The Messerschmitts behind followed suit.

At the controls of B-17 'Jeannie Marie' Les Rentmeester of the 91st watched the incoming Me 110s grow larger in his windshield. 'A dozen twin-engined Messerschmitts came straight at my squadron. Dirty smoke from the firing of their cannons was easy to see but we tried to ignore it. Suddenly pieces of steel came ripping through the aircraft skin, something slammed me back in my seat and everything went black. The sounds of Mickey's twin fifties firing inches above my head told me that I was conscious . . .' Desperately Rentmeester felt his body to discover where he had been hit and if he was bleeding. Then with enormous relief he found the cause of his 'black-out': the shock of the hits had unlatched the small window in front of him, which slammed back and had knocked his steel helmet over his eyes! The pilot had escaped injury. In the rear of the Fortress Sergeant Phil Lunt loosed off at the Me 110s as they flashed past his tail gun position: 'I opened fire at the bunch at about 150 yards and fired 100 rounds at them. One started smoking . . .'

The action opened at 12.42 pm, almost over the small town of Tangerhuette 20 miles to the north of Magdeburg.

Following close behind Kogler's Gruppe came the main force of rocket-carrying Me 410s and 110s. But now the P-51s of Blakeslee's 4th Fighter Group were hurtling out of the sun to block the German attack. Nick Megura fired head-on at one formation of destroyers and saw them dive away. 'I jumped three other Me 110s just as they let go their rockets, which burst behind the last of the bombers. I raked the three Me 110s which were flying wing-tip to wing-tip. As the No 1 enemy aircraft broke into me, I saw strikes all over the cockpit and both engines as he disappeared beneath me,' he afterwards reported. 'I cleared my tail, noticing a P-51 covering me behind and to the side. I closed in, firing on the No 2 Me 110 and saw pieces falling off and an explosion in the cockpit. I pulled up over him and last saw him in a vertical dive pouring black smoke.'

Lieutenant Cecil Manning of the 4th also engaged at this time. 'Several twin-engined enemy aircraft came in to attack the bombers from the port side, Me 110s with Me 109s for top cover. They were all firing rockets at the bomber formation.' Manning followed one section of twin-engined fighters as they dived away after attacking. 'I got real good strikes on the first one, from his port engine clear back to the rear gunner.' The Messerschmitt caught fire and fell away into a spin; Manning saw two parachutes blossom behind it. 'I swung over and lined up on another twin-engined fighter and after I had raked him with strikes I last saw him going down in a smoking spiral.' During the engagement the German rear gunner had kept up an intermittent return fire and Manning felt his Mustang judder as something hit the starboard wing. Everything seemed still to be working however, so he continued the fight.

Almost immediately afterwards Tom Hayes led the P-51s of the 357th in to engage. Lieutenant Don Bochkay, leading three of the Mustangs, afterwards reported: 'I saw three Me 110s off my left wing at about 20,000 feet flying line abreast toward the bombers. We dove after them, coming up behind them. The two Me 110s on the right must have seen us as they peeled off and down. I closed in on the remaining Me 110 on the left. Just before I fired he let loose his rockets towards the bombers but without any effect. I then gave him a long burst and hits were scored on his right engine and wing, pieces came off and he caught fire.' The burning Messerschmitt spun out of the sky.

Lieutenant Leroy Ruder, also of the 357th, was flying as wingman to Lieutenant John Carder as the Me 110s attacked. 'Lt Carder immediately broke to the left to intercept one that was getting into position to fire rockets at the bombers. The Me 110 immediately broke away downwards with Lt Carder and myself following. At 14,000 feet Lt Carder fired a burst. He broke to the right after excessive speed caused him to over-run the enemy aircraft. I then started firing at the Me 110 from a deflection of 15 degrees at about 300 yards and continued firing until breaking was necessary to avoid collision.' Pieces fell away from the crippled Messerschmitt which steepened its dive. Carder then closed in and fired a short burst; he noticed the enemy fighter's left engine windmilling and the canopy shattered. As the descending chase passed 5,000 feet Captain William O'Brien of the same unit moved in to short range and his rounds finished off the enemy fighter which dived straight into the ground.

Trailing black smoke the rockets from the German twin-engined fighters streaked towards the bomber formations. The aggressively handled P-51s forced many launching aircraft to break off attacks prematurely; and those German pilots brave enough to hold their positions found it almost impossible to judge the range and deflection accurately enough for rockets to explode close to the bombers. As a result almost all the hundred or so rockets burst harmlessly clear of their intended victims. According to American records only one bomber suffered damage from an exploding rocket and that was not serious.

But, lethal or not, the rockets sizzling through their formations had a devastating psychological impact on the bomber crewmen. 'We had people shooting at us, rockets coming at us, planes coming at us. And the crew hollering over the intercom. It wasn't like in the movies, I can tell you, they really screamed,' recalled Ed Curry. 'We had one kid, a gunner, he had a high shrill voice and when he got excited he spoke very quickly. As one of the German fighters came past I can still remember him shouting excitedly over the intercom to one of the other gunners: "Pick him up Paul, pick him up Paul, Paul get 'im, get 'im, get 'im Paul!" Then the other gunners joined in. You wanted to keep discipline over the intercom but once the battle got going it was almost impossible.'

After firing his rockets and engaging one B-17 with cannon, Oberleutnant Friedrich Stehle led his Me 410 Gruppe through the bomber formation. They passed so close that his radio operator, Feldwebel Alois Slaby, was able to hear the roar of engines above those of the Messerschmitt. Following the Me 410s came the Me 110s of Destroyer Geschwader 76. Oberleutnant Herbert Schob hit a B-17 with cannon fire and saw it swing away from the formation.

One of the first bombers to go down at this time was the Fortress piloted by Lieutenant Douglas Harding of the 91st Bomb Group. The right inboard engine burst into flame then fuel ignited and the fire became general. Harding gave the order for his crew to bail out. The radio operator, Sergeant Hubert Peterson, moved to the rear door and pulled the handle to jettison it. The door should have fallen clear immediately but to his surprise it remained firmly in place. Peterson was wondering what to do next when a blurred image flashed in front of him: another of the crewmen had charged past, pushed out the door and disappeared out of the hole all in a single movement. Peterson followed. The left waist gunner, Sergeant Wallace Beyer, went out soon afterwards and after a short fall pulled his ripcord without noticing that a testicle had lodged between the thigh strap of the parachute harness and his body. When the parachute opened the testicle took the full shock and, in Beyer's words, 'I let out a scream they must have heard on the ground a couple of miles away!'

Lieutenant Paris Coleman's B-17, leading Harding's squadron, also went down at this time. In the squadron above, Les Rentmeester watched its death throes: 'Fire was pouring out of the squadron leader's plane directly under my left wing, it was even coming out of the cockpit and from the radio-gunner's hatch on top of the aircraft. A figure crawled out of this top hatch, his parachute already half open and on fire. He bounced off the horizontal stabilizer where his chute briefly caught, ripped and was torn free. The plane, losing speed rapidly, went out of sight . . .'

While some Mustangs had been able to get through and engage the lumbering destroyers with ease, others found themselves embroiled with Me-109s covering the attack formation. Lieutenant Richard Turner of the 354th Fighter Group, flying P-51 'Short Fuse Sallee', suddenly observed Me 109s diving on his squadron. 'I ordered the squadron to drop tanks and break to the right and started to haul on the stick. At this moment my engine went quite cold! My blood chilled as I slumped down in the cockpit to grab my fuel switch, knowing instantly that I had forgotten to switch from drop tanks to internals before releasing,' he afterwards wrote.* 'After four or five seconds the engine restarted and I nosed down to gain flying speed and looked to the rear – straight into the guns of four 109s coming down fast on my tail! I was cold meat. At minimum flying speed with no Flight to help, I couldn't think what to do. Some subconscious instinct must have moved my hand to the flap lever handle. As the flaps hit the slipstream, the Mustang almost hung in mid-air, full power keeping it from spinning. The 109s flashed by without scoring a hit.'

Almost immediately afterwards Turner's P-51 came under attack from another Messerschmitt closing rapidly from above. 'With his speed advantage the 109 was soon in range, and in desperation I prepared to skid violently down to the left as soon as I saw his guns start blinking. The 109 was in perfect range and yet he didn't fire. As I waited for the sight of those blinking muzzle flashes the suspense was terrific. He seemed to fall back a little and hesitatingly bob his left wing slightly as if he were undecided,' Turner continued. 'Puzzled, I took a quick glance around and saw the most beautiful sight in the world. Two Mustangs were rushing toward me from eleven o'clock high. No wonder the 109 was hanging back! I started to turn to the left hoping to suck the German after me to give the two Mustangs a better shot at him, but he was no fool. Over and down he went, making tracks for the Fatherland.'

Lieutenant Dick Floyd, piloting a B-17 of the 92nd Bomb Group, observed the scene: 'Just before we made our turn north to make our bomb drop I saw one of the damndest dogfights of the war. It was off to the right of us as we headed east and several thousand feet higher – about one and a half miles away. It looked like a giant swarm of bees, P-51s, Me 109s, FW 190s. The swarm would go round and round, up and down.'

As the German twin-engined fighters emerged from the bomber formations after attacking, several came under attack from P-51s. Hans Kogler cleared the bombers and looked around to see how many Me 110s were with him for the next attack, when he was horrified to see three Mustangs diving on one of them. This was the first he had seen of enemy fighters in the area. Then his radio operator, Officer Cadet Feldwebel Kluepfel, excitedly called there was a Mustang coming in to attack their aircraft also. Their assailant was Tom McKinney of the 357th Fighter Group flying P-51 'Round Trip'. McKinney had seen the Me 110s pop out of the bomber formation below and with his wingman dived to engage three of them. The twin-engined fighters immediately split up. McKinney picked the one which had been leading and closed rapidly to 400 yards where he opened fire. The Mustang pilot observed his rounds strike the right wing and fuselage and he also saw the muzzle flash of Kluepfel's gun firing back at him. Kogler felt his Messerschmitt shudder under the impact of the hits then heard the radio operator cry 'We're trailing white smoke from the right side!' That meant that the radiator had been hit. Kogler glanced at the engine temperature gauge and saw that it had not yet begun to over-heat; that was good – if he was to stand any chance of throwing off the Mustang he would need all the power he could get. The German pilot pulled the heavy fighter into a steep descending turn. McKinney followed. As the turn continued Kogler heard a plaintive voice over the intercom: 'Herr Major,

*In his book *Mustang Pilot*, Doubleday and Co, New York.

please will you ease the turn a little so I can get back to my gun?' In an effort to increase his field of fire Kluepfel had slackened his seat straps; but the severe G forces had pulled him off his seat on to the floor of the cabin and now he could not get up. Kogler saw the only salvation for the Messerschmitt lay in holding the tight turn; the radio operator would have to stay where he was for the time being. McKinney noticed his opponent was no longer returning his fire, though many years were to pass before he learned the reason. Now the American pilot closed to short range and loosed another accurate burst into the diving Messerschmitt. In Kogler's aircraft there was a huge bang, the anguished crack of breaking metal and flying plexiglas and the smell of burned cordite. It was as well for Kluepfel he was on the floor, for one of McKinney's rounds had passed close over his head and clean through the back of his seat before it detonated against Kogler's back armor. The American pilot fired a further burst at the Messerschmitt but without effect. 'It wouldn't have been any problem for a sharp shooter to have got him. But I was early in the game and I just could not get my sight on him for long,' he later explained. Then before the Mustang could deliver yet another attack, an Me 109 suddenly appeared above curving around behind the two escort fighters. McKinney broke off the attack and as he did so his wingman glanced back at the Me 110; it appeared to be going down in a spin trailing smoke. Certainly it had been hit hard; the American pilots thought it was 'probably destroyed'.

After getting the destroyers through to the bombers those German single-engined fighters not involved in dogfights with the escorts now moved into position to carry out their own attacks. Leutnant Hans Weik, leading a Staffel from IVth Gruppe of Fighter Geschwader 3, pulled his Me 109 out in front of the bombers. 'The attack was from out of the sun so the enemy fighters could not engage us. We attacked the formation with our Gruppe exactly from head-on. I fired at an aircraft in the upper part of the enemy formation and scored hits on the fuselage, the left engines and the left wing,' he afterwards reported. 'Looking back, I saw the aircraft I had hit pull left away from the formation and lose altitude. As we pulled around for a further attack the the the aircraft broke up. I saw four parachutes.'

Leutnant Hans Iffland attacked with Weik's Staffel. 'During the firing run everything happened very quickly, with the closing speed of about 500 mph. After firing my short burst at one of the B-17s I pulled up over it; I had attacked from slightly above, allowing a slight deflection angle and aiming at the nose. I saw my rounds exploding around the wing root and the tracer rounds from the bombers flashing past me,' he remembered. 'As I pulled up over the bomber I dropped my left wing, to see the results of my attack and also to give the smallest possible target at which their gunners could aim. Pieces broke off the bomber and it began to slide out of the formation.'

Lieutenant Dan Knight, piloting B-17 'Mary Alice' of the 401st Bomb Group, found the head-on attacks by the single-seaters an unnerving experience. 'During one fierce head-on fighter attack Rusty Rustand, the copilot, and I both ducked down for a split second as the Me 109s came straight at us and through the formation. Our eyes met but nothing was said until much later when I asked Rusty "What were you doing down there, anyway?" He said "I was picking up cigarette butts. What were you doing?!'' But it wasn't so funny at the time.'

Friedrich Stehle led his Me 410s in for a second head-on attack on the bombers. As the destroyers flashed over the top of the B-17s Stehle's radio operator, Alois Slaby, saw Feldwebel Willi Bonnecke's Me 410 suddenly swerve and, either accidentally or deliberately, crash into one of the bombers. The whole thing was over in an instant and both aircraft plunged out of sight.

The B-17 Bonnecke hit was that flown by Lieutenant Eugene Whalen of the 457th Bomb Group, part of whose tail was knocked off in the collision. The bomber had been flying on the right side of the High Squadron. Now it swung out of control in a sharp diving turn to the left. It narrowly missed several bombers in the formation before it rammed into Lieutenant Roy Graves's aircraft on the left side of the Low Squadron. The force of the impact was so great that wreckage of Whalen's B-17 was later found scattered over four miles; there were no survivors. From Graves's aircraft there was only one survivor, tail gunner Sergeant Eldon Williams, who landed by parachute with a fractured skull.

Hauptmann Heinz Wurzer, leading the eight Me 109s from Fighter Geschwader 302, also made a head-on attack on the bombers. But as he recalled 'The newer pilots with little flying experience had little chance of scoring hits during the head-on attacks. So after we passed through the enemy formation we pulled up and around for an attack from the rear. That way we were likely to achieve more kills but risked greater losses to ourselves. The enemy formation had closed up after our initial attack and put up a furious defensive fire.' During his attacks Wurzer was able to hit two bombers, before he was forced to break away.

Other German fighters also carried out rear attacks at this time. From the rear gun position of B-17 'My Darling Also' of the 91st Bomb Group, Sergeant Walter Davis watched three FW 190s moving into firing positions. He concentrated his fire on the leader and saw hits. The Focke-Wulf descended a little, then climbed relentlessly towards the bomber seemingly ignoring the return fire. Immediately after it passed out of view to Davis's left there was a loud bang which sent a shudder through the entire bomber: the Focke-Wulf had rammed it, knocking off the entire right stabilizer. In the left waist position Sergeant Dana Morse also felt the aircraft lurch as the German fighter struck and was hurled away from his gun. Even before the collision enemy cannon shells had caused fearful destruction to that part of the aircraft. 'I had a burning sensation to my left thigh. The right waist gunner was holding his stomach and had been hit bad. I looked out of the right waist window and saw we were on fire and sliding off to the right going down. Due to the smoke I could see no movement at all in the forward part of the plane. The intercom was knocked out.' Morse moved forward to try to help the ball gunner out of his turret but it seemed the unfortunate man was either unconscious or dead. By now the other waist gunner had collapsed, lifeless, on the cabin floor. As the Fortress started to tumble out of the sky the 'G' forces became stronger and Morse knew that if he did not get out quickly he would go down with the dying bomber. He moved to the rear door, pulled the jettison handle and gave it a hefty kick but the door remained firmly in place – the shock of the collision had distorted the frame. With increasing desperation Morse kicked and kicked at the door until it finally fell away. Then he dived after it. In the rear gun position Walter Davis had a similar problem getting his escape hatch open before he was able to get out also.

The only unit with FW 190s engaged in this part of the action was Sturmstaffel 1, which operated the special heavily armored version of this fighter. It would seem that it was one of these aircraft that had rammed 'My Darling Also'.

As well as the bombers going down out of control there was the usual crop of stragglers forced to leave their formations. For those thus isolated deep over enemy territory life was often short and brutal. Dick Floyd watched the end of one of them. 'The enemy really worked on any of our boys who dropped out of formation. It was tough sitting there watching and not a darn thing one could do about it. Over to my left was a single B-17 that had dropped out of the formation. Behind him came a twin-engined German fighter and a single-engined one. They must have hit him with a rocket or something because he just blew right up. Afterwards there were just pieces falling earthwards.'

Sometimes escorting P-51s were able to intervene in time to save stragglers, which meant they survived a bit longer. Captain Davis Perron of the 357th Fighter Group was up at 24,000 feet when he sighted one of the bombers in difficulty, straggling below at 18,000 feet under attack from a pair of FW 190s. Perron dived to engage followed by his wingman Lieutenant Rod Starkey who later wrote: 'We had not been out of formation more than 10 seconds when Captain Perron flew through a group of Messerschmitt 109s. In concentrating on where he was going he had not seen these enemy planes!' Perron told Starkey to try to hold off the Messerschmitts while he continued down to drive the Focke-Wulfs away from the bomber. To Starkey there seemed an air of unreality about the scene: 'Another 109 went under my nose, so close I could look into the cockpit and see the pilot's suit. But if we were not aware the 109s were there in force, the German pilots were not aware of us either. The pilot that passed under my nose never bothered me and I never saw him again.' Meanwhile Perron saw the Focke-Wulfs break away from the B-17 as he plunged down to engage. He opened fire at the leader with three long bursts, starting at 600 yards and continuing down to 300 yards and saw his rounds striking home. There was an explosion, the FW 190 caught fire and went spinning down.

Starkey then became embroiled with one of the Messerschmitts and scored hits on it. But during the engagement his guns had jammed one after the other until of the four only one was working; it was a familiar problem with the new Mustangs. 'As I looked around I could see three or four 109s nearby. I got on the radio immediately asking for help. The squadron commander answered and said he would be glad to help – if I could tell him where I was! I didn't know where I was! I knew I was somewhere to the south of Berlin but having chased the 109 I had no idea exactly where I was,' Starkey later recalled. 'However the sight of the 109s nearby was enough to stimulate me to lift the little latch on my throttle arm for War Emergency Power. This gave me a little more power but only for about 5 minutes or the engine would suffer severe damage. It was strictly an emergency measure – but at that moment I deemed it to be something of an emergency!' Using maximum power Starkey beat a hasty retreat from the scene.

After knocking down one of the B-17s Leutnant Hans Weik led his Me 109 Staffel around for a second head-on attack on the bombers. 'I opened fire at a range of 500 meters from dead ahead and fired at one of the enemy aircraft on the left outer side of the formation. I scored several hits on the right outer engine and the right wing. As I pulled up over the aircraft I saw the outer part of the right wing was badly hit. The aircraft pulled away steeply to the left and went down in a spiral. I saw two men bail out.'

Close behind Weik, Hans Iffland picked out another of the bombers and closed rapidly for a head-on attack. But the American pilot saw him coming and, since the formation had opened up considerably following earlier attacks, he had room to maneuver. As Iffland was about to open fire the B-17 pulled to one side and his rounds passed safely clear. Then his guns fell silent: 'Once one was out of ammunition it was important to join up with other German fighters, because it was very dangerous if one now came under attack from the escorts. On breaking away from the bombers we went down in a rapid descent to about 200 meters above the ground, to get well clear of the enemy fighters. At that altitude our camouflaged aircraft were very difficult to see from high above, while we could see the enemy machines silhouetted against the sky.' Hugging the ground the German fighters leveled out and headed back to Salzwedel.

Lieutenant Kenneth Hagen of the 357th Fighter Group led an element of four P-51s which chased an Me 110 from 23,000 feet to ground level, where it burst into flames and crashed. Hagen and his wingman, Lieutenant Arval Roberson, were climbing back to altitude when suddenly the leader sighted another Me 110 slightly below and the pair swung to engage it. The German fighter dived into a small patch of cloud and, opening out slightly, the two Mustangs followed. Then, in Roberson's words: 'Coming out of cloud, Lt Hagen was gone but the Me 110 was 50 feet in front of me. About all I had to do was press the button. I commenced firing from 50 feet range and closed still more, using short bursts. I saw numerous strikes on his fuselage and left wing. Suddenly he exploded like a big sky rocket and I went through the flame. My tail was gashed a bit from flying debris. I looked down to see a mass of fire plummeting earthwards and crash into the woods below.'

Oberleutnant Herbert Schob, flying an Me 110 of Destroyer Geschwader 76, had earlier knocked one B-17 out of its formation. During his second attack he knocked down a second bomber. But then his fighter was caught by the American escorts. 'My radio operator reported Mustangs coming down on us from behind. Of course they were much faster than we were. Two came at us from below, two from above, behind and to the right. I put my aircraft into a steep turn to the right and dived but we had not got far when enemy rounds hit us and the right wing caught fire.' With minor injuries Schob and his radio operator Johann Horning bailed out.

One of the last bombers to go down during this phase of the action was B-17 'Hell and High Water' piloted by Clyde Mason of the 91st Bomb Group. After one of the enemy attacks he saw his left wing well ablaze; the Fortress was obviously doomed. Mason engaged the autopilot and ordered his crew to bail out then made his way to the open bomb doors. 'I had always wondered whether I would be afraid to jump if the time came. But in the event I just pulled my feet together, pulled my arms against my sides and dropped out.' The pilot did a long free fall drop then pulled his ripcord. As the parachute opened he saw his aircraft going down in a shallow descent, the blazing left engines trailing a sheet of flame that extended well past the tail.

Although most engagements during this phase of the action were concentrated around the 1st Bomb Division leading the attack, there were also some hit-and-run attacks on bombers in the divisions behind. Lieutenant John Flottorp, piloting a B-17 of the 390th Bomb Group with the 3rd Bomb Division, came under attack from an FW 190 shortly before the target. 'I felt and heard some hits and the No 3 engine oil pressure dropped to zero. I retarded the throttle and rpm and hit the feathering button but the propeller would not feather. The ball turret gunner reported the oil cooler mostly missing and the nacelle and under-wing covered with oil. The loss of power caused me to drop back in the formation and I had the three good engines at maximum continuous power to try to catch up.' Flottorp eased his aircraft on to a more northerly heading to cut off the turn before the target and so rejoin his formation; but as he was doing so other German fighters attacked. 'In the turn the top turret gunner called out two Me 110s attacking from 3 to 4 o'clock. I turned hard into them and they overshot, passing close enough for me to make out the brown helmets, black oxygen masks and dark goggles of the pilots.' No sooner had the pilot overcome one problem, there was something else to worry about. 'Suddenly the No 3 engine seized from lack of oil, the reduction gears sheared and the prop was running out of control in extreme fine pitch. This increased drag considerably and the vibration became so severe the instruments in the shock mounted panel were all but unreadable.' Flottorp was forced to throttle back to slow the bomber and decrease the vibration, but as he did so the safety of his formation receded into the distance.

Hans Iffland was elated. With other pilots of IVth Gruppe of Fighter Geschwader 3 he had just taken part in his first air defense mission over the German homeland and he had scored a kill. As he returned to his base at Salzwedel at low altitude he saw an Me 109 in front rock its wings to indicate its pilot had made a victory. Then he flew low over the airfield rocking his wings also. He landed and taxied to his Staffel dispersal area where his beaming mechanic was waiting to meet him. 'He had seen me rock my wings and when I shut down the engine and opened the hood he stood by the wing. He clapped his hands above his head, shouted "*Gratuliere, Herr Leutnant!*" and offered me a cigarette.'

Wallace Beyer parachuted to earth in a sparsely inhabited area to the north of Magdeburg, after bailing out of his B-17. After it had been crushed by the parachute harness his testicle was excruciatingly painful. Nevertheless his first thought was how he might escape from Germany. Quickly he hid his parachute and life jacket. Then he took a compass bearing and started walking in the direction of the Baltic, 120 miles to the north. He hoped he might be able to sneak on board a ship bound for Sweden.

Hubert Peterson, the radio operator in Beyer's crew, came down in a wood a few miles away with his parachute caught up in a tall tree and his feet dangling some 15 feet above the ground. By pulling on the rigging lines he was able to swing himself from side to side, as he tried to grab the trunk of the tree so he could climb down. But in mid-swing the parachute slid off the branch supporting it and he fell hard on his rump suffering a fractured vertebra. The white nylon canopy dropped silently on top of him. In some pain Peterson struggled out of the harness and hid the parachute in a patch of snow. Then he took out his compass and began walking in the direction of the French border, more than 300 miles to the southwest.

John Frawley, top turret gunner in the same crew, made a normal parachute landing some distance from the other two and, after burying his parachute and life jacket, set out for the most ambitious walk of all: in the direction of Switzerland nearly 400 miles to the south.

Following the timely intervention of the Me 109, which had prevented Tom McKinney from finishing off his Me 110, Hans Kogler had continued his dive and leveled out just above the ground. There he shut down the damaged right engine and his radio operator was able to struggle off the floor and get back into his seat. Kogler took the battered Messerschmitt to the nearest airfield, Magdeburg, and lined up for the landing. With only one engine and battle damage whose full extent he could only guess, Kogler came in fast and put the wheels on the ground. The aircraft ran across the frozen ground and when Kogler applied his brakes, they had little effect. The fighter crashed through the boundary fence on the far side of the airfield and came to rest with its nose dug in the ground and tail pointing in the air. Giving thanks for their narrow escape the two airmen scrambled to the ground.

B-17 pilot Clyde Mason landed by parachute in a snow-covered field south of Berlin, to see three or four cars stop on the road a few hundred yards away and their occupants start running towards him. Mason quickly threw off his harness and tried to out-run them, but after a chase lasting over a mile he was finally cornered and forced to surrender.

Oberleutnant Herbert Schob parachuted to earth beside the small village of Letzlingen, to the west of Tangerhuette, having bailed out of his Me 110 after it was attacked by Mustangs. As always he had on his brown leather flying suit; it was quite different from those normally worn by Luftwaffe aircrew, made in Spain where he had fought during the Civil War. Now, however, the unusual outfit proved an embarrassment. A party of farmers from the nearby village advanced on the pilot and, taking him for an American, began to beat him with fists and sticks in spite of Schob's protestations that he was German. Only after several painful blows was the pilot able to convince his assailants of his nationality, then everyone became apologetic; he was taken to one of the farm houses and plied with food and drink.

The most ferocious part of the Tangerhuette action ended within 25 minutes of its beginning, as German fighters began to run short of fuel and ammunition and were forced to break away. There would, however, be minor skirmishes for up to half an hour after that. The 41 destroyers and 72 fighters put up by the Luftwaffe 1st and 7th Fighter Divisions represented a far more powerful force than that which had gone into action over Haseluenne. But this time the German ground direction had not been so good and the escorting P-51s had been in the right place at the right time to deflect the worst of the blow. During the action eight B-17s had been shot down and three more destroyed in collisions; several others suffered damage, in some cases sufficiently serious to force them to leave their formations. Four escorting P-51s were also shot down in the Berlin area. But while inflicting these losses the defenders had also suffered; the twin-engined destroyer units, in particular, had been very roughly handled by the escorting Mustangs. Hans Kogler's Gruppe, IIIrd of Destroyer Geschwader 26, had lost five Me 110s destroyed and two damaged of seven which engaged. Friedrich Stehle's IInd Gruppe lost six Me 410s destroyed and two damaged of ten which engaged. Herbert Kaminski's Me 110s from Destroyer Geschwader 76 lost five destroyed of 24 which engaged. In comparison with the destroyer losses those of the German single-engined fighter units were light: five Me 109s and two FW 190s destroyed.

Two further German aircraft were lost during the engagement, whose crews had not intended to take part: an Arado 96 and a Heinkel 111 on training flights in the area, whose crews had somehow missed the repeated radio broadcasts warning all such aircraft to land at the nearest airfield. Both were summarily dealt with by the marauding Mustangs.

As the bombers continued to their designated Initial Points south of Berlin then turned northeast to begin their bomb runs, there was an unreal calm as most German fighters broke away. But nobody in the bombers doubted this was anything but the calm before the storm, as the capital's powerful flak defenses waited to receive them.

The first warning of possible danger to the German capital had been issued at 12.09 pm, while the Haseluenne battle was in full swing. Then the vanguard of the raiding force came within 160 km of the city and, in accordance with the usual procedure, Air Danger 30 was issued for the Berlin area. This was a non-public warning issued by telephone to military, party, civil defense, industrial and police establishments, and hospitals and schools, that enemy bombers were within thirty minutes' flying time.

On receipt of the fore-alarm Berlin's gun defenses had sprung to readiness. Sixteen-year-old Luftwaffenhelfer Gottfried Gottschalk, serving with Light Flak Abteilung 722 defending the Siemensstadt district, was in a classroom receiving lessons when Air Danger 30 was issued. 'One of the boys came in and shouted ''*Voralarm!*'' We all jumped up and dashed out of the room, grabbing steel helmets and gasmasks as we did so, and ran to the guns.' Gottschalk's unit manned three 37 mm guns all within 100 yards of the classroom. On reaching their weapons the boys unstrapped the heavy canvas covers, tensioned the cocking springs and placed a six-round clip of shells into the breech of each gun. Then the elevation layer wound the barrel to 80 degrees to prove the mechanism was functioning, then back to the horizontal. As each gun became ready for action its commander shouted '*Geschutz frei! Feuer fertig!*' When the last gun called in the troop commander ordered all weapons to swing to the west, the direction from which the enemy force was approaching.

There were similar scenes at the heavy gun sites, though there crews had much more equipment to check out. Luftwaffenhelfer Dietrich Scheibel, 15, served with an 88 mm battery of Heavy Flak Abteilung 307 situated in the Tempelhof district. Working in the command post he heard the gun crews check in by telephone that they were ready for action: '*Anton, alles in Ordnung!*', '*Berta, in Ordnung!*', '*Caesar . . .*', '*Dora . . .*', '*Emil . . .*', '*Friedrich . . .*'. There too, when all guns had checked in, the battery commander ordered them to swing to the west.

Now the young defenders were left, each with his own thoughts, waiting for the enemy to come to them. Many times previously fore-alarms had been issued for the Berlin area during the day and no attack had developed; few gunners thought this occasion would prove any different. During the period of waiting young minds began to wander. 'The fore-alarm went just before lunch and we all ran to our guns and got them ready for action. As we waited for the bombers I remember feeling a bit annoyed they should choose this time to attack, when I wanted my lunch!' commented Oberhelfer Hans Ring serving with Heavy Flak Abteilung 437 in the Spandau district.

At the same time other, less military, preparations were in train. Police Oberwachtmeister Wilhelm Winkler, 54, left his station and climbed the high tower in the Mexicoplatz overlooking the Zehlendorf district; if there was an attack his duty was to report by telephone the positions of exploding bombs so his headquarters could send in the necessary fire and rescue services.

At the Telefunken plant in the Steglitz district 14-year-old apprentice radio engineer Horst Krieger heard the announcement of the fore-alarm on the loudspeakers. The firm was busily mass-producing the latest *Mannheim* flak control radar but now this ceased as all machinery was shut down. At the same time other workers began carrying the more important prototype and experimental components and drawings away to an especially heavily constructed bunker in the grounds. This was a continual source of annoyance to the workers: the components and drawings went in the only really secure bunker, while the workers had to use the less-strongly constructed dug-out shelters. Nobody seemed to think an attack on Berlin was likely now, however, and Krieger and his workmates waited beside their benches for the all-clear so they could resume production.

In the Rittberg Hospital nearby 21-year-old Marianne Wittstock lay in bed; shortly before midnight she had given birth to a 7-pound daughter. On the fore-alarm two burly hospital porters came into the ward and lifted her into a wheel chair. She was then pushed into the corridor with other patients, to await developments. She had not seen her baby since the birth and now began to worry about the safety of the youngster.

At 12.43 pm the public warning of imminent danger sounded in Berlin: the *Fliegeralarm*, full alarm, a series of two-second siren blasts whose warbling note echoed across the city from Potsdam in the west to Lichtenburg in the east, from Reinickendorf in the north to Tempelhof in the south. Trains and streetcars halted to disgorge passengers; men, women and children streamed out of factories, offices, shops and schools and hastened to the shelters.

At the Telefunken factory Horst Krieger and his workmates strolled to their shelters, dug-outs with a few concrete slabs covered with soil to give top protection. Still nobody really expected an attack and the men stood outside waiting for something to happen.

At the Rittberg Hospital Marianne Wittstock was taken in her wheelchair to the ground floor by elevator, then along a corridor to the sloping ramp leading to the cellar. On her way she passed the wards containing those patients too ill to be moved; these unfortunates, and the nurses assigned to look after them, had to remain above ground while everyone else made for the shelters.

In the Prenzlauerberg district 34-year-old housewife Gertrud Tappert had been doing the housework when the siren sounded. Together with others living in the block of apartments she hastened to the cellar. Each woman carried a previously packed holdall or suitcase containing the things without which life in wartime Germany could be very difficult: identification papers, ration books and medical papers, family documents, money, jewelry or small treasured possessions and as many clothes as could be squeezed in (by 1944 new ones were almost unobtainable). Frau Tappert's husband and daughter were at work and her two young sons were at school; she could only hope that they were taking shelter also.

In Friedrichstrasse near the center of Berlin 16-year-old apprentice telephone engineer Gert Mueller and his classmates moved in orderly file to the basement of the Reichs Post Office technical school. The boys chatted about the chances of this being a real attack, rather than yet another false alarm. Surely the Berlin defenses were far too strong for enemy bombers to get through by day?

For those who had come to Berlin unwillingly, the many thousands of workers deported from countries occupied by Germany, the wail of the sirens was almost welcome. To 23-year-old Leon Butticaz at the Deutsche Waffen und Munitionsfabrik in the Reinickendorf district, the warning meant a break from the grueling 12-hour shift assembling 37 mm anti-tank and anti-aircraft guns. Nobody liked being bombed, but the prospect was softened by the knowledge that it would bring one step nearer the defeat of Germany and a return to his native France.

With most of its population under cover and the civil defense and flak batteries stood to and ready for action, the sixth largest city in the world was as ready as it would ever be to meet its fiery ordeal.

CHAPTER 5

THE BATTLE AT BERLIN

1.04 to 2.07 pm

The cannons have their bowels full of wrath
And ready mounted are they to spit forth
Their iron indignation.
                    Shakespeare: King John

In front of the vanguard of the raiding force, a smudge on the horizon, lay Berlin. Shortly after 1 pm the forty-three surviving B-17s of the 1st Combat Wing turned northeast at their Initial Point and were now closing formation for the bomb run. At first it seemed their target, the Erkner ball bearing works, would be clear of cloud. Then, when the wing was well into its bomb run, a ridge of cloud slid across to blanket the aiming point. This placed the leader in a difficult position: a visual bomb run was now impossible and Erkner was too small a target for attack using radar; and it was now too late to realign the entire 1st Bomb Division for a radar bomb run on the Friedrichstrasse railway station in the center of Berlin. The leader abandoned the bomb run and ordered succeeding groups to attack whatever they could in the Berlin area.

Thus the first group to carry through a bomb run was the second in line, the 381st, whose 17 Fortresses made a bee-line for Zernsdorf 7 miles southwest of the primary target. At 1.10 pm the lead aircraft released its smoke markers and bombs and the other aircraft followed suit. Forty seconds later the bombs burst in and around the village tearing out a swathe of destruction.

As the 381st swung away to the east after bombing, its B-17s closed on the 88 mm flak battery at Gosen. The predictor operators had aligned their sighting telescopes on the lead aircraft in the formation and the predictor's mechanical computer began working out the necessary firing information for the guns. To reach bombers flying at 19,500 feet at a maximum slant range of $5\frac{1}{2}$ miles an 88 mm shell took 19 seconds; and in that time a B-17 covered 1,900 yards. The task of the predictor was continually to work out the distance in front of the target aircraft the shells had to be aimed, for them to burst close to it. Three seconds before the bombers came within range of his battery the commander shouted '*Achtung*!' At each gun the shell was lifted out of the fuse-setter and passed to the loader, who thrust it up into the chamber and closed the breech. Exactly as the bombers came within range the commander shouted

'*Gruppe*!' Each gunner opened his mouth to equalize the pressure on his ear drums and the loaders pulled the firing levers of their guns. With a united 'Woomph' the eight guns belched forth their salvo of 20-pound shells.

There was no time for the gun crews to admire the results of their work; the bombers would not be in range long and while they were there the gunners had to get off as many aimed rounds as possible. Loosing off one salvo every 3½ seconds the battery put 48 shells into the air before the first rounds burst with a cluster of black smoke clouds that pock marked the sky around the bombers. Passing almost over the Gosen battery, the B-17s remained in range for nearly two minutes. Then they came within the engagement zone of the double-battery at Ruedersdorf just to the north, with sixteen 88 mm guns. By then the action had become general, with almost the entire 1st Combat Wing being engaged by one battery or more; nearly two-thirds of its Fortresses suffered flak damage.

Watching the approaching bomber stream from one of the buildings at Tempelhof airfield to the northwest, 16-year-old Luftwaffenhelfer Guenther Schulze could hardly believe his eyes: that so many enemy four-engined bombers could reach the German capital in broad daylight. Like most Berlin defenders, this was the first time he had had a clear view of an attacking bomber force (at night the defenders caught only fleeting glimpses of individual raiders). Worst of all there was not a single German fighter anywhere to be seen – he had no inkling of the savage battles fought on the way in. The bombers were too far away and far too high to be engaged by the 40 mm guns of his unit, Light Flak Abteilung 979. But from the trails of smoke in the distance it seemed some flak units were hitting bombers. Only later would he learn the smoke really came from marker bombs dropped by the raiders – it was the first time the Berlin defenders had seen these.

Seventeen-year-old Luftwaffenhelfer Alexander Witzigmann watched the action from the 88 mm double-battery at Gross Zeithen, which also went into action at this time. It was his first day at the flak site, and since he was untrained, he was told to take cover in one of the slit trenches and keep out of everyone's way. 'I was so frightened by the display of strength by the enemy I began to shake. It was probably because I had nothing else to do but watch the bombers; later, serving as a gun layer in far more dangerous situations, I was never so frightened.'

The 91st Bomb Group, leading the 1st Combat Wing, continued past the Erkner primary target and released its bombs on the small village of Eggersdorf eight miles to the north. Twelve-year-old Norbert Kelling, on his way there home from school, watched the scene crouching in a roadside ditch. Then he heard the whistle of falling bombs and hurled himself flat and covered his head with his hands. What possible reason could the Americans have for dropping bombs around his village, he wondered?

One Fortress of the 91st, piloted by Lieutenant Bryce Evertson, managed to stay with the formation until the bombs were released. But then the left outboard engine, badly damaged during the fighter attack east of Tanger-huette, caught fire. 'I had come to think of my B-17 as indestructible. But now it was on fire and all sorts of bad things were happening, it just wasn't going to keep flying for much longer.' Evertson ordered his crew to bail out and followed through the nose hatch.

The 1st Combat Wing had clipped the eastern side of Berlin and somehow managed to pick its way between the more powerful flak defenses. The 94th, coming up behind, was less fortunate; its fifty-one B-17s followed a more westerly heading which took them much closer to the center of the capital. As a result it came under fire from several batteries. The double-battery at Biesdorf, manned by Heavy Flak Abteilung 326, loosed off 185 rounds from its sixteen 88 mm guns at the Wing concentrating on the 401st Bomb Group in the lead. Then Heavy Flak Abteilung 605 carried on the engagement; two of its double-batteries, each with sixteen 88 mm guns at Lindenburg and Karow to the north, fired a further 300 rounds at the formation as it came past. 'I'd been to Oschersleben, the Ruhr, but I'd never seen flak as heavy as that they had over Berlin. It wasn't just the odd black puff, it was completely dense; not just at one altitude, but high and low. There was a saying that you see the smoke only after the explosion; but that day we actually saw the red of the explosions,' recalled Ed Curry, deputy lead bombardier of the 401st. 'One shell burst near us and we had chunks of shell tear into the radio room and the bomb bay. One large splinter smashed into the swivel mounting of the gun at one of the waist positions and severed it clean through.' Lieutenant Dan Knight's B-17, 'Mary Alice', also of the 401st, was hit in the radio room too: 'We had a shell blow out the radio hatch and severely injure my radio operator, Charlie Archer. He was hit in the head and chest and the concussion collapsed one of his lungs. We made him as comfortable as possible on the floor of the radio room.'

One of the early salvoes wrecked the bombing radar of B-17 'Chopstick K', the pathfinder from the 482nd Group leading the wing. As a result the intended radar bomb run had to be abandoned.

Leutnant Dittmer, directing the Lindenburg double-battery during the engagement, afterwards reported: 'After the eighteenth salvo we hit a machine flying in the middle of the formation. Leaving a trail of smoke it fell away.'

The unfortunate bomber was that piloted by Lieutenant Claude Kolb of the 401st. Losing height the B-17 curved away to the east with two of its engines shot out, a third on fire and the tail almost shot away. Unable to hold the crippled bomber in the air much longer Kolb ordered his crew to abandon it. One by one the ten men jumped clear.

On the ground Norbert Kelling had got out of his ditch when the bombs ceased exploding. Now the twelve-year-old watched Kolb's bomber spiralling down. 'I could make out some parachutes in the sky. My main hope now was that none of those Americans would land near me!' For a young boy it was all very unnerving, but the wind obligingly carried the parachutes well away from him. The plunging B-17 smashed into the ground near the little village of Biesow, ten miles to the northeast of Kelling.

Because of the cannonade and damage to the pathfinder aircraft the 94th Combat Wing was unable to pick out and attack another target before it reached the northern edge of Berlin. Its B-17s headed away to the north, bomb bays still full. The ground gunners had concentrated their fire on the 401st Bomb Group in the lead position; of the 18 aircraft in the group formation at the beginning of the engagement one, Kolb's, had been shot down and thirteen others damaged.

Succeeding bomb groups of the 1st Air Division released their bombs on other targets on the eastern side of Berlin. The 41st Combat Wing, comprising the 303rd and 379th Bomb Groups, bombed the Koepenick district. The 40th Combat Wing, comprising the 92nd and 306th Bomb Groups, pressed in closer to the city center than any other unit and bombed the Weissensee district. This took them within range of numerous gun batteries, including the 128 mm super-heavy guns on top of the Humbolthain flak bunker which loosed off 36 rounds at the raiders. The Wing suffered accordingly: of the 46 aircraft which attacked 38 were damaged by flak, in some cases seriously. The 40-41 Composite Wing at the end of the 1st Division put down its bombs on the Mahlsdorf district.

Tom Hayes had the shock of his life. Most of the German fighters and American escorts kept out of the flak-defended area immediately around Berlin, though there were exceptions. In his Mustang, Hayes was gaining nicely on the Me 109 ahead twisting and turning as it dived towards the capital in an effort to escape. The American pilot was concentrating on bringing his sight to bear when: 'Suddenly something large flashed past my aircraft. I looked around and there was a whole God-damned string of bombs, 500 pounders, going down! They looked like the rungs of a ladder except they were somewhat blurred. I looked up and all I could see were B-17s above me! I thought "To Hell with everything!", let the 109 go, rolled out of the way and split-S'd for the deck!'

As the 1st Bomb Division pulled away to the north of Berlin a few Messerschmitt 110s of Night Fighter Geschwader 5 closed in to pick off wounded bombers. Leutnant Guenther Wolf, leading a loose gaggle of four of the slow night fighters later recalled: 'We caught sight of the enemy bomber formation and, keeping a wary eye for enemy fighters, wondered how we were going to tackle them. Then we saw one bomber all by itself, straggling below the formation. "Now," we thought, "here is our chance!" ' Not a word passed on the radio but all four Messerschmitts swung after what looked like an easy target.

Wolf closed on his prey from behind. 'Suddenly when I was at about 600 meters, just outside firing range, my aircraft shuddered under the impact of bullets. The canopy was smashed and glass flew in all directions. I never saw what hit us.' Wolf's assailant was the P-51 flown by Lieutenant Leroy Ruder of the 357th Fighter Group. At the time Ruder had been flying clear of the main body of escorts, covering Captain William O'Brien whose engine was running rough. Then Wolf's Me 110 was sighted about 3,000 feet below the pair and, with O'Brien covering his tail, Ruder had dived out of the sun to a point immediately behind the Messerschmitt before pulling up to attack from underneath. 'I started firing and observed numerous strikes on the left engine. Debris flew from it and it immediately started smoking. My next burst was from about 150 yards and I observed hits all along the fuselage from nose to tail. The third burst I fired was slightly low but the fourth struck the right engine which immediately gushed forth a great deal of smoke and oil,' Ruder afterwards reported. 'The oil from the enemy aircraft covered my canopy and I broke away.'

Werner Wolf's Messerschmitt was now in severe trouble. 'My right engine burst into flames, streaming oil back across the wing and trailing black smoke. There was a terrible noise in the cockpit, with the wind whistling through the holes in the canopy,' he remembered. 'I shouted to my radio operator, Unteroffizier Hein Hafemeier, "Hein get out, quickly!" He shouted back "No! I can't! My parachute is ruined!" He was sitting on the pack but a couple of bullets had torn into it from the side, slashing away the cover and leaving him with the canopy spilling out underneath him. So he couldn't bail out and I couldn't leave him there to die; I decided to take the aircraft down and crash-land it.'

Wolf put the Messerschmitt into a steep diving turn, throttling back as he did so. He could not understand why the enemy fighter did not attack again, 'I should have been easy meat for him if he had done so. Probably he thought I was finished anyway.' It was an accurate assumption. To Ruder it looked as if the German fighter was in an uncontrollable spin; he followed it to 11,000 feet and lost sight of it spiralling down. The American pilot claimed the Me 110 destroyed. At the last moment Wolf leveled the aircraft out and made a wheels-up landing in fields near the small village of Albertshof to the northeast of Berlin.

When the Mustangs caught up with the lumbering night fighters they did great execution. Leutnant Hermann Hagen was leading a pair of the Me 110s when P-51s of the 357th hit and destroyed them both. Captain Joseph Broadhead dived after Hagen and scored many hits, which ignited fuel streaming from the Messerschmitt's wing tanks. The German pilot escaped into cloud and crash-landed in a snow-covered field near Erkner where the crew abandoned the aircraft to burn itself out. Leutnant Hermann Muth, Hagen's wing-man, was killed during the initial attack and his radio operator bailed out of the tumbling fighter.

Night Fighter Geschwader 5 was unable to claim a single kill during the action but suffered terribly at the hands of the Mustangs: of the 16 Me 110s sent to engage the raiders eleven were shot down and eight crewmen killed.

As the 1st Bomb Division was attacking the eastern side of the German capital leading elements of the 3rd Division were closing from the south on their primary target, the Robert Bosch electrical works at Klein Machnow. There too, however, the lead bombardiers found their target blanketed by a cloud bank and had to switch to secondary targets in Berlin itself. Just to the right and beyond Klein Machnow was an area clear of cloud through which parts of the city could be seen. The leaders headed for that.

The A and B Formations of the 4th Combat Wing, leading the 3rd Division, had both overshot by several miles their planned Initial Point west of Treuenbrietzen. Three of the four leading Combat Boxes cut the corner with the result that, instead of running in to bomb in line astern, they approached their bomb release points almost in line abreast.

Dietrich Scheibel, serving with Heavy Flak Abteilung 307 in the Tempelhof district, gazed at the approaching bomber formations in awe. To him it seemed the line-abreast approach was a clever ploy on the part of the Americans, for it was not immediately clear which box of bombers his battery should engage. The task of the battery was to protect the Daimler Benz tank engine plant nearby so the commander, Oberleutnant Mueller, selected the box heading for the plant and ordered his predictor crew to align on that one. As the bombers came within range the six 88 mm guns opened fire with rapid salvoes.

The box Mueller had selected comprised eighteen B-17s of the 447th Bomb Group. During the cannonade one of the Fortresses, piloted by Lieutenant Socolofsky, had two shells burst almost immediately under the fuselage. The blast blew out the hatch above the radio compartment and with it the unfortunate radio operator who fell to his death. Sergeant Ed Leighty, manning the waist gun in one of the unit's B-17s, hated this sort of flak more than anything: 'Although the fighter was the deadlier of the two you could do something back to him and that relieved the tension. But whenever there was a heavy concentration of flak all you could do was squeeze yourself into a ball and hope they wouldn't hit you.'

With the other boys manning the predictor at his battery, Dietrich Scheibel concentrated on holding his sighting telescope on the B-17 at the head of the 447th formation. Suddenly, without warning, Wachtmeister Saenger commanding the predictor detachment shouted '*Deckung!*' – take cover! Saenger, an old soldier from the eastern front, knew that if a bomb made a whistling sound there was nothing to worry about; if there was no whistle but just the sound of rushing air that meant the bomb was heading for him. He had heard the sound of rushing air and hurled himself to the ground, as did the boys. Even before everyone was down there was a huge bang and a blast wave threw everyone into a heap in one corner of the predictor pit; loose debris rained from above. One by one the men and boys picked themselves up and dusted themselves down. Then someone noticed one of the boys lying in the corner. He had a large bomb splinter embedded in his back and had been killed instantly. Probably part of a stick jettisoned by a damaged aircraft, three bombs had hit the battery site. Two exploded safely clear of the guns, the third fell about 5 yards from the packed-sand blast wall surrounding the predictor. With its predictor now out of action the battery had to cease firing.

The four leading boxes of bombers continued towards the area clear of cloud, under which lay the Steglitz district of Berlin, with a total of 75 B-17s: two pathfinders from the 482nd, and the remainder from the 94th, 385th and 447th Bomb Groups. Several flak units engaged the bombers during their attack runs and from German records it is clear that seven of the batteries, drawn from Heavy Flak Abteilungen 126, 307 and 662, fired off 300 rounds of 88 mm and 228 rounds of 105 mm during this part of the engagement.

From B-17 'Blitzin' Betsy', in one of the following Wings, Lieutenant Lowell Watts of the 388th Bomb Group watched the fusillade. 'A dark, puffy veil that hung like a pall of death covered the capital city. It was the heaviest flak I had ever seen. It almost seemed to swallow up the bomber formations as they entered it.'

Just before it reached the bomb-release point the lead pathfinder-aircraft, carrying the 3rd Division air commander Colonel Russell Wilson, suffered severe damage from a shell exploding nearby. With one engine on fire the pilot, Major Fred Rabo, held it on the bomb run until the smoke markers and bombs had been released, then ordered everyone to abandon the crippled machine. A few seconds later the bomber blew up. The copilot, Lieutenant 'Red' Morgan who had won the Congressional Medal of Honor some months earlier for bringing back a bomber with a dying pilot, suddenly found himself falling through space with his parachute pack tucked under his arm – he had not had time to clip it to his harness. As Morgan collected his wits he tried to pull the pack in with his left arm and clip it on, but found it almost impossible to do so. 'I couldn't figure out why it was taking so long, until later. I was pulling awful hard with my left hand but I was holding on even harder with my right arm. I guess I didn't want to drop it!' Morgan's terrifying predicament lasted about a minute before he finally succeeded in clipping on the pack. He pulled the ripcord at the last possible moment for survival: with a jerk the parachute slammed open and immediately afterwards he crashed into the top of a tree.

The German flak report on the engagement bears testimony to the narrowness of Morgan's escape:

> The enemy aircraft, trailing dark smoke, lost height and fell away from the formation. Shortly afterwards it exploded in a sheet of flame and pieces fell to the ground. Two dead crewmen came down north of Heinersdorf, one engine and various bits landed near Lichterfelde, the fuselage of the aircraft, the nose, the remaining engines, other pieces and four dead crewmen were later found in Section 97 of the Grunewald.

The distance from Heinersdorf to Section 97 of the Grunewald is 7 miles.

Lowell Watts observed the tussle with admiration and growing apprehension. 'One ship blew up and three others dropped away from their formations. But still the formations went in to drop their bombs. It didn't seem that anything could fly through that. But there they were, Flying Fortresses sailing proudly away from the scene of devastation. It wasn't too comforting to realize that soon we would enter that Hellish scene.'

Of the 75 bombers in the leading four boxes, one had been shot down and 49 suffered flak damage.

The bombs from the 4th Combat Wing exploded across the Steglitz district, a mainly residential area. One chance cluster of bombs landed immediately to the south of the Hauptkadettenanstalt, the barracks of the *SS Division Leibstandarte Adolf Hitler* the Fuehrer's personal bodyguard, but without causing any serious damage to the buildings.

At the Telefunken works nearby, Horst Krieger and his workmates had taken shelter in their dugouts when they saw the bombers approaching. Huddled in the semi-darkness, they felt the walls shudder as bombs exploded nearby.

Marianne Wittstock, in the cellar of the Rittberg Hospital with those patients who could be moved, now began to get frantic for the safety of her new-born daughter as the sound of exploding bombs came closer. One of the doctors tried to comfort her, saying that her baby was with the others in an especially strong concrete bunker nearby and would come to no harm. But his words did little good: so far as Marianne Wittstock was concerned a young baby could be safe only with its mother.

In the cellar of his house, one mile away to the west, 66-year-old estate agent Adolf Echtler sat with his wife Alma listening to the whistles and crumps of the bombs. Then there was a colossal bang and everything shuddered, the room filled with dust and loose sand. Coughing and gasping for air Echtler and his wife struggled up the staircase on all fours. At the top he pushed open the door leading outside and saw that where the neighboring house had been was only a pile of rubble. His secretary had taken shelter there. Fearing for her safety he dashed to the remains shouting her name but there was no reply. He tried to pull away the rubble with his bare hands but the task was too much for an old man. Then he heard yet more bombers approaching and had to run back to his own shelter.

Attacking with the 4th Combat Wing, Lieutenant Roy Menning piloting B-17 'Casey Jones' of the 94th Bomb Group told his crew to keep a sharp watch on a nearby Fortress bearing another group's markings, which had slipped into their formation about half an hour earlier. Like everyone else he had heard rumors of bombers flown by enemy crews trying to infiltrate formations and to Menning it seemed this aircraft might be one of them. 'A captured B-17 manned by Germans followed us around the Berlin area except in the heavy flak. I realized it had to be a German B-17 when he pulled away when the flak started getting close. I ordered my crew to shoot him down if he came in again, but he kept his distance . . .'

In fact the B-17 was 'Our Gal Sal' of the 100th Bomb Group, a fugitive from the shattered 13th Wing B Formation which had moved forward and joined up with the 4th Wing in front. Bob Shoens at the controls of the Fortress had a good idea of what the crews of the aircraft around him were thinking: 'I knew we had a lot of gunners looking at us, because we had been warned to watch out for Germans flying captured aircraft and joining the formations.' After the bomb run Shoens decided to leave the formation, though not for the sinister motives ascribed by Menning: 'For some reason, after bombing, the group turned left which took them right into the heaviest flak. Since we were not part of the group we went the other way and, once again, found ourselves alone.'

The other combat wings of the 3rd Division continued up the western side of the capital and bombed targets there; for the most part the bombardiers lined up on holes in the cloud through which anything of Berlin could be seen. The 13th Combat Wing A Formation released its bombs in the Spandau district. There Army Gefreiter Guenther Lemm was working at the Falkenhagener Chaussee Depot fitting radios to armored half-track vehicles before they were shipped to the battle fronts. When the sirens sounded the men had gone outside their workshops and on the approach of the thirty-five B-17s they gazed up curiously at the parading bombers. Suddenly a line of gray smoke appeared behind the aircraft and one of the soldiers, who had seen it before and realized its dreadful significance, bellowed 'Take cover!' There were no shelters or dugouts nearby so the soldiers dashed for cover in bomb craters left by an earlier RAF night attack. Then came the shrieks of falling bombs followed by loud explosions, hot waves of blast and clouds of dust and sand falling from above.

INTENDED TARGETS, AREAS BOMBED AND POSITIONS OF WITNESSES IN AND AROUND BERLIN

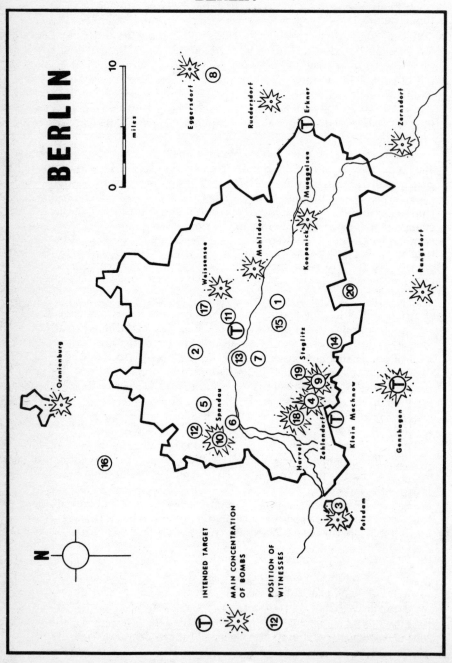

BERLIN

There was a short silence, shattered by the screams of wounded men. A stick of bombs had fallen across one of the earlier craters, burying several soldiers and injuring others. Lemm and his comrades set about trying to dig the men out of the loose gray sand with their bare hands; in many cases they were successful, though four of the buried had suffocated before they could be reached. The bombs set on fire two workshops and damaged two others. Lemm and some of the other soldiers tried to extinguish the blaze but it was a hopeless task; the forty half-tracks inside were destroyed.

Listening to the bombs exploding nearby, from a public air raid shelter in the Wilmersdorf district, was 27-year-old university student Ursula Kath. Although it was strictly forbidden to take pets into public shelters an old lady sitting opposite had brought a large sheepdog. On the sound of exploding bombs the old lady became more and more agitated, then collapsed in a faint. The other

The primary targets for the mission were the VKF ball bearing plant at Erkner, the Robert Bosch electrical equipment works at Klein Machnow and the Daimler Benz aero engine plant at Genshagen. If any of these targets were concealed by cloud, the raiders were to make radar bomb runs taking the main Friedrichstrasse rail station, in the center of Berlin, as their aiming point. In the event cloud banks prevented attacks on Erkner and Klein Machnow and allowed only a few bombers to attack Genshagen. And in each case the decision to abandon the attack on the primary target was made too late for the formations to realign themselves for radar bomb runs on the Friedrichstrasse station. Individual bomb wings and groups were then left to attack whatever they could in and around Berlin and bomb concentrations were scattered over a wide area. The numbers on the map refer to the positions of witnesses, as follows:

1. Arthur von Brietzke, Foreign Ministry Official, Keukolln district.
2. Leon Butticaz, French forced laborer, DWM factory, Reinickendorf district.
3. Hans-Joachim Dombrowski, schoolboy, Potsdam district.
4. Adolf Echtler, estate agent, Zehlendorf district.
5. Luftwaffenhelfer Gottfried Gottschalk, Light Flak Abteilung 722, Siemens-stadt district.
6. Elfriede Grasser, housewife, Spandau district.
7. Ursula Kath, university student, Wilmersdorf district.
8. Norbert Kelling, schoolboy, Eggersdorf.
9. Horst Krieger, Telefunken company apprentice, Steglitz district.
10. Gefeiter Guenther Lemm, Falkenhagener Chaussee Army Depot, Spandau district.
11. Gert Mueller, Reichs Post Office engineering apprentice, Central district.
12. Luftwaffenoberhelfer Hans Ring, Heavy Flak Abteilung 437, Spandau district.
13. Kriegseinsatzfuehrer Werner Schaeffer, Zoo district flak bunker.
14. Luftwaffenhelfer Dietrich Scheibel, Heavy Flak Abteilung 307, Tempelhof district.
15. Luftwaffenhelfer Guenther Schulze, Light Flak Abteilung 979, Tempelhof district.
16. Luftwaffenhelfer Werner Synakiewicz, Heavy Flak Abteilung 422, Marwitz.
17. Gertrud Tappert, housewife, Prenzlauerberg district.
18. Police Oberwachtmeister Wilhelm Winkler, Zehlendorf district.
19. Marianne Wittstock, housewife, Rittberg Hospital, Steglitz district.
20. Luftwaffenhelfer Alexander Witzigmann, Flak Grossbatterie, Gross Zeithen.

shelterers tried to assist her but the dog fiercely held them off and, in trying to defend his mistress, lashed out and bit Ursula Kath on the cheek. After this the shelterers decided to leave the old lady alone and let her recover by herself.

Serving as an observer with Heavy Flak Abteilung 437 also in the Spandau district, Hans Ring was another of those distressed to see so many American bombers over the capital: 'The sky over Berlin seemed full of American aircraft, and no German ones at all!' To the south he saw bombs exploding in the Steglitz and Spandau districts, hurling skywards great curtains of smoke, dust and the distinctive light-gray Berlin sand.

The opportunity to engage enemy bombers with optically laid fire by day was a new and unaccustomed one for the Berlin defenders, though this gave rise to some problems. 'Working the range-finder on the predictor at our battery we had an adult, a very stupid Obergefreiter. Suddenly in the middle of one of the engagements he threw himself to the ground and covered his head with his hands. Denied ranging information, the predictor could not function and the battery had to cease firing,' recalled Ring. 'Everybody stared at the man who got off the ground looking very sheepish. Peering through the powerful x32 telescopes of the range-finder, he had been watching the bombers with their bomb doors open and had seen the bombs falling away. And he thought the bombs were coming at him!' The youths, at an age when they were critical of adults at the best of times, made no allowance for human frailty. 'From that day on we boys had no respect for him at all,' Ring continued.

The 13th Combat Wing B Formation, reduced to 33 bombers after the vicious fighter attack near Haseluenne, put down its bombs northwest of Potsdam. There it came under accurate flak and other bombers suffered damage. Sergeant Harold Stearns, top turret gunner of B-17 'Rubber Check' of the 100th Bomb Group, felt his aircraft rock as a shell exploded nearby and the right outboard engine started to burn. 'We fell out of formation and Frank Granack, our pilot, called Major Elton leading the flight and asked if he could slow the formation by at least 5 mph so that we could catch up. Elton said it was impossible but wished Frank luck. We watched the formation of B-17s disappear from sight. We were all alone.'

The 45th Combat Wing, B Formation, drifted out well to the east of Berlin and put down its bombs on stone quarries near Ruedersdorf.

The A Formation failed to find a clear target on the south side of the capital and continued across the most heavily defended part of the city. 'Our Group leader opened his bomb doors and we followed suit,' recalled Lowell Watts. 'However the turn into the target was not made. Instead we were making a wide sweeping circle to the left over the city. Precious seconds mounted into minutes and still we did not begin our bomb run.' That curve saved the Wing from a terrible beating; it made prediction difficult and most of the flak shells burst safely outside the formation. But this did little to assuage the fears of the men now loitering over one of the most dangerous places on earth. Watts continued: 'Tempers mounted and the radio crackled with curses and challenges to the men aboard our lead plane. "Get that damn thing headed towards the target!" "What in Hell do you think this is? The scenery may be pretty, but we're not one damned bit interested in it!" "If you ain't got the guts to fly through that, let somebody else lead this formation!" '

Finally, to the northeast of the target, the A Formation leveled out and started its bomb run on the Oranienburg district. 'Then the flak hit us. They didn't start out with wild shots and work in closer. The first salvo they sent up was right on us. We could hear the metal of our plane rend and tear as each volley exploded. The hits weren't direct. They were just far enough away so they didn't take off a wing, the tail, or blow the plane up; they would just tear a ship half apart without completely knocking it out,' Watts commented. 'Big, ragged holes appeared in the wings and the fuselage. Kennedy, the copilot, was watching nothing but the instruments, waiting for the tell-tale indication of a damaged or ruined engine. But they kept up their steady roar, even as the ship rocked from the nearness of the flak bursts.' The guns below were served by 15- to 17-year-old schoolboys, but these certainly seemed to know their business.

One shell burst buffettingly close to 'Blitzin' Betsy' and knocked out part of the oxygen system to the rear crew members. By connecting up to reserve bottles, the men kept going. 'The flak was coming up as close as ever, increasing in intensity. Above and to the right of us a string of bombs trailed out from our lead ship. Simultaneously our ship jumped upwards, relieved of its explosive load as the call "Bombs away!" came over the interphone. Our left wing ship, one engine feathered, dropped behind the formation,' Watts continued. 'Shortly afterwards, it seemed like a long time, the flak stopped. We had come through it and all four engines were purring away.'

The gunners on the ground, of course, saw no effect of their fire unless an enemy aircraft fell away from the formation in a spectacular manner. Serving with a double-battery of Heavy Flak Abteilung 422 at Marwitz, south of Oranienburg, 15-year-old Luftwaffenhelfer Werner Synakiewicz tracked a passing bomber formation through his rangefinder telescopes. During the engagement the sixteen 88 mm guns loosed off more than a hundred rounds and Synakiewicz watched the shells detonating in exactly the right place just below the aircraft. But the salvoes seemed to have no effect at all; the bombers, seemingly made of steel and impervious to the fire, droned on as if nothing had happened. He had no idea of how terrible it was to be on the receiving end of such a bombardment.

Bringing up the rear of the attack were the B-24s of the 2nd Division. At 1.20 pm the 389th Bomb Group, part of the 2nd Combat Wing at the head of the division, aimed its bombs at the partially obscured aero engine plant at Genshagen; it was the first of the attacking units to make a serious attempt to hit its primary target. The other two bomb groups in the wing, the 445th and the 453rd, aimed their bombs into the southern and western sections of the city. Both units were heavily engaged by the flak defenses, including the 128 mm super heavy guns on the flak towers. Lieutenant Hubert Cripe of the 453rd struggled to hold his B-24 in formation as shells burst all around: 'Jerry had the most intense flak barricade I'd ever seen. It was solid black smoke and red flashes. We continued on course, all bombers had their bomb bays open, the lead plane in the wing was using its bomb sight and making corrections. Flak bursts were everywhere. We rolled from concussion and spent particles rattled off our airplane like BBs*'. The 445th came under attack from several Heavy Flak Abteilungen including Hans Ring's (the 437th), the 211th and the special Flak Batterie 5552 whose guns were mounted on railway flatcars. One B-24, 'God Bless Our Ship', had two engines knocked out and a third set on fire; it fell away from the formation losing altitude and trailing smoke. One by one, parachutes plopped open behind the stricken bomber.

Of the second B-24 Wing, the 14-96, the 44th and 458th Bomb Groups aimed their bombs at Genshagen. The third group, the 392nd, put down its bombs on the Potsdam district of the city. In the past there had been cases of bomb doors of B-24s inching closed during bomb runs; if they went too far, a safety switch operated to prevent the bombs releasing. Until aircraft could be modified to cure this fault the radio operators had to position themselves over the front of the bomb bay and press the lever to hold the bomb doors fully open. As he did so Sergeant Don Chase of the 44th Bomb Group looked down hoping for a glimpse of Berlin: 'I remember seeing a lot of clouds and flak bursts; there were some great rifts in the cloud, but I don't remember seeing anything of the city.'

The last to attack the capital was the 20th Combat Wing, which put down its bombs on the Zehlendorf district. Perched high on his watch tower Police Oberwachtmeister Wilhelm Winkler saw the first sticks of bombs exploding some way from him and reported their locations to his headquarters by telephone. Through his binoculars he saw a fire starting on the roof of the nearby Rheingold Hotel and as a result of his report the fire brigade was able to extinguish the flames before they could take hold. Then a salvo of bombs burst all around his tower, causing the structure to rock on its foundations. The blast shattered the windows and hurled Winkler to the floor with broken glass and bits of equipment flying around the observation room.

As the B-24s curved away from their targets the flak gunners followed them with their salvoes. The 128 mm guns of Heavy Flak Abteilung 123 on the Humbolthain and Zoo bunkers joined in this engagement, loosing off 91 rounds at the B-24s of the 93rd Bomb Group. Later Oberleutnant Maschewski, directing the fire from the Humbolthain bunker, reported how his guns had engaged a formation of Liberators to the southwest:

The bombers were engaged with repeated salvoes from all eight 128 mm guns. During the course of the engagement the altitude of the targets reduced from 6,400 m to 6,000 m, velocity 130 meters per second. Tracked by the Em 10m R 43 [optical rangefinder] the formation flew without taking any evasive action, from Direction 7 [south-southwest] to Direction 9 [west]. Fire was opened at maximum effective engagement range and soon after the detonation of the initial salvo a machine in the middle of the formation began to trail dark smoke from both outer motors.

The aircraft was 'De-Icer' of the 93rd, which had suffered severe damage to the nose and the left inboard engine. As it fell away from the formation the pilot gave the order to bail out. Breaking up, the aircraft spun to the ground and crashed in the Spandau district narrowly missing a house. Hans Ring, concentrating his attention on the main formation being engaged by his

*Ball Bearings

battery, was suddenly astonished to see a complete B-24 fin and rudder assembly coming down like a falling leaf near his gunsite.

Wilhelm Winkler was in agony as he eased his badly cut and shaken body slowly down the long spiral staircase of his watchtower and went in search of medical treatment. Already the last of the bombers had pulled away to the north and the sounds of aircraft engines and gunfire quickly receded. Back on the ground he saw numerous bomb craters near the tower, but the houses there were well spaced and few had suffered major damage. Sand from the bomb craters had been blasted over many of the buildings, leaving them with a covering of fine gray powder.

At 2.07 pm the all-clear sounded in Berlin and the city began to return to normal. At Siemenstadt Gottfried Gottschalk and his light flak troop received the order '*Feuerbereitschaft aufgehoben!*' – readiness cancelled! Throughout the entire attack not one of the hundreds of bombers passing overhead had come within reach of their 37 mm guns. Now the ammunition clips were removed from the breeches and returned to the lockers, the firing springs were released and the canvas covers replaced on the guns. 'Then we walked back to our billets feeling tired and disappointed.'

In the Potsdam district 13-year-old schoolboy Hans-Joachim Dombrowski and his friends ran from their shelter as soon as the all-clear sounded. The great attraction for them was the bomb and shell splinters left after the attack, avidly collected by the boys and traded between them. The initial search of the immediate area revealed none, then Dombrowski chanced to look up and noticed a couple of parachutes seemingly stationary in the sky. Awestruck, the boys watched their descent. The nearer of the two came closer and closer until it touched down about a hundred yards from them. Cautiously the boys advanced on the parachutist, fearful he might have a gun. But when they reached the man they found him lying dead on the grass with the parachute streamed out beside him. Dombrowski did not dwell on the body long, his mind was on other things: dress material was hard to come by at this stage of the war and a panel from the parachute would be a valuable prize for his mother and sister. But before he could slice one out with his knife some men from the nearby flak site came running up shouting 'Don't touch anything!' 'Go home you kids!' 'Scram!' Reluctantly the schoolboys left the gruesome scene and sauntered off looking for other, less useful, booty.

Long after the last bomber had passed out of sight and sound there was one final legacy of the raid: hundreds of thousands of propaganda leaflets began to descend on the city after their long flutter to earth. Squads from the Hitler Youth and the League of German Girls were immediately detailed to pick them up. Anyone caught reading the offensive literature was liable to be punished.

In the Wilmersdorf district Ursula Kath emerged from the shelter still bleeding from her cheek where the dog had bitten her. Once outside she found the sky so full of smoke and dust it was almost dark as night. Her first priority was to get an anti-tetanus injection so she walked to the hospital in the nearby Nikolsburger Platz. There she received first aid but no injection; there had been such a run on the serum the supply had run out.

Horst Krieger climbed out of his dug-out shelter beside the Telefunken works in the Steglitz district to see that some of the factory buildings had been hit and badly damaged. Nearer to hand a stick of bombs had exploded close to one of the shelters; the blast had blown away the concrete slabs on top and collapsed the sides on those inside. Already the firm's rescue service had gone into action, with frantic efforts to scoop the loose Berlin sand from the unfortunate mens' heads. But in many cases the rescuers were too late and the men had suffocated. Now the heads of the dead protruded above the ground in a line, looking like so many grotesquely distorted footballs.

In the cellar of the Rittberg Hospital nearby, Marianne Wittstock was getting more and more frantic about the safety of her new-born baby. Halfway through the attack a bomb had severed the electrical supply cable to the area, dowsing lights in the cellar. Until the harassed nurses had been able to light candles the patients were in darkness. After the all-clear the patients had to remain in the cellar because without electricity the hospital's elevator would not function.

In the Zehlendorf district Adolf Echtler summoned police and civil defense workers to the wrecked house next door, where his secretary and another woman had been sheltering. Soon a 30-man rescue team arrived and began tunneling into the rubble.

Gert Mueller and his classmates emerged from the basement of the Post Office technical school in the center of Berlin flabergasted at the day's events. No enemy bomb had fallen anywhere near their shelter but they had clearly heard them exploding in the distance. 'I thought "My Gosh, if they can do that once they can do it again!" It was a serious development – enemy bombers were not supposed to be able to get through to Berlin by day!'

With two engines knocked out Lieutenant George Lymburn struggled to maintain control of his extensively damaged B-24 'God Bless our Ship' of the 445th Bomb Group as it rapidly lost height. After it had been hit by flak over Berlin all of the other crewmen, apart from the tail gunner, had bailed out. Lymburn set the aircraft down on open ground near Neuruppin, 25 miles northwest of the capital. He was watched by Nazi party member Guenther Kuenst who afterwards reported:

On 6 March at about 13.45 hours, during the period of the alarm, I observed a four-engined machine coming from the south with its left inner motor on fire. The aircraft lost altitude and flew over Brandishof, then landed on the Karwar meadows 300 meters from the forest. I saw that the aircraft had lowered its left wheel. From the south, whence the aircraft had come, I observed many flak bursts. I did not see any parachutes. After the landing I inspected the aircraft and saw flak damage.

Heil Hitler!
(signed) G. Kuenst

After Guenther Wolf and Hein Hafemeier had collected their wits, following the crash-landing of their Me 110 night fighter near Albertshof after their brush with Mustangs, the two set out to walk to the village half a mile away. About half way there they met a small crowd of old men, women and boys armed with farm tools and staves who advanced on them menacingly. Quickly the two Luftwaffe men assured the villagers that they were German, upon which the mood changed to one of helpfulness. Wolf's first care was for the security of the highly secret SN-2 radar carried by the fighter. While Hafemeier and one of the men returned to the aircraft to guard it, Wolf was taken to a telephone to call the nearby Luftwaffe unit. A truck soon arrived to pick up the two-man crew, the radar boxes were pulled out of the Messerschmitt and loaded on board. Wolf and Hafemeier were dropped at the railway station at Bernau to make their way back to Leipzig, more than 100 miles away, by train. Waiting on the platform they smoked cigarettes, looking conspicuous in their yellow life jackets and gray flying helmets and suits; at their feet lay their parachute packs, Hafemeier's with great bullet tears and part of the silk canopy hanging out. 'We were standing there, feeling self-important at the stares from the civilians on the station, when I noticed something odd about the top of Hein's helmet,' Wolf remembered. 'He pulled it off and a great handful of hair came away with it. Across the top of the helmet was a long slash. I had a look at his scalp and saw a thin weal, as though made by a finger nail. One of the enemy bullets had grazed the top of his head leaving a red swelling. The skin was not broken, there was no blood. That was the sole injury suffered by either of us!'

After bailing out of his Fortress Bryce Evertson landed immediately to the east of Berlin. There was quite a lot of snow on the ground but no trees or cover of any sort. Evertson decided to try and merge with his surroundings and hide until nightfall. 'I just rolled myself up in my parachute and thought "The Germans will never find me here, the parachute is the same color as the snow." Well, it took all of five minutes for a German army patrol to find me!'

With both right engines knocked out by flak over Berlin, B-17 'Liberty Lady' of the 306th Bomb Group limped northwards away from the German capital. Obviously it would not be possible to regain England but the pilot, Lieutenant Charles Smith, thought he might be able to reach Soviet occupied territory – though the navigator carried no maps of that part of the world. Smith eased the damaged bomber into a bank of cloud to conceal it from enemy fighters and headed on instruments to the northeast.

Lieutenant Charles York's B-24, 'Hello Natural' of the 448th Bomb Group, had an engine shot out by flak and also some of its fuel tanks punctured. It broke away from the formation and its pilot headed north trying to make Sweden.

During the cannonade over Berlin two B-17s and three B-24s were shot down and crashed in the target area; and about half the bombers which reached the capital suffered flak damage of one sort or another, in several cases sufficient to force them to leave the protection of their formations and so become especially vulnerable to· fighter attack. Two damaged bombers headed north and northeast away from Berlin, their crews hoping to reach Swedish and Soviet territory respectively.

As the citizens of Berlin emerged from their shelters and began to take stock of the damage their city had suffered, the day's battle was far from over. The

CHAPTER 6

THE LONG WAY HOME

2.08 to 5.48 pm

In battle most men expose themselves enough to satisfy the needs of honor; few wish to do more than this, or more than enough to carry to success the action in which engaged.

François de la Rochefoucauld

It was 2.08 pm and as the 'All Clear' finished sounding throughout the German capital the bomber wings streamed away to the northwest to re-form into their divisional formations. Due to cloud and technical problems, the B-17s of the 94th Combat Wing and the Lead Box of the 45th Wing had failed to find suitable targets in or near Berlin. These aircraft still had bomb loads on board. The 94th Wing now carried out a long bomb run on the small town of Templin, 25 miles north of Berlin. There the thirty-seven B-17s of the Lead and Low Boxes, drawn from the 401st and 351st Bomb Groups respectively, put down their high explosive bombs. They caused considerable damage. The town's hospital was hit and parts razed to the ground; fifty patients were killed and numerous others injured. The High Box of the Wing, comprising sixteen B-17s of the 457th Bomb Group, failed to receive the bomb release signal however; its aircraft came away from this secondary target still with bombs on board.

As the raiding force left Berlin it trailed numerous stragglers, damaged aircraft which made inviting prey for German fighters. One was B-17 'Rubber Check' of the 100th Bomb Group, which had had an engine knocked out by flak over the capital. Sergeant Harold Stearns, manning the top turret, felt very lonely and vulnerable 'I was looking for bandits when I heard the radio operator, Grant Scott, call over the interphone "Fighters at 3 o'clock!". I turned my turret to 3 o'clock and sure enough there was an Me 109 blasting away. I think Scott must have been killed instantly. I fired from my turret and could see smoke coming from the enemy fighter . . .' The B-17 had suffered further damage however and Lieutenant Frank Granack ordered his crew to bail out. 'We were losing altitude, smoke pouring from Nos 3 and 4 engines,' Stearns continued. 'I bailed out from the bomb bay doors, waited until I had cleared the plane, then pulled open my chest chute. In the distance I could see "Rubber Check" chugging along, black smoke trailing from its damaged engines.'

All of the crew apart from the radio operator and one of the gunners, who had been killed during the fighter attack, successfully jumped from the crippled bomber. Descending slowly under autopilot the B-17 continued northwest-wards until the No 3 engine failed also. Then the crewless bomber began to go down faster in a series of wide turns. On the ground Otto Weichert watched the aircraft circle several times almost over the small town of Halenbeck. It came down so gradually that to him it seemed a human pilot was flying it. 'After losing altitude it finally attempted a belly landing 300 meters north of Halenbeck. During this maneuver the aircraft struck some trees and boulders scattered around the area. It overturned several times and was smashed to pieces.'

Flight Officer Bernie Dopko, piloting B-17 'Little Willie' of the 388th Bomb Group, had two engines damaged by flak and had also been forced to leave the protection of his formation. He too came under fighter attack soon after he left Berlin. The bomber suffered several 20 mm hits and the rear gunner received severe head injuries. 'As the Germans were circling for another pass, I maneuvered the plane as best I could to appear that we were out of control and headed down to the deck. I guess it worked as the attack was broken off and we leveled out below 50 feet,' Dopko later recalled. The crew was now some 350 miles inside enemy territory, alone and at low altitude, in a badly damaged aircraft with two engines knocked out and unable to exceed 115 mph in level flight. Too busy controlling the bomber to consider the full implications of his plight, Dopko pointed the nose of the B-17 due west for England.

Having earlier had to use maximum war emergency power to pull his P-51 away from the Me 109s all around him, Rod Starkey found he had taken even the rugged Merlin engine beyond its limits: 'I found that every time I tried to retard the throttle the engine would suddenly quit, and every time I advanced the throttle it would quit.' Ahead Starkey could see bombers moving northwest away from the target and he moved to join them. He closed on the bombers with the utmost caution, necessary when approaching gunners who tended to shoot first and ask questions afterwards. Everything had to be done slowly. 'You went in sideways showing your silhouette, never approaching the bombers from behind, above, or in any manner that could be thought threatening, but taking plenty of time and showing the silhouette of the wings. I was able to get in underneath the wing of a B-17 and flew back to England, not escorting the bombers but with the bombers escorting me.'

After he had shot down an Me 110, Lieutenant Archie Chatterley of the 4th Fighter Group went down to low altitude with Lieutenant John Godfrey to shoot up a train. Still keeping low, the pair found themselves approaching the Henschel works airfield at Johannisthal on the southern outskirts of Berlin; both made strafing attacks and scored hits on at least one of the brand-new Junkers 88 bombers parked around the perimeter. Shortly afterwards they came upon a train which they shot up also.

Now beginning to run low on fuel, Chatterley and Godfrey headed west for home. They had not gone far when the exertions of the day caught up with Chatterley and he had to urinate. A makeshift tube was carried in the cockpit for this purpose, but before it could be used a great deal of strap-loosening, unzipping and general fumbling was necessary. 'I was just beginning to relieve myself when tracers passed on each side of me, converging in front. I could hear the firing and I thought my guns were running away. Lt Godfrey called to break, which I did without putting any of the relief equipment back in place.' As Chatterley pulled into a steep turn to avoid the assailant his P-51 was hit in the wings and tail and two of his propeller blades were pierced by machine gun rounds. Godfrey engaged the attacker, an Me 109, and allowed Chatterley to pull away; none of the damage impaired the flying ability of the Mustang and Chatterley continued homewards.

The three bomb divisions came together at the Rallying Point almost over the small town of Kyritz, northwest of Berlin, then turned west for England. For the return flight the bomb divisions flew almost in line abreast, with the 1st to the north, the 3rd in the center and the 2nd Bomb Division in the south. The combat wing formations were now bunched together in a relatively compact mass which made easier the task of the escort fighters.

At the Rallying Point the P-51s which had given such valiant support to the bombers in the target area began to run short of fuel and one by one sections had to break away and head for home. Now the escort was taken up by 23 P-38s of the 20th Fighter Group, followed soon afterwards by 32 more from the 364th. There should have been more P-38s to cover the bombers but the 55th Fighter Group, which had put up 47 P-38s for this phase of the escort, had sixteen develop defects; most of the failures occurred over enemy territory and the need to provide aircraft to escort them back to England prevented the 55th from playing any effective part in screening the bombers.

One of those keeping watch on the bombers' homeward flight at this time was Leutnant Rudolf Thun, piloting an old Me 110F of Night Fighter Geschwader 5. Thun's orders were to report the bombers' movements to the headquarters of the 1st Fighter Division at Doeberitz; keeping out of harm's way close to the ground, some 18,000 feet beneath the bombers, the Messerschmitt crew passed back the required information.

Just past the Rallying Point the sixteen B-17s of the 388th Bomb Group, which still had their bombs on board, carried out an attack on the Kurmaerkische Zellwolle textile factory just outside the town of Wittenberge on the Elbe river. Their bombs straddled the works and caused severe damage to a large warehouse and several smaller buildings.

Captain Glendon Davis of the 357th Fighter Group was in one of the last of the target support P-51s to leave the bombers. He was on the point of heading for home when he caught sight of a straggling B-17 some way below with an FW 190 sitting on its tail. Davis and his wingman, Lieutenant Tom Harris, dived to engage the enemy fighter which broke away from the bomber and turned into the attackers. 'We turned into him and then he started for the deck in a tight spiral. We followed him down indicating from 450 to 500 mph. We were forcing him to keep a tight spiral by cutting on the inside of him whenever he tried to widen it out,' Davis afterwards reported. 'At 10,000 feet he dropped his belly tank. At 5,000 feet his plane appeared to be stalling as he tried to pull out. His canopy flew off but the plane went right on into the ground without the pilot ever getting out.' In fact the FW 190 was one of the especially heavily armored aircraft operated by Sturmstaffel 1; burdened by the additional weight it had stalled out trying to turn with the American fighters. The Focke-Wulf crashed into the ground near its base at Salzwedel and the pilot was killed, without either P-51 pilot being able to loose off a shot at it.

Relieved of the need to safeguard the bombers, those P-51s with ammunition left now rampaged westwards across northern Germany looking for targets in the air or on the ground. Major Tom Hayes of the 357th was returning with his flight at low altitude when he spotted a single Me 109 out to one side. Hayes curved into an attacking position, opened fire from 300 yards and observed the Messerschmitt begin to smoke. Then an airfield hove into view. 'I was pulling up on him and suddenly he put his flaps and landing gear down. I was concentrating on getting my sight on him and all of a sudden he seemed to be backing up. I opened fire and shot him down,' Hayes later recalled. The airfield was Stendal, home of IInd Gruppe of Fighter Geschwader 302 and the Messerschmitt had belonged to that unit; the pilot was killed. Hayes and his flight stayed in the vicinity long enough to work over some Heinkel 111 bombers dispersed around the airfield perimeter, then continued their homeward flight.

After his one-wheeled landing at Wunstorf earlier in the afternoon, Heinz Knoke of Fighter Geschwader 11 was preparing to get airborne in another Me 109 for his second mission of the day. Knoke was strapping himself in with the canopy open; on the right wing of the fighter stood a couple of mechanics, slowly turning the huge crank handle of the flywheel to start the engine. A true fighter pilot's instinct for survival never leaves him and something caught Knoke's eye out to the left: a pair of black specks against the eastern horizon. They were approaching aircraft, fast and low: American fighters coming in to strafe the airfield! 'I threw off my straps and scrambled out of the cockpit, shouted "*Tiefangriff!*" at the mechanics and dived into a small ditch nearby. One of the mechanics followed a few steps behind. But the second remained on the wing, looking around and wondering what was happening,' Knoke later recounted. 'At that moment bullets started flying around us. The Messerschmitt was hit several times in and around the cockpit, the canopy was smashed. Then the Mustangs flashed close overhead and were away, they did not come back. Immediately afterwards we heard agonized cries from the second mechanic, the poor man had three fingers shot off his right hand and had taken a round through his buttock.

The assailant had been Lieutenant John Carder of the 357th Fighter Group, flying as part of Tom Hayes's flight, who afterwards reported: 'We came upon an airfield which was very well camouflaged, even at close range. The planes had netting over them. I fired a long burst at an Me 109 and detected numerous hits and believe I may have hit one or both crew members on the wing of the enemy aircraft.'

Knoke helped carry the wounded man to the pilots' readiness room nearby and he was laid on the table on his stomach. He was bleeding quite badly and Knoke told one of his men to telephone for an ambulance. Then the pilot ordered yet another Messerschmitt to be made ready so he could go into action.

Still Hayes's Mustangs had not finished. Passing south of Bremen after

gaining altitude, the P-51s came upon another lone Me 109. Hayes ordered
Lieutenant John Howell, with Carder covering him, to go down and engage.
'Lt Howell fired on the enemy aircraft from 300 yards down to close range,
breaking off to the left as he rapidly overran,' Carder later wrote. 'Then I closed
to 100 yards and opened fire, observing strikes. The enemy aircraft then dove to
the ground from 5,000 feet and I followed at close range, firing numerous bursts
and observing strikes. The enemy aircraft cut its throttle and pulled up to
approximately 2,000 feet. He released his canopy as I continued to fire, getting
strikes.' The pilot bailed out of the shot-up Messerschmitt, but as his parachute
opened the harness came apart and he fell to his death. The unfortunate
German was Oberleutnant Gerhard Loos of Fighter Geschwader 54, a leading
ace with 92 victories to his credit.

Not all P-51 pilots were in a position to behave so aggressively during their
return flight, however. Lieutenant Cecil Manning of the 4th Fighter Group had
suffered engine damage during his fight with Messerschmitt 110s near Berlin.
He succeeded in limping more than 250 miles across northern Germany with an
engine running progressively rougher, protected by his comrades. 'I kept going,
trying to get as far west as I could. Then, just before the Dutch border, the
engine began to get really hot and the cockpit started to fill with smoke. I knew
the time had come to bail out.' As the engine died completely Manning released
his canopy and followed the normal bailout drill: selecting full nose-down trim
he rolled the aircraft on to its back holding it straight and level, then released
the stick and the straps at the same time. The nose of the aircraft should then
have swung up sharply and he should have been thrown out cleanly. 'But,
because there was no power on, the nose immediately fell and I failed to clear
the aircraft. I struggled back into the cockpit and turned the aircraft right way
up. In the process I lost quite a lot of height and the second time I tried to get out
I was kind of desperate. I just stood on the seat and kicked out – and found
myself falling clear. After a short fall I pulled my ripcord and as the chute
popped I saw my aircraft hit the ground.'

At 2.10 pm, as the bombers passed north of Brunswick on their way home,
the escort was bolstered by 26 Mustangs of Nos 19, 65 and 122 Squadrons of the
Royal Air Force. These fighters lacked the rear fuselage tanks fitted to the US-
operated P-51s and so had been unable to penetrate deeper into Germany. Still
there was little Luftwaffe fighter activity around the raiding force.

The lull in the fighting did, however, make it possible for one German pilot to
sneak in and attack unobserved. Oberleutnant Hermann Greiner of Night
Fighter Geschwader 1, flying a radar-equipped Me 110, had already picked off
one damaged B-17 earlier in the day. Now he was able to position himself
exactly underneath one of the formations of B-24s then, with the stealth of a
pickpocket and exploiting the light night-fighter camouflage of his aircraft
which merged against the clouds below, he slowly edged closer to the bombers.
'If they had seen me they would have fired at me, but they did not. I managed to
get into position under one of the bombers, pulled up and fired a short burst.
The entire tail unit of the B-24 was literally "sawn-off". The bomber went into a
steep dive, spinning out of control without catching fire, and crashed.'
Immediately after his sneak attack Greiner too dived away; if the escorts saw

him he knew he would have stood little chance. The B-24 he hit belonged to the 458th Bomb Group and it crashed beside the German Army munitions plant at Munsterlager. Two crewmen were killed, the other eight bailed out and were taken prisoner.

After the attack on Templin the High Box of the 94th Combat Wing, comprising sixteen B-17s of the 457th Bomb Group, still had bombs on board and was looking for a 'target of last resort'. Finally, at 2.20 pm, the formation found one: the small city of Verden to the southeast of Bremen. The bombers released their six hundred 100 pound-incendiaries across the built-up area and continued west.

The lack of activity around the bombers meant American fighters had fuel and ammunition left for other mischief over Germany when they broke off the escort. Lieutenants Peter Pompetti and Luther Abel of the 78th Fighter Group were returning in their P-47s when they spotted a freight train chugging southwards near Cloppenburg. The pair went down to beat up the train and scored numerous hits on the engine, which stopped in a cloud of steam. About two minutes later, still keeping low, the two Thunderbolts came upon another freight train, attacked the engine of that one also and brought it to a steaming halt. As he pulled up to pass close over his target Pompetti felt his aircraft jolt, but as he climbed away it seemed to handle normally and he thought no more of it. Only much later would he learn that a large piece of steel hurled from the locomotive had struck his P-47 and smashed in the supercharger.

The period of relative calm around the bombers was soon to end. Already the Gruppen of Fighter Geschwader 2 and 26, pulled back earlier to airfields in the Wiesbaden and Frankfurt areas from eastern France, had been scrambled and were heading north to engage the raiders.

Also scrambled at this time were ten Me 109s of the Ist Gruppe of Fighter Geschwader 300 at Bonn Hangelar, a night fighting unit whose pilots had only a little ground instruction in day fighting. 'Since we had no previous experience in fighting by day we were to go into action against the bombers on their way home when it was hoped there would be some stragglers for us to pick off,' recalled Leutnant Lothar Sachs who flew with the Gruppe. As the Messerschmitts assembled in formation after taking off, one ran into trouble. 'He passed too close to one of the other Me 109s and ran into the propeller wash as the formation was climbing at low speed. The fighter rolled on to its back and spun into the ground. It smashed into a house beside the airfield, the pilot and four people living there were killed.' After this chastening experience the remaining nine Messerschmitts continued their climb to the north to engage the enemy.

As well as the fresh German units now moving to intercept the raiding force, all those which had taken part in the Haseluenne action earlier sent contingents making their second sorties of the day. In all there were more than a hundred fighters airborne and being vectored into position for the last big action of the day.

After the hard-fought actions on the way to and over Berlin, to many American crews the return flight so far was a considerable anti-climax. Lowell

Watts of the 388th Bomb Group was on his 25th and final mission of his combat tour; when he landed he would be due to return to the USA for leave. He later wrote:

> As we settled down into the routine of the trip home I began to feel a glow of happiness. We had come through Hell without injury to the crew. Shot up as we were, the plane was still flying smoothly. Now we were heading for home. There was an immeasurable relief in knowing that a target had been crossed for the last time, at least in our present combat tour. No longer would we have to worry about the alerts that meant fitful sleep before another mission.
>
> On into the west we flew while the minutes turned to hours and the miles clocked beneath us in endless and fatiguing procession. The sun swung low into our faces, streaming through the windshield in a bright but eerie light. Off to our right we could now see the much-bombed cities of Bremen and Hamburg. In a few minutes Holland would be beneath us.
>
> The interphone came to life: 'Fighters at 10 o'clock high. . . . Hey! They're 47s!' Oh what a beautiful and welcome sight they made as they swooped over us, dipped their wings and wheeled away. With our first sight of them a terrific sense of relief swept away the horrible feeling of alone-ness and danger that had ridden the skies with us all the way from Berlin. We were now protected and would soon be over the English Channel. I began to think about the buzz job I was going to give at base for my crew chief and also to wonder how I'd word the cable home to my wife Betty when we landed.

For those unfortunate enough to be singled out by the defenses, however, death could still come at any time with little warning. As the bombers trundled over northern Germany they were engaged by those flak batteries which happened to be in their path. Defending the small town of Vechta and the nearby airfield were the 1st, 3rd and 4th Batteries of Heavy Flak Abteilung 231 with a total of twelve 105 mm guns. Between 2.30 and 2.32 pm these loosed off 141 rounds at a B-17 formation which passed almost overhead. Their shooting was accurate. Rounds burst almost immediately under one of the bombers, a B-17 of the 92nd Bomb Group, which broke in two and both sections tumbled out of the sky. The sole survivor was Sergeant Orlando Maiocco, the tail gunner, who managed to scramble out of the falling tail section and parachute to earth.

While this was happening the German fighter controllers were passing final vectors to concentrate interceptors just in front of the Dutch-German border for the next action. But to reach this point some units had to fly from their bases in the east almost alongside the US formations. As a result some Luftwaffe pilots found themselves embroiled with the enemy prematurely.

One such unit was the IInd Gruppe of Fighter Geschwader 11, down to only four usable Me 109s at Wunstorf after the noon action and led by its commander fighter ace Major Guenther Specht. With him was Heinz Knoke who had been in action during the noon battle and returned with a damaged aircraft, then later had vaulted out of his Me 109 on the ground at Wunstorf seconds before it was shot up by a strafing P-51. Accompanying these battle-hardened pilots were wingmen Feldwebel Michael Hauptmann and Unter-offizier Franz Zambelli. Early on Knoke's wingman, Zambelli, became separated then succumbed to the temptation to try to pick off a straggling B-17. The intended victim was not so helpless as it seemed, however, for above it

hovered Captain Wayne Bolefahr with three P-47s of the 359th Fighter Group.
'He evidently did not see our flight for I closed to 300 yards dead astern before
opening fire,' Bolefahr later wrote. 'My number two and three men positioned
themselves perfectly on each side of me. I gave the enemy aircraft about a two
second burst observing strikes on both sides of the fuselage, canopy and wing
roots. Many pieces fell off and the enemy aircraft began smoking.' Bolefahr
lined up for a second attack but before he could open fire 'something black'
came out over the left side of the Messerschmitt: Franz Zambelli, who
parachuted to earth.

Meanwhile the other three Messerschmitts were coming under attack from
P-47s of the 359th: the American unit had some forty Thunderbolts in the area.
'Suddenly Specht called out "Achtung! Enemy fighters!" As usual he saw the
enemy first. He had lost an eye in combat early in the war but with his
remaining one he could see better than most men could with two,' Knoke
explained. Specht led his small force into a tight turn to avoid the P-47s, then
into the cover of cloud below. But the cloud puffs were small and each time the
Messerschmitts emerged there seemed to be P-47s ready to pounce on them.
Having returned to altitude after shooting down Zambelli, Wayne Bolefahr
joined in the rough and tumble of the chase. 'I spotted three more Me 109s
below going east. The third one was being attacked by a P-47 and ducked into
the clouds. I then made a bounce on the starboard enemy aircraft of the other
two at 6,000 feet. We were in a starboard turn and I fired a four second burst
from 400 yards without observing strikes, when another P-47 cut me out. The
enemy aircraft ducked into a large patch of cloud. They broke out of the clouds
but were chased back into the same patch at least twice more by myself and
several other P-47s in the vicinity.'

During one of the lunges at the Messerschmitts Lieutenant Raymond Janney
of the 359th was able to press home his attack. 'Yellow 4 initiated the attack, I
followed him until I saw three Me 109s then made my own attack on them.
Overshot 3, and continued to attack 1 and 2. Opened fire at approximately 500
yards and held a short burst until both enemy aircraft ducked into cloud,' he
later wrote. 'I pulled up and waited for them to come out and attacked again
and again in a similar manner, each time losing them temporarily in clouds.
Got a dead astern shot at the No 2 man as he was disappearing into cloud.
When he came out the other side he was rolling to the left and trailing white
smoke.' Janney's victim was Michael Hauptmann's Messerschmitt.

Now only Specht and Knoke were left and the two German aces, fearfully
outnumbered, were having to use all the cunning and adroitness they had
picked up during their fighting careers merely to stay alive. Though ignorant of
the identity of his opponents Bolefahr recognized their skill and later noted:
'These two enemy aircraft maintained their two-ship formation well during
these attacks and made no effort to hit the deck, but utilized the protection
afforded by the clouds.' Nevertheless, if it continued much longer the pursuit
could have only one outcome for the German pilots. Picking his moment
carefully, when temporarily none of the tormentors was in a position to bounce,
Specht suddenly called 'Let's go home!'; skilfully the pair used a cloud to shield
them from the enemy as they dived to ground level and sped away from the scene.

It was 2.40 pm and the leading bombers were now almost at the German –
Dutch border in the general area of Lingen. But so too were the fighters
assembled by the German controllers for the final onslaught of the day. The
Gruppen were to attack in ones and twos, there was no time to assemble the
huge attack formations used during the earlier actions. Coming from the south
Lothar Sachs caught sight of the mass of bombers in front of him. 'It was
enormous, the first time I had ever seen one of the American formations from
the air. It looked like a swarm of hornets, a breathtaking sight.' Leading the
Gruppe was Oberleutnant Waldemar Grafe, the only man with previous day-
fighting experience. The Me 109 night fighter unit had been briefed to hunt
straggling bombers but Grafe seemed to be leading them straight towards the
enemy and continued climbing. Sachs wondered what was going on but
dutifully followed. Grafe led the nine Messerschmitts into position almost over
the enemy bombers. 'Then he waggled his wings, rolled on his back and pulled
into a vertical dive. We did the same. We were now a good 1,000 meters above
the bombers and we dived straight on them.' In fact Grafe had led his
inexperienced pilots well: he had positioned them for an attack out of the sun on
a bomber formation lacking fighter cover. Sachs fired bursts at a couple of the
B-17s in front, then aimed his Messerschmitt through a gap in the formation. In
the vertical dive his fighter built up speed rapidly and as it exceeded 500 mph
the aircraft began to shudder and was barely controllable. Sachs had to throttle
back and use the elevator trim to ease himself out of the dive.

Other German units went in to attack at about the same time. Major Kurt
Buehligen led in 17 Me 109s of IInd Gruppe of Fighter Geschwader 2;
Hauptmann Josef Wurmheller of IIIrd Gruppe attacked with 10 FW 190s.
Major Heinz Baer brought 4 FW 190s of IInd Gruppe of Fighter Geschwader 1.
Hauptmann Anton Hackl led a similar force from IIIrd Gruppe of Fighter
Geschwader 11.

One of the first bombers hit during this phase of the action was B-17 'Junior'
of the 95th Bomb Group. Lieutenant Elton Skinner, its navigator, watched the
enemy fighters looming larger in front of him. 'Their guns looked like head
lights, blinking on and off as they came in,' he recalled. Then the B-17 was hit.
'Rus Allman, our bombardier, caught a bullet through the wrist. When I laid
him out on our small walkway I could see his hand was almost entirely severed.
The only thing holding it on was two narrow strands of skin. One thing stands
out in my mind about this wound: it had not bled a drop. There was bone and
flesh spattered over our stations, but no blood.' Skinner made the wounded
man as comfortable as possible and helped administer a shot of morphine to
deaden the pain. At first it seemed the damage to the aircraft might be only
superficial. But then Skinner noticed something streaming back from the right
wing tip: either smoke or fuel and of the two he hoped it was the latter. 'I
immediately notified the crew and we all looked at it and discussed it for a
while. The gas cap had come off which made me think it was gasoline; but when
the skin started to bubble up we knew there was a fire.' The pilot, Lieutenant
Garland Lloyd, ordered his crew to abandon the aircraft. Skinner's first
thought was that he would have to jump with the injured bombardier and when
the pair were clear of the aircraft he would pull his friend's ripcord. But Allman

THE OPPOSING FORCES AT 2.45 pm

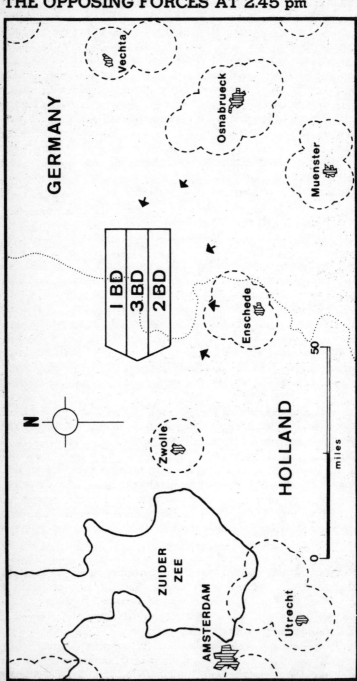

Approximate positions of the opposing forces at 2.45 pm. The majority of the bombers were now flying the planned route in the planned order of formation with bomb divisions side by side in line abreast, the 1st to the north, the 3rd in the middle and the 2nd to the south. Behind the orderly formations, however, came numerous stragglers unable to keep up because of battle damage or technical failures. Escorting the bombers at this time were 160 P-47s and eight P-51s from the 352nd, 355th, 359th and 361st Fighter Groups. Also at this time numerous small formations of German Fighters, with between two and 30 aircraft, were moving towards the raiders from the south and the east for the final large interception of the day.

showed he was perfectly capable of pulling his own ripcord with his good hand; he was helped out of the escape hatch and Skinner was relieved to see his parachute start to open. Then it was the navigator's turn to follow. 'The feeling I got when I opened that chute is impossible to describe (for some reason, I had no doubts about it opening). After the roar of the engines, the racket of the guns, the chatter on the interphone, the fear and anguish of the fire and the bail out into God only knew what, then suddenly dead silence and a peace I had never before experienced. I wanted to float on forever . . .' All ten crewmen succeeded in jumping clear of the stricken bomber before it smashed into the ground southwest of the Dutch town of Assen.

B-17 'Lil Opportunity' of the 94th Bomb Group was also hit at about this time. One 20 mm round came straight through the windscreen and struck the copilot in the face, killing him instantly. A fire started in the cockpit, filling the fuselage with dense smoke. Lieutenant Paul Sullivan, the navigator, was in the nose when he saw the pilot scramble out of the burning cockpit without his parachute; he had had to leave it behind. There was a sudden flash and a bang as one of the oxygen bottles exploded and Sullivan saw a huge gash, more than seven feet long, where the outer skin of the fuselage had been blown away by the explosion. Sullivan moved towards the pilot. 'There was no conversation between us, we just wanted to get out. We grabbed each other, moved to the hole in the nose and jumped. I counted up to eight to get us clear of the aircraft, then pulled the ripcord.' Sullivan's thoughts of thanksgiving as the parachute started to deploy immediately turned to horror. The shock of the opening caused the pilot to lose his grip and slide down Sullivan's body, taking the latter's boots with him as he fell to certain death.

'Flakstop', a B-17 of the 452nd Bomb Group, was yet another bomber which went down at this time. Lieutenant Alan Willis, the copilot, watched the German fighters sweeping in to attack. 'I remember a head-on pass with the bullets raking our fuselage – the very same ah-ah-ah-ah noise we used to make as kids when we played at dogfighting (this particular ah-ah-ah-ah killed the tail gunner). The number 3 and 4 engines had been hit and evidently the oil lines had too, because the props wouldn't feather no matter how I fiddled with the switches,' he continued. 'Next we were hit in the leading edge of the port wing, probably by a 30 mm shell which flattened out a section about 30 feet long. So now on the port side we had two engines and no airfoil, and on the starboard side an airfoil but no engines. Numbers 1 and 2 engines were at full rpm, numbers 3 and 4 were windmilling and the vibration began. Wagner and I were both at the controls trying to hold "Flakstop" steady but it was like trying to hold a trip-hammer . . .' Steadily loosing altitude the Fortress continued west, its crew hoping beyond hope to keep it in the air long enough to reach England or at least the sea. Then the left wing burst into flame, the bomber's fate was sealed. Lieutenant Chuck Wagner, the pilot, gave the order to bail out and Clyde Martin, the navigator, went out of the nose exit first. Willis went out after him. 'I missed the bomb bay doors by an inch or so, counted to ten – leaving out 3 through 9 – and pulled the ripcord. To my rather frantic surprise nothing happened. The snap cords pulled open the pack, but the pilot chute and the neatly folded pile of white nylon just lay there on my chest. Thinking "Its not supposed to work this way!", I grabbed handfuls of material and fed it into the wind. This worked, and the chute opened with a shoulder-rending jerk.' Hanging on his parachute during the lengthy descent Willis's mind began to wander. 'I had purchased a uniform greatcoat in London, a real classy one. Orberg, a bombardier in another crew who shared our hut, coveted that coat. I had said to him "Well, if I get shot down, you can take the coat before the adjutant comes for my belongings." What crazy thoughts people have. There I was, floating down into occupied Holland, thinking "Orberg, keep your hands off my coat!" ' Lieutenant Hank Gladys, the bombardier, followed Willis through the nose exit. 'When I jumped the chaos and Hell changed to Heavenly peace. I thought I had died and gone to Heaven until I saw the tree tops – then I realized I still hadn't pulled my ripcord!' Gladys's parachute opened in the nick of time and a few seconds later he hit the ground. Chuck Wagner bravely went down with the blazing Fortress; in holding it straight long enough for his crew to bail out he forfeited his own chance of survival.

In 'Blitzin Betsy' Lowell Watts watched the attack on his formation. 'The interphone snapped to life: "Focke-Wulfs at 3 o'clock level!" Yes, there they were. What seemed at a hurried count to be about 30 fighters flying along just out of range beside us. They pulled ahead of us, turned across our flight path and attacked from ahead and slightly below us. Turrets swung forward throughout the formation and began spitting out their .50 caliber challenge,' he later wrote. 'Some Focke-Wulfs pulled above us and hit us from behind while most dove in from the front, coming in from 11 to 1 o'clock to level, so close that only every second or third plane could be sighted on by the gunners. Still they came, rolling, firing and diving away, then attacking again. As the first of these vicious attacks began to ease off, flames shot out of Grindley's plane flying on our left wing. Chutes began dropping, one after the other, from it. "Those poor guys," somebody said, "they've got in 21 missions, too . . ."'

During the moments immediately following the attack Grindley's bomber had been transformed into a private Hell for those unfortunate enough to be on board. The left waist gunner had been struck by a 20 mm round and killed instantly. The ball turret gunner had most of his right arm blown off by an exploding cannon shell, but somehow managed to get out of his turret and bail out. The copilot was almost unconscious from severe head and throat injuries; his parachute was clipped on and he was pushed out of the escape hatch by the top turret gunner but the ripcord was never pulled. The blazing aircraft went down steeply and the bombardier and tail gunner were still on board when the flames reached the fuel tanks and it blew up; both escaped, however, and parachuted to safety. The burning wreckage rained down outside the small village of Schoeningsdorf, just east of the German – Dutch border.

Another of the 388th's B-17s, 'Suzy Sagritz' piloted by Lieutenant Monty Givens, was also knocked down. Both its right engines were set on fire and the crew began to abandon it; all did so successfully apart from one of the waist gunners. The aircraft crashed at New Amsterdam just inside the Dutch border.

Then Lowell Watts's B-17 was hit. 'Brassfield called from the tail position "I've got one! I've got one!" Then, almost with the same breath "I've been hit!'' No sooner had the interphone cleared from that message when an even more ominous one cracked into the headsets: "We're on fire!" Looking forwards I saw a Focke-Wulf coming at us from dead level at 12 o'clock,' Watts recalled. 'The fire from our top and chin turrets shook the B-17. At the same instant his wings lit up with fire from his guns. The 20 mm rounds crashed through our nose and exploded beneath my feet amongst the oxygen tanks. At the same time they slashed through some of the gasoline cross-feed lines. The flames which started here, fed by the pure oxygen and the gasoline, almost exploded through the front of the ship. The companionway to the nose, the cockpit and the bomb bays was a solid mass of flame.' Watts ordered his crew to bail out and tried to hold his bomber level so that they could do so. Unable to see ahead because of the flames, however, he had no way of knowing his B-17 was edging dangerously close to that of the formation leader above him. There was a sudden flash as the two aircraft collided, then both slowly began tumbling earthwards.

The rammed B-17, piloted by Captain Paul Brown of the 388th, immediately caught fire. 'A ball of flame extended from the No 3 engine back beyond the right elevator. The only intercom chatter I remember after we were hit was Paul Brown's order to bail out. I handed the pilot his chute and he buckled it on,' Sergeant Roy Joyce, the top turret gunner afterwards wrote. 'I buckled on my chute and headed for the bomb bay. After opening the door I backed off – it was full of flaming gas. I vaguely remember some of the crew at the radio room door and saw one man jump through the bomb bay.' Joyce was still considering how best to get out of the plunging inferno when the bomber exploded and he was knocked unconscious. Five crewmen succeeded in getting out of the aircraft either before or after the explosion. Joyce himself came to as he was falling through space and pulled his ripcord.

Lowell Watts knew nothing of the collision but he was left in no doubt about its effects. 'I could tell we had rolled upside down. My safety belt had been unbuckled. I fell away from the seat, but held myself in with the grasp I had on the control wheel. After a few weird sensations I was pinned to the seat, unable to move or even raise my hand to pull off the throttles or try to cut the gas to the inboard engines,' Watts later wrote. 'My left foot had fallen off the rudder bars while we were on our back. I couldn't even slide it across the floor to get it back on the pedal. Flames now swept past my face, between my legs and past my arms as though sucked by a giant vacuum. Unable to see, I could tell only that we were spinning and diving at a terrific rate.'

As Watts struggled with his controls the G forces began to ease off and the bomber straightened out though it was still going down fast. The pilot glanced above and was amazed to see the entire roof of the cabin gone, as far back as the top turret (it had been smashed off during the collision with Brown's B-17). Still Watts fought to hold the aircraft straight so his crew could get out. 'That wild eerie ride down the corridors of the sky in a flaming bomber still haunts my memory. But it wasn't just the terror of death, it was the unending confusion and pain of a hopeless fight and the worry for the nine other men that were my responsibility. Contrary to the usual stories, my past life failed to flash in review through my mind. I was too busy fighting to keep that life.'

Then, suddenly, Watts found himself hurtling through space; he had been thrown out of the open cabin roof. At first he found his body was spinning so fast he could not pull in his flailing arms and legs. His flak jacket, oxygen mask, goggles and helmet all tore away; then the spinning slowed and he was able to grasp his ripcord. 'I jerked the ripcord and waited. Nothing happened. I thought "Hell! The whole day is screwed up!" I jerked it harder. There was a soft swish, then a hard sharp jerk and I was suspended in space, hanging in the most complete silence I have ever known.' Watts glanced up anxiously, half expecting the parachute to be on fire; but mercifully the white nylon canopy was intact. Then he noticed the wreckage from his aircraft falling earthwards. 'A few pieces of metal wrinkled on down and further away I caught sight of the bright yellow of the dinghy radio falling through space. What a screwy time to notice that radio! But ever since the sight of it has stayed in my mind more clearly than anything else.'

Leading two out of the four FW 190s of IIIrd Gruppe of Fighter Geschwader 11 against the enemy formations, Hauptmann Anton Hackl found that each time he tried to set up a head-on attack on the bombers P-47s intervened at the critical time and forced him to break away. The pilot leading the other pair, fighter ace Oberleutnant Hugo Frey with 22 heavy bombers already to his credit, was more successful. Frey was able to press home four attacks to short range and during each his wingman saw a B-17 go down; it is likely that some or all of these aircraft came from Lowell Watt's Group, the 388th. Then Hackl heard Frey's voice cry over the radio 'I've been hit!'; they were his last words.

Hanging under his parachute, Watts noticed a Focke-Wulf curving towards him in a slow deliberate circle. His first fear was that the German pilot intended to shoot him up and he felt terribly vulnerable. Then he noticed the turn develop into a spiral dive; the enemy fighter gathered speed rapidly until it smashed into the ground. Looking down, Watts observed the smoke columns rising from three other crashed aircraft.

Almost certainly Hugo Frey was knocked down by defensive fire from bombers of the Low Box of the 45th Combat Wing B Formation; several gunners from the 388th and 452nd Bomb Groups later reported shooting down an FW 190 at about 2.50 pm near the Dutch border town of Coevorden; German records confirm Frey's Focke-Wulf crashed there.

The savage mauling of the 45th Combat Wing was cut short by the arrival of the P-47s of the 361st Fighter Group. Lieutenant Charles Keppler was flying east along the bombers' track past the 3rd Bomb Division when: 'I saw the last box of B-17s under attack from 12 to 16 FW 190s and a few scattered Me 109s. I attacked an FW 190 but he saw me and took evasive action and I observed no hits from a short burst. Then I broke off and attacked 3 FW 190s which were lining up to attack the bombers. One broke off and went into a steep climbing turn. I tried to get deflection and closed to about 75 yards but could see no hits. I was then bounced so I broke off the attack and was separated from my wingman . . .'

The calls for assistance from Keppler's squadron drew in Thunderbolts of the 361st from all directions. Captain Robert Sedman approached the rear box of B-17s with his squadron to find the dogfight already breaking up and the

Above left: Major Hans Kogler, the commander of IIIrd Gruppe of Destroyer Geschwader 26, who led the
German attack formation which engaged over Tangerhuette. During the action Kogler's Me 110 was shot up by
Mustang and he forced landed near Magdeburg. **Above right:** Oberleutnant Herbert Schob of Ist Gruppe of
Destroyers Geschwader 76 was credited with one B-17 destroyed and another shot out of the formation, before
was shot down and wounded on 6 March 1944. **Below:** Schob's slip giving official confirmation of one of
victories on 6 March; it took until 10 September for the Luftwaffe Claims Commission to issue the confirmation.
Kogler, Schob.)

Oberkommando der Luftwaffe

Chef f. Ausz. u. Diszpl. (V)

Az. 29 Nr. 519 /44

Berlin, den 10.9.44.

An 1./Z.G.76

Der 1./Z.G.76

wird der Abschuß eines **amerikanischen Kampfflugzeuges vom Typ**

Boeing " Fortress II " am 6.3.44, 12.38 Uhr

durch Oblt. S c h o b

als dreizehnter (13.) Luftsieg der Staffel. Gruppe anerkannt.

I. A.

B 5221. 8. 44. S

The escorting P-51s did great execution of German twin-eng[ine] fighters during the action sou[th] west of Berlin on 6 March. **Left:** Lieutenant Arval Roberso[n] the 357th Fighter Group was [one] of the successful pilots.

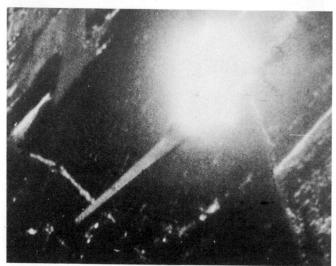

Left and below: two stills fro[m] combat film that day when his rounds set off an explosion in [the] Me 110 he was chasing. (Roberson.)

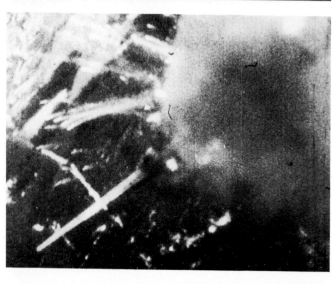

7s of the 41st Combat Wing, comprising the 303rd, 379th and 384th Bomb Groups, photographed on the tern side of Berlin on 6 March 1944. **Above:** aircraft releasing their bombs on the Koepenik district of the , at 1.21 pm. The bombers in the foreground are dropping 100-pound incendiaries. Below the aircraft can seen the trails from the smoke markers dropped by the lead Pathfinder aircraft. **Below:** the same formation w minutes later being engaged by flak; more than twenty bursts are visible in the photograph. (USAF)

Above left: a Pathfinder B-17 of the 482nd Bomb Group, leading the 3rd Bomb Division, going down after be[ ] hit by flak at 1.22 pm on 6 March 1944 over the southern outskirts of Berlin. Shortly afterwards the aircraft b[ ] up and Lieutenant 'Red' Morgan, **(above right)** who won the Congressional Medal of Honor the previous y[ ] was thrown clear. He opened his parachute moments before he hit the ground. **Below left:** the twin-128m[ ] gun, the most powerful weapon used by the German flak units. **Below right:** the Friedrichshain flak bunker n[ ] the center of Berlin, whose four twin-128mm guns engaged the raiders on 6 March 1944. (USAF, Bundesarch[ ] Schliephake.)

Above: bombs from the 4th Combat Wing exploding in the Steglitz district of Berlin at 1.23 pm. Immediately to the right of the bomb bursts is the Hauptkadettenanstalt, the SS barracks housing Hitler's personal bodyguard; the barracks escaped damage. **Below left:** Horst Krieger, who was in a shelter at the Telefunken works (arrowed, A) at the time of the attack. **Below right:** Marianne Wittstock and her new baby Sabine were in the cellar of the Rittberg Hospital (arrowed, B). (USAF, Krieger, Wittstock.)

Left and below: 500-pound bombs going down from B-24s the 446th Bomb Group at 1.40 on 6 March 1944. At the time o release the bombers were flying northeast; to the top of the lowe photograph can be seen Lake Harvel, with the Zehlendorf autobahn cloverleaf junction in t bottom right corner. (USAF)

Above: those same bombs exploding in the Zehlendorf district of Berlin about 40 seconds later. **Right:** Police Oberwachtmeister Wilhelm Winkler whose watchtower (arrowed), was badly shaken by bombs. (USAF, Winkler)

Above: 'Flak you could walk on' was a phrase often used by returning bomber crew. This is what it meant to those in the B-24s of the 2nd Combat Wing as they passed over the Spandau district on 6 March 1944. The photograph was taken looking west and the line of the Harvel canal can be seen in the center. **Below:** B-24 'God Bless our Ship' of the 445th Bomb Group was seriously damaged during the cannonade and Lieutenant George Lymburn crashed landed it near Neuruppin, 25 miles northwest of Berlin; the aircraft is seen here being inspected by German officers. **Inset:** Luftwaffenoberfelfer Hans Ring served with Heavy Flak Abteilung 437 in the Spandau district, one of the units credited with the destruction of Lymburn's B-24. (Cripe, Holmes, Ring)

nt: Lieutenant Archie
tterley of the 4th Fighter Group
t down an Me 110 near Berlin
went down to low altitude to
e the Henschel Company
ks airfield at Schoenefeld. In the
from his combat film taken on
arch 1944, **below,** his rounds
be seen striking one of the
d new Junkers 88 bombers
iting delivery to the Luftwaffe.
atterley.)

The last American over Berlin on 6 March 1944 was Major Walt Weitner of the 7th Photo Group in Spitfire 'High Lady', **right**. Weitner made several photo runs over the city from altitudes around 40,000 feet; one of the pictures he brought back, **below,** shows smoke rising from fires in the Zehlendorf district. (Weitner, USAF)

ɔve: a deceptively peaceful
ʋ of B-17 'Flakstop' of the
ɲd Bomb Group photographed
he homeward flight as it
sed south of Bremen at about
ᵓ pm on 6 March 1944. About
minutes later she was shot
ʋn by German fighters. **Right:**
ʳman fighter aces Hauptmann
ɪɔ Frey (left foreground, without
, Oberst Walter Oesau (facing
ɪera, center) and Major Anton
ᴋl (back to camera). During the
ɔn on 6 March 1944 all three
ᵉ credited with victories. Frey
credited with shooting down
B-17s in combat near the
ɲan-Dutch border at about
ᵓ pm, one of which may have
ɲ 'Flakstop', then Frey was
ɩelf shot down and killed by
ɲ fire and aircraft of the 388th
452nd Bomb Groups. (USAF,
ᴋl.)

Above left: Lieutenant Norman Fortier, who flew
P-47 of the 355th Fighter Group and **(above)**
Oberleutnant Gerd Schaedle of IInd Gruppe of Fig
Geschwader 2 whose Me 109 Fortier forced dow
following a long chase at low altitude.
Left: Oberleutnant Hermann Greiner of Night Figh
Geschwader 1, who shot down a B-17 immediate
after he took off from Quakenbrueck and later on
March 1944 shot down a B-24. (Fortier, Schaedle
Greiner)

The raiders return from battle on 6 March 1944. **T
right:** Lieutenant Ned Renick's B-17, 'Big Mike' of
381st Bomb Group, on its belly after running off t
runway at Ridgewell with the brakes shot away. T
aircraft suffered only minor damage. **Center right**
loading into the ambulance the wounded top turre
gunner, Sergeant Steve Kovacik, from B-17 'Schi?
Skonk' of the 390th Bomb Group after it landed a
Framlingham. This bomber had suffered extensive
battle damage; the dinghy hatch behind the cockp
had been blown open and the left inboard propell
feathered. **Right**: P-47 brought back by Lieutenar
Farmer of the 356th Fighter Group. (USAF)

After the 6 March mission. **Left:** post-flight debriefing of Lieutenant John Lawlor's crew, 379th Bomb Group, at Kimbolton. **Below:** seen during the celebration at Leiston the evening of the 6th, four successful P-51 pilots of the 357th Fighter Group: left to right, Capt Davis Perron (claimed 3 enemy aircraft destroyed during the mission), Major Tom Hayes (1), Captain Glendon Davis (2) and Lieutenant Don Bochkay (2). (USAF, Hayes)

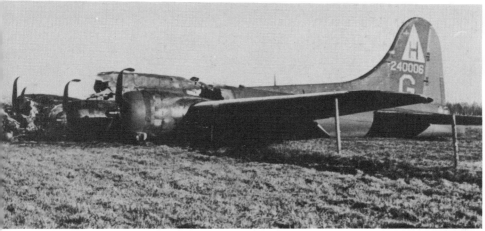

ɔve: Lieutenant Charles Smith's B-17 'Liberty Lady' of the 306th Bomb Group burning out and burned out
the Swedish island of Gotland. The aircraft had been damaged by flak over Berlin and Smith tried to reach
sian-held territory but ran short of fuel and was forced to crash land. Thinking themselves in enemy territory,
crew set fire to the bomber. **Below:** Lieutenant Charles York's B-24 'Hello Natural' of the 448th Bomb Group
damaged by flak over Berlin and is seen after it landed at Bulltofta in Sweden. The right inboard propeller
athered. (Courson, Olausson)

Above: Jeffrey Ethell discussing point with General James Dool and, **left,** General Adolf Gallan explaining the operation of the German fighter force to Alfred Price, during the research for t book.

German fighters scattering in front of him. 'At this point I saw one FW 190 flying 180 degrees to me about 3,000 - 4,000 ft below me. Calling my wingman, Lt Moore, to cover me I cut my throttle and split S'd on to his tail at 14,000 ft. At approx. 700 yards I opened with a short burst observing no hits. I then closed to about 250 - 300 yards and opened fire with a very long burst, observing many hits around the cockpit and wing roots. Very large pieces of the FW 190 were breaking off and several small explosions were seen around the cockpit. Sedman followed the German fighter down through cloud and saw it dive straight into the ground and explode.

Sedman's wingman, Lieutenant Wayne Moore, watched his leader knock down the FW 190 then he saw another to his left about 1,500 feet below. He broke away and, after clearing his tail, attacked from behind: 'I opened fire at 250 yards with a short burst and observed the right wheel drop. The enemy aircraft rolled over and split-S'd down and I followed. Enemy aircraft went into a tight spiral and I was unable to get him in my sight so I pulled up at 3,000 feet and enemy aircraft leveled off at about 1,000 feet. I again attacked from astern but before I came into range he rolled over, going straight down and crashed.'

The two Focke-Wulfs claimed by Sedman and Moore link with the loss of FW 190s flown by Feldwebel Werner Dotzauer and Unteroffizier Alfred Haupt of Ist Gruppe Fighter Geschwader 1, which crashed in eastern Holland near the German border; both pilots were killed.

Elsewhere other German fighters were also finding it difficult to get at the bombers because of the escorts. Oberleutnant Gerd Schaedle, flying an Me 109 of IInd Gruppe of Fighter Geschwader 2, joined in a head-on attack on one of the B-24 formations but did not see any hits on his target. Then P-47s pounced on the German fighters and he became embroiled in a dogfight. With fuel and ammunition beginning to run low, he pulled out of the fight with two of his comrades and dived for the ground.

As Schaedle's Messerschmitts broke away from the fight they were seen by Captain Walter Koraleski leading three P-47s of the 355th Fighter Group. 'When he spotted the 109s they were way, way, below us. They couldn't have been more than a couple of thousand feet at that time and we were right up over twenty thousand. I don't know how in the world he saw them. We went down like bats out of Hell,' remembered Lieutenant Norman Fortier who was flying on Koraleski's wing tip. After the lengthy high speed dive Koraleski swung into a firing position behind one of the Messerschmitts as it was pulling out of its dive. 'At 300 yards or less I fired a burst at great deflection as the 109s pulled up. The 109s passed under me in a steep dive and I found out later from my wingman, Lt Fortier, that I had hit the 109 all over the canopy and wing roots and with clouds of smoke pouring from it the Me 109 went into an almost vertical diving turn.' The Messerschmitt Koraleski hit was piloted by Oberfeldwebel Willi Morzinek, who succeeded in getting out just before the aircraft plunged into the ground.

Koraleski then pulled his aircraft around and with his two comrades sped after the two remaining Messerschmitts. 'They were right on the tree tops and we headed for them. My first burst missed the No 2 Me 109 but my second burst of about two seconds at 300 yards distance and a deflection of about 10 degrees hit him all over the cockpit, engine and fuselage and along the wing roots on the right side. A burst of flame shot out from the right side of the fuselage and the enemy aircraft flipped over to the right.' In his earphones Gerd Schaedle heard his wingman, Unteroffizier Gustav Sens, call 'I've been hit, bailing out!'; Sens got out just before the Messerschmitt struck the ground, dug in its left wing and cartwheeled to destruction.

That left just Schaedle, alone, hurtling low over the ground with three P-47s thundering after him. 'The chase continued, passing low over trees, meadows and farm buildings. They fired at me whenever they could and my aircraft began to take hits. I kept as low as I could, 3 or 4 meters high. To make things as difficult as possible for the enemy pilots I jinked each time they came into attack, all the time keeping very low and holding maximum speed. But my aircraft took more hits and I felt if the chase continued any longer they would get me.' Not that Schaedle was the only one with problems, as Fortier later recalled: 'The guy kept going. It looked as if he was trying to put some trees between us and him. He was making pretty good time, too. It seemed like every time we got close enough to fire a burst, the recoil from those eight .50s would slow us right down! We were awful low, of course, almost as low as he was, so we had not only to try to get him in the gunsight but also we had to be careful not to fly into the ground.'

Schaedle was too low to bail out and had no doubt that if he pulled up to gain altitude the Thunderbolts would immediately smash him out of the sky. 'Then, suddenly, beyond the small wood in front of me there appeared ahead a long meadow. As I passed over the trees I cut the throttle and pushed my Messerschmitt on to the ground. There was a series of hefty bumps as my fighter decelerated rapidly, then the Thunderbolts came screaming past.' The deceleration had indeed been rapid and unexpected. Koraleski, concentrating on following the Messerschmitt as he moved in close behind to finish it off, had to pull up sharply to avoid colliding with his victim. As his fighter jerked to a halt Schaedle scrambled out of the cockpit and bolted to the cover of a small ditch nearby. From its safety he watched the enemy fighters pull up and circle the scene, then turn west for home.

There were numerous small skirmishes at this time, as German pilots in ones and twos tried to press home attacks against the bombers. Lieutenant Kenneth Lyell, copilot on B-24 'Shifluss Skunk' of the 446th Bomb Group, recalled one such action: 'Our formation was attacked by a lone Me 109 which made several head-on and broadside attacks. The pilot was a very bad shot, he did not hit any of our aircraft. On one of his passes he came over our aircraft so close that a spent 20 mm case crashed through the plexiglas dome of the top turret. The gunner, Sergeant Charles Lamarca, had the hot case fall between the sheepskin collar of his flying jacket and his bare neck, which gave him quite a scare!'

Trailing the main bomber formations came the numerous stragglers, those forced to drop back by battle damage or technical failures. Some bombers only just made it as far as Holland, where their crews opted to bail out and take their chances with the Dutch resistance. One such was that captained by Lieutenant Beverly Ballard of the 458th Bomb Group, whose B-24 had suffered flak damage and lost an engine during the return flight. Sergeant Victor Krueger, the ball turret gunner, was making his way to the rear escape hatch when suddenly he was thrown against the side of the fuselage: 'The pilot had set the autopilot but it must have clicked out for some reason because the bomber went out of control and started to spin. With the other gunners in the rear I was thrown about and it was a terrible struggle to get to the hatch. In the end I managed to reach it. But I think I must have struck my head against the side because the next thing I knew I was coming to as the parachute was opening. I don't remember pulling the ripcord.'

On the ground watching the Liberator spin out of the sky and its crew jumping clear, was 21-year-old Niek Klaassen at his home in the small village of Wormer. At first he thought the bomber was going to come down on his village, but it swung away and fell some way to the east. Also watching was 14-year-old schoolboy Cees Bakker, standing beside his father's farmhouse. The spinning aircraft plunged into the ground not far from the house and was completely wrecked.

Many stragglers owed their survival to the timely appearance of escorts sweeping behind the main bomber formations. Lieutenant Thurman Spiva, bombardier on B-24 'Little Max' of the 446th Bomb Group returning alone with one engine feathered, recalled his feelings as he saw a pair of Messerschmitts curving around to finish off the bomber: 'We were a sitting duck and everyone knew the fighters would continue to attack until we were shot down. We had watched this drama played out too many times not to know what the outcome would normally be. The lone cripples always lost. The lucky crews were allowed time to bail out after the fatal blow was delivered. The unlucky crews were killed or went down with the aircraft as it blew up or went into its final spin.' All of this time, however, Spiva's pilot had been broadcasting desperate appeals for help. 'It must have been our lucky day, because the Me 109s were still in their descending turn below our aircraft when two P-47s came out of nowhere and dived straight after the enemy fighters. We could also look up and see two other P-47s as they flew an S pattern back and forth to stay near our speed.'

Lieutenant John Flottorp, piloting a B-17 of the 390th Bomb Group with both right engines damaged, had a similarly close shave as his straggling bomber came under attack from Me 109s: 'I banked hard into them in evasive action and heard several hits. The aircraft jolted and I momentarily lost elevator control. One of the fighters had hit the left life raft compartment, blowing out the raft which struck the left horizontal stabilizer, hung up for a short while disrupting control, then fortunately blew off,' he later wrote. A 20 mm round then exploded against the hydraulic control panel and set it on fire but the top turret gunner was able to put out the blaze with a hand extinguisher. 'The fighters were queuing up for a gunnery pattern. All stations were about out of ammo, I was out of ideas and was thinking it was a Hell of a note to get shot down now as the coast was in sight. As I straightened out on course for home two more flights of fighters were diving from up sun. As they closed, the oval snouts of P-47s became apparent...'

Sometimes the escorts' intervention was not timely enough. Lieutenant Hubert Cripe of the 453rd Bomb Group was returning in company with another B-24 straggler when the pair were attacked and hit by a couple of Me 109s. 'I got busy right away on the radio and called up our fighters: "Denver, Denver, I need help, I'm being hit!" Back came the reply in a Texas drawl "Don't get excited Sonny, Pappa's coming!" A pair of P-47s appeared and forced the Messerschmitts to break off their attack.' But the rescuers had come too late. 'My engineer called and said we were on fire in the left wing. Sure enough, smoke was coming from a hole you could walk through.' Cripe dived the Liberator in an attempt to blow out the flames but it was no good, the fire began eating its way towards the left outboard engine. Cripe ordered his crew to bail out, then followed: 'I forced my way through to the bomb bay, then stepped into 12,000 feet of space. The 170 mph slipstream hit me and I tumbled in midair but managed to pull the ripcord and the canopy opened with a thwack. Then silence. I was in thick overcast and did not see the plane crash. As I came out of the bottom of the overcast I could see only water beneath me: the Zuider Zee.'

From the German point of view, however, even a wounded bomber could sometimes present a dangerous adversary. Me 109 pilot Leutnant Lothar Sachs, flying his first intercept mission by day, nearly came to grief trying to finish off one of the stragglers. Separated from his comrades after the high speed dive on the bombers, Sachs caught sight of a lone B-17 some way behind the formation and moved in to attack. In his inexperience the German pilot opened fire at too great a range and scored no hits. Then, before he could get into position for a second attack, the bomber vanished into a thin bank of cloud. Sachs went below the cloud and saw nothing, then climbed back through it and caught sight of the bomber again some distance to his left. He ran in to attack again and fired a second long burst but again did not see any hits. Now the bomber was in the clear on the far side of the cloud bank; but Sachs was out of ammunition.

The B-17 Sachs had attacked was piloted by Lieutenant A. Adams of the 306th Bomb Group; it had suffered flak damage over Berlin and the right outboard engine had been knocked out; the propeller had been damaged and would not feather, causing considerable drag which forced the bomber out of formation. On the return flight the B-17 had come under further attack from fighters; the intercom was shot out and the left outboard engine stopped and its propeller would not feather either – fortunately it balanced out the drag on the opposite wing. Sachs had no inkling of his opponent's problems but obviously the bomber was in trouble or it would not have become a straggler in the first place. Now it was firing red flares in an effort to summon help. The German pilot searched the sky for enemy fighters but there seemed none in the vicinity. The Americans had no way of knowing he was out of ammunition, perhaps he could bluff them into abandoning their machine? He pulled in behind the bomber for a dummy firing pass, then watched an escape hatch fall away and four of the crew leave by parachute. Congratulating himself on his first victory by day Sachs closed in to inspect his victim as it continued west. 'I flew past it very close, about 10 meters over the top. As I passed the nose I dropped my left wing to take a closer look – and found myself gazing into the faces of the two pilots and the top gunner who were staring back at me! I pulled my wing up and tried to accelerate away but as I did so my Messerschmitt shuddered under the impact of bullet hits.'

Wondering what to do next Sachs pulled to a respectful distance and watched the bomber descend gradually. Still he hoped it might go down and crash so he could claim it. But 50 feet above the Zuider Zee the B-17 leveled out; still it headed west and there was nothing the German pilot could do about it. Then Sachs noticed white smoke streaming from his left radiator: the glycol system had been hit! He looked into the cockpit and saw the needle of the engine temperature gauge starting to climb dangerously. Instinctively he throttled back, turned for one of the airfields in eastern Holland and kept a running tally of those fields within gliding distance suitable for a crash landing, should the need arise.

At the very rear of the bomber formations and their stragglers came B-17 'Little Willie' of the 388th Bomb Group. This was the bomber piloted by Bernie Dopko with badly damaged engines, returning from Berlin 50 feet above the ground at a speed of 115 mph. Remarkably, the crew made their flight across Germany with no molestation from fighters and very little from ground fire. The only serious trouble occurred immediately before the Dutch coast. 'We would have reached our Waterloo if the Germans had held their fire for another 30 seconds or so, as my line of flight would have put me directly over their battery of light flak about 8 feet off the ends of their barrels,' Dopko later commented. 'Their premature firing allowed me to bank sharply to the left, taking advantage of some buildings I was able to put between me and the Germans.' Dopko picked another point to cross the coast and this time encountered no defenses.

While the mass of American bombers and fighters rumbled over the Dutch coast and out to sea, a lone aircraft was speeding eastwards to Berlin to complete the mission. This was Spitfire 'High Lady' of the US 7th Photo Group piloted by Major Walt Weitner. The Spitfire had been stripped of all armament and armor, part of the wing had been converted into a huge fuel tank and in the rear fuselage were two large aerial cameras with 36-in telephoto lenses. Weitner's orders were to take post-strike reconnaissance photographs of the target.

Flying at 39,000 feet with a ground speed of about 350 mph, Weitner's Spitfire left behind a long white condensation trail to point out its presence. 'The Germans must have known I was there but at first nobody paid me any attention. It was a big sky and all the other trails I could see were well away to the southeast of me,' Weitner recalled. 'Anybody coming up after me would have had to leave a trail too so I knew I would get plenty of warning.'

For the reconnaissance pilot survival depended upon avoiding enemy fighters and Weitner continually scanned the sky around his aircraft; from time to time he rolled on to one side to search below and also to check his navigation. Then during one such search he suddenly realized he was not alone. 'I saw three black forms, also trailing, following mine closely an uncomfortable 1,500 yards away, their altitude just below my own.' Weitner eased forwards his throttle, selecting maximum power without resort to 'War Emergency'; the latter guzzled fuel he could not spare and he resolved to keep it up his sleeve in case things became really desperate. Then the American pilot eased up his nose, letting the Spitfire convert the extra power into greater altitude. Glancing behind he saw his pursuers had split: one was behind to his right and the other two were to his left. They were boxing him in, in case he tried to turn and run for home. Slowly the Spitfire gained height, passing through 40,000 feet then 41,000 feet. Weitner leveled out at 41,500 feet and peered behind to see what was going on. He saw the pursuers well below and losing ground the whole time; they were no match for the Spitfire at high altitude. Within a couple of minutes they were out of sight.

By now the Spitfire speeding through the rarified air was almost at Berlin. Away to the north Weitner could make out the huge Lake Mueritz, which he knew was some 50 miles west northwest of Berlin; but still he could not see the capital itself for the layer of smoke and haze. Keeping a wary eye for other enemy fighters he lined up to pass over the capital from the north eastern side; this would enable him to make his photographic run downwind without having to compensate for drift. 'There was quite a layer of haze but I could see the sun glinting off the red brick and tile houses as I rolled the Spitfire on to its side to line up on my check points. Then I leveled out as accurately as I could using the artificial horizon, switched on the cameras and began the first photographic run,' Weitner later recounted. 'My orders were to photograph the bombers' targets and I had aerial photos of the city taken previously with the targets marked on them. I could see the smoke rising from places other than my assigned targets so I decided to photograph these also.'

Weitner flew several runs over the German capital during the 25 minutes that followed, crossing it on different headings and taking in most of the sources of smoke on the ground. In his honor the entire Berlin flak defenses had been brought to readiness though only the 128 mm guns on the flak towers could engage aircraft at such an altitude with any prospect of success. 'Some flak came up when I was over Berlin. It wasn't heavy but I could see the smoke bursts mushrooming,' Weitner remembered. 'I could see that somebody below did not appreciate my being up there!' Then, his task complete to the extent his limited fuel allowed, the American pilot pointed his Spitfire west for England.

Cecil Manning made a painful landing just inside Germany after he bailed out of his Mustang. 'I came down on top of a fence and suffered a wrenched hip. With some difficulty I was able to stand. I released my parachute, bundled it up and took it to a small hut by the side of the field to hide it. But just then a couple of German soldiers found me.' Manning was taken to the nearby town of Sogel where several civilians eyed the hobbling pilot curiously. 'Then a woman walked along beside me and asked in English if I was an American. When I said I was, she asked if I knew a Mr Kroger in America.' Amused, Manning said he did not know the man; but it turned out the 'Mr Kroger' referred to was owner of the Kroger chain of grocery stores. 'She said she had a sister in the US working for Kroger and she wanted to know whether her sister was being mistreated, as she had read was happening to Germans in America. She said Mr Roosevelt must be a terrible man to order such a thing. I told her "No, it isn't like that in America", but she would not believe me.' Manning was taken to a government office in the town, where officials telephoned for instructions on what to do with him.

After the cooling system of his Messerschmitt had been hit, by return fire from the Fortress he attacked over Holland, Lothar Sachs headed east looking for somewhere to land. Somehow his sorely tried Daimler Benz engine kept going until the fighter base at Twente appeared. He extended the landing gear and set the fighter down on the grass, then shut down the engine. Even before Sachs had time to climb out, the fire truck was screeching to a halt beside him and the crash crew were smothering the steaming engine with foam to prevent it bursting into flames.

Elton Skinner came down near the German-Dutch border after bailing out of his B-17 and hid his parachute. Then, a couple of hundred yards away, he saw his bombardier being led away by an old lady; the last time Skinner had seen the man, Rus Allman, was when he had jumped from the bomber with one hand almost severed. Concerned for his friend, Skinner ran over and caught up with the pair. Allman's wound was bleeding badly so Skinner improvised a tourniquet using his scarf. Still the Americans did not know in which country they had landed. 'Dutch?' Skinner asked the woman in English. But he did not know the word sounded like the local words for 'German': *Deutsch* or *Duits*. '*Nee!*' the woman indignantly replied and Skinner's jaw dropped. Then she continued '*Niet Duits! Hollands!*' So he had landed in Holland after all! Skinner felt a great burden had been lifted off his shoulders. 'She took us to a barn nearby where we met a small group of people one of whom spoke English. He told me they would have to turn Rus over to the Germans so he could receive proper medical attention. And I should hide in one of the fields nearby until they came for me,' Skinner moved to a small depression some 400 yards from the barn and waited there. 'There was snow on the ground but in my flying clothing I was not uncomfortable. I lay there the rest of the day, watching the smoke rising from our crashed aircraft some distance away and wondering what had happened to the rest of my crew and what was going to happen to me.'

A few miles away B-17 pilot Lowell Watts came down on snow and hastily hid his parachute. Watts stayed close to cover and after about half an hour a man and his wife out walking saw the American pilot; they indicated he was 4 kilometers inside Holland but were afraid to assist him further. Nevertheless it was comforting news and Watts resolved to wait until nightfall, then make his way west until he found someone prepared to help.

B-17 pilot Monty Givens came down in the same general area and had quickly joined up with Ken Betts and Dan Walstra, his navigator and tail gunner. The trio were wondering what to do next when a couple of teenage Dutch boys arrived and led them to a nearby farm house. At the house were two men and several women and children; although the fugitives were given bread and coffee and treated kindly the language barrier proved insurmountable. There was nothing to do but wait and find out what the Dutch had decided to do with them.

B-17 copilot Alan Willis landed by parachute to find a small crowd of Dutch civilians waiting for him. As he was getting rid of his parachute one came up to him and to his surprise said in perfect English 'Will you come with me please.'

He was led away and joined his navigator, Hank Gladys, then the Dutchman took them away from the scene; on the way the trio had to duck behind cover to avoid a squad of German soldiers on their way to where the Fortress had crashed. The Americans were taken to a farm house where they were given bread and milk, and two other members of the crew were brought in.

B-24 bombardier Alvis Roberts came down in western Holland and saw three teenage boys come running towards him. 'They couldn't speak any English but they were very friendly. Then a fellow on a bicycle came along the nearby trail, jumped off and came running towards me. When he reached me he said in English "My name is Arnold, I lived in Chicago!" and shook me by the hand.' The man pointed to a windmill on the skyline about three quarters of a mile away and told Roberts to make his way there, go inside and wait. 'Arnold' said something to the boys, who rolled up the incriminating parachute and carried it away, then went back to his bicycle and rode away. Keeping a wary eye for German patrols Roberts started towards the windmill.

B-24 ball turret gunner Victor Krueger came down in a plowed field near the Dutch town of Pummerend. As soon as he landed he bundled up his parachute and ran quickly to hide in a small clump of bushes. From his hiding place he cautiously surveyed the landscape; in the distance was a solitary farmhouse but there was no evidence anyone had noticed his arrival.

Not all of those who came down in the area had much chance to avoid capture, however. Hanging from his parachute B-24 pilot Hubert Cripe saw his crewmen drop one after the other into the Zuider Zee, then it was his turn. 'Splash! Man, the water was cold. With my heavy clothing and boots I was pulled right under. But God was merciful and permitted me to live and not die. It had to be God's miracle that on one grab I found the string which operated the carbon-dioxide bottle and inflated the Mae West. Suddenly my head was supported above water and I sucked in the sweet breath of life. Thank you, God, that I am yet among the living and I shall never forget this day.' After a few minutes a Dutch fishing boat pulled alongside the shivering pilot and hoisted him out of the water; only two other members of the crew were picked up alive. Then a German launch arrived to take off the American survivors who were informed, in broken English, 'For you the war is over . . .'

On the ground at Wunstorf Guenther Specht and Heinz Knoke, exhausted after their combat with the P-47s, ambled slowly away from their Messer-schmitts. Each of the German aces' thoughts were with the wingman he had just lost. 'Specht was a very brave man, one of the bravest I have ever known,' recalled Knoke. 'But on this day he had just had enough of fighting. Wearily he turned to me and commented "We did not show ourselves to be particularly great fighters!" '

As the raiding force streamed across the North Sea the Royal Air Force rescue service was ready for those for whom, inevitably, the hundred-mile sea crossing would prove an insurmountable final obstacle. Mid-way across was a line of high speed rescue launches, circling slowly as they awaited the call for assistance. Backing the launches, and already airborne, were a score of Hudson, Warwick and Anson search aircraft and small Walrus amphibious flying boats.

The first to go down in the sea was B-24 'Major Hoopo' of the 446th Bomb Group. This aircraft had suffered damage during a fighter attack just before it reached Berlin, which knocked out an engine and forced the crew to abort the mission. The bomber crossed Germany and Holland at low altitude and suffered further damage from both flak and fighters. The unfortunate Liberator was riddled with holes; 'I don't know what kept it in the air!', commented tail gunner Sergeant Richard Denton. Finally, shortly after crossing the Dutch coast, a second engine gave out and although everything moveable had been thrown overboard to lighten the aircraft, pilot Lieutenant Bob Paltz was forced to set it down on the water. The B-24 was a particularly difficult aircraft to ditch. The fuselage was liable to snap like a carrot just aft of the wing then the forward section, weighed down by the four large engines, would sink rapidly taking with it any crewmen who had not got out in time. That was what happened to Paltz's aircraft. Denton was in his ditching position in the rear fuselage: 'We hit the water the first time and bounced, then the second time we hit the water the plane broke in half at the trailing edge of the wing. The front end of the plane nosed over and started to sink. I struggled out of the waist window and came out at the back end of the fuselage, then managed to scramble aboard a life raft that had inflated.' The pilot, with both legs broken, and the top turret gunner with an injured shoulder, both swam over to the raft and Denton helped them board it. The rest of the crew went down with the aircraft, which sank rapidly. Fortunately for the survivors Lieutenant John Bentley of the 361st Fighter Group, in a P-47, had watched the ditching and was reporting their predicament by radio. Denton and the others watched the fighter circling them: 'He flew around us two or three times, then the pilot waved and headed off to the west. As he disappeared we felt very lonely.'

The second bomber to ditch was a B-24 of the 453rd Bomb Group which came down some 30 miles off the coast of England. The ditching was seen from a patroling Hudson of No 279 Squadron which was over the scene within minutes. The pilot, Flight Lieutenant D. Butt, later reported: 'The aircraft's back had broken and the nose was well down, with only the wing trailing edge above the water. No dinghies were seen but some survivors (number uncertain) could be seen clinging to the wreckage.' The Hudson dropped dinghies and rescue equipment beside the floating wreckage but its crew could only watch in despair as the men in the water struggled unsuccessfully to reach the yellow canisters. Next on the scene was a Walrus amphibian of No 277 Squadron. Pilot Officer Bill Greenfield flew low over the wreckage and saw three men swimming towards each other. 'We alighted well down wind and taxied to the three men in the water. As we moved in we passed a fourth clinging on to an oxygen bottle, who waved to us. I decided to pick up the other three first, then go for him. The waves were about five feet high and the water was very cold.' The drill for picking an airman out the water was to taxi the aircraft slowly past him, attach a line to him from the nose hatch and pay him back to the rear hatch which was somewhat lower and from which the survivor could be lifted into the fuselage. But as he was being paid back the first man, barely conscious with the cold, slid his arm around one of the landing gear struts under the wing and could not be moved. Greenfield shut down the engine then reached out of his side window and grabbed the collar of another of the survivors bobbing in the water beside him; the man was barely conscious. 'Now we were stuck. Leighton climbed on the left wing to try and free the man and Carpenter went to join him. They tried to pull the man forward to release his grip but were unable to do so. While this was happening the man I was holding suddenly died. He stiffened up completely and ceased breathing. I had to let him go and he started to float away.' Greenfield went to the rear hatch and, using a boathook, joined in the efforts to free the man under the wing. After several minutes' pulling and pushing his arm was dragged clear and he was hauled back to the rear hatch and pulled in. By that time the third man in the group was floating several yards away face down, obviously dead. 'I then re-started the engine and we went for the man we had seen first. We approached him from down wind but as we got close he let go of the oxygen bottle and went under. We were there right away, however, and pulled him out and managed to revive him.' The two men were wrapped in blankets and Greenfield took off and flew them to his base at Martlesham Heath. On arrival the survivors were rushed to the base hospital but in spite of efforts of the medical teams one of the men succumbed that evening.

The third bomber to go down in the sea was another B-24 of the 453rd Bomb Group, piloted by Lieutenant Elmer Crockett. One engine had been knocked out and two others damaged by flak over Berlin. During the return flight the bomber had come under fighter attack and a further engine was knocked out, then one of the damaged engines packed up as it crossed the Dutch coast. In a remarkable display of airmanship Crockett kept the bomber airborne on only the damaged left inboard engine, escorted by P-47s of the 358th Fighter Group. Then, just five miles short of the coast of England, Crockett's remaining engine gave out. 'We had no power and no flaps and the bomb bay and nose wheel doors were open, so it was thought best to jump and hope to be picked up,' explained Lieutenant Orvis Martin, the bombardier. Martin went out through the bomb bay of the silent aircraft and after his parachute opened he saw boats and a Walrus moving in and P-47s circling the survivors. 'Upon hitting the water I was amazed how far I went down, but when I surfaced I got out of the parachute harness quickly and it sank almost immediately. I then tried to inflate my Mae West but my hands were so numb I couldn't untangle the cord to the carbon dioxide bottle; in the end I blew it up by mouth. The air trapped in the heavy flying suit helped me keep afloat and I was a good swimmer, but I had never been in water as cold as this before. We had been told half an hour was all a person could survive there and I can confirm that.' Martin watched a minesweeper about a hundred yards away rescue one of his comrades, then it began to move away from him. He could feel his life ebbing away and in desparation he yelled at the top of his voice for help, but the launch continued to move away. Martin became frantic in his efforts to attract attention when something caught his eye to one side: another rescue boat sliding up beside him! Martin was hoisted out of the water and dumped on the deck. 'The crew stripped me, wrapped me in blankets and took me to the galley where they held my feet and hands in the oven for warmth. They gave me dry clothes and brandy I couldn't even taste – it went down like water.' In spite of the presence of rescue boats where the Liberator crew came down only five of the men were picked up alive; one body was recovered, those of the other four men were never found. The North Sea was as formidable as any human adversary.

Four badly damaged bombers sought safety in the east rather than the west, three making for neutral Sweden. The first to reach the haven was B-17 'Barrick's Bag' of the 100th Bomb Group, with two engines knocked out during the action near Haseluenne. As the aircraft crossed the Swedish coast bombardier Sergeant James Brady heard one of the gunners call 'Fighters at 3 o'clock!' 'I looked over and saw two odd looking planes bearing strange markings with three crowns. I shouted over the intercom. "For Christ's sake don't shoot, they're Swedish!" The fighters moved into position about 500 yards out, one on each wing tip, then rocked their wings as a signal for us to follow.' The Swedish fighters led the B-17 to the grass airfield at Bulltofta near Malmoe where Sam Barrick made what was, in the circumstances, a good landing. But as the left wheel touched down the leg collapsed and the Fortress swung in a wide turn pivoting on the skidding wingtip. As it came to rest the crew threw open the hatches and scrambled out. Then, in Brady's words: 'Some rather grim looking characters advanced on us carrying sub machine guns. We all raised our hands but the guys just laughed at us. That was a great relief and we slowly lowered our hands. We were taken to their headquarters and given a meal; it wasn't to gourmet standards but it was very welcome.'

Later in the afternoon B-24 'Hello Natural' of the 448th Bomb Group also landed at Bulltofta, with one engine knocked out by flak over Berlin. And B-17 'A Good and Happy Ship' of the 388th Bomb Group came down on Rinkaby airfield near Kristianstad.

The fourth aircraft took a more adventurous route. B-17 'Liberty Lady' of the 306th Bomb Group had two engines knocked out by flak over Berlin and pilot Lieutenant Charles Smith descended into cloud and headed northeast in an attempt to reach Soviet-held territory. After a couple of hours the cloud cleared and the crew found themselves over water. Obviously it was the Baltic but where? The navigator's maps did not cover that part of the world. Fuel was beginning to run low when an island appeared ahead and Smith decided to put the Fortress down there. In fact the island was Gotland, part of Sweden, but the airmen did not know or even suspect this.

Smith made a wheels-up landing on farm land and the crew climbed out; then, assuming he had come down in German-held territory, he ordered one of the men to ignite the incendiary bomb in the radio room to destroy the aircraft. The fire took hold and the bomber started to burn encouragingly. It was not long before the rising column of black smoke summoned attention. Strangely uniformed soldiers arrived on the scene carrying automatic weapons. Clearly the men were not Russian though they seemed friendly enough. 'The soldiers spoke no English so we couldn't speak with them,' recalled Sergeant Don Courson one of the waist gunners. 'They took us to the nearby hospital where one of the doctors asked in broken English if anyone was injured. Nobody was. Then he told us we were on Gotland, but nobody in the crew realized the significance of that. We thought we had been captured by the Germans and our good treatment was all part of some elaborate trick to get us to talk.'

During the withdrawal German fighters had caused the loss of eighteen B-17s and B-24s: 15 were shot down, one was destroyed when it was rammed by another set on fire during a fighter attack, one which suffered flak damage over Berlin was finished off, and one was damaged and came down in Sweden. Two of the escorts, a P-47 and a P-38, were shot down by German fighters and a P-51 damaged during the previous action near Berlin came down near the German-Dutch border. Flak accounted for six more bombers, two of which came down in the North Sea. For its part the Luftwaffe lost seven Me 109s and four FW 190s during the action.

In the course of this phase of the action the raiding force lost more bombers than during the initial furious clash over Haseluenne, though the later engagement had of course been more protracted and spread over a far greater area. Only the A Formation of the 45th Combat Wing, comprising B-17s of the 388th and 452nd Bomb Groups, came under concentrated fighter attack during this phase and it lost seven bombers in rapid succession. The remaining bombers lost had been picked off, usually one at a time, either out of their formations or as they straggled behind them. Considering the large numbers of stragglers it is a tribute to the effectiveness of the escorts that many more bombers were not lost during the withdrawal.

Three B-24s had come down in the North Sea as a result of battle damage, two from flak and the other from unknown causes. Ditching in these terribly cold waters was a hazardous enterprise, as evidenced by the fact that of the thirty crewmen on board the bombers only 8 survived. Four bombers reached the safety of Sweden, one damaged by fighters during the Haseluenne action, two by flak over Berlin and one by fighters during the withdrawal.

The first US aircraft to regain their bases in England after the action around Berlin were the P-51s of the target support groups, which had broken off the escort just to the west of the German capital. Soon after 3.15 pm these began to land at their airfields in East Anglia. Tom Hayes, who had led the 357th Fighter Group, swooped low over his base at Leiston then pulled into a climbing roll to show that he had knocked down one of the enemy. 'The guy you did the roll for was your crew chief, that made him feel on top of the world,' Hayes explained. 'We had maintained radio silence so I did not know how many Germans the others had hit or how many of our own guys had gone down. We had gone out as a formation but returned in ones, twos and fours. I knew there had been one Hell of a fight. But as I landed my concern was not "How many of the enemy have we destroyed?" but "How bad has it been for us?" ' Hayes taxied to his dispersal point to receive congratulations from his beaming crew chief. 'I saw other P-51s coming in and doing victory rolls, some even did two before going into the landing pattern. Everyone was getting more and more elated,' the commander recalled. On arrival at the debriefing room each pilot received the usual shot of whiskey. As the returning aircraft were counted and the pilots made their initial reports, the degree of the group's success during the mission became clear: of the 48 Mustangs that had taken off only 33 reached the target area; but in the ensuing action their pilots claimed 20 enemy aircraft destroyed, one probably destroyed and 7 damaged – and all of the P-51s had returned safely.

The 4th Fighter Group, based at Debden 70 miles to the west, had also been successful during the action: of the 35 Mustangs which had set out 25 reached the Berlin area and their pilots claimed 15 enemy aircraft destroyed and 11 damaged; but the unit had lost 4 P-51s and a fifth returned with battle damage.

The 354th Fighter Group based at Boxted had put up 45 Mustangs of which 34 reached the target area. These claimed 8 enemy aircraft destroyed and 2 damaged for the loss of one P-51.

As the bombers crossed the coast of England the stately wing formations split into their constituent bomb groups, which then made their way individually to the bases. The first bombers to land were always those with wounded on board, firing red flares during the landing approach to announce their plight. Next down were the so-called 'hot photo ships', those bombers fitted with strike cameras whose films had to be processed as rapidly as possible. Then the rest of the bombers followed.

There were always difficulties during this phase of the mission as tired pilots fought to land damaged aircraft. That afternoon General Doolittle was at Kimbolton to see the return of the 379th Bomb Group. The unit had done well: of the 23 B-17s that had set out only two returned early and one had been shot down. As Doolittle and his staff watched from the control tower, however, B-17 'Dragon Lady' piloted by Lieutenant Frederick Sommer swung into the landing pattern with one engine feathered and firing red flares. The damaged bomber came in fast and rather too close to the aircraft in front, ran into the turbulent wake and curved dangerously out of control across the airfield. It narrowly missed the control tower with the party of senior officers before Sommer was able to regain control and take the bomber around for a more normal landing approach.

Lieutenant John Flottorp of the 390th Bomb Group also had problems putting his badly shot-up B-17 down at Framlingham. First the landing gear had to be hand-cranked down; he had no hydraulic pressure – and therefore no brakes – and one of his tires had been badly burned when the right inboard engine caught fire. Preparing for the worst Flottorp ordered his crew to take up their crash-landing positions: the pilots in their seats with straps tightened, the remaining crew members in the radio compartment which was considered the safest part of the aircraft. The pilot then made a long approach and eased the bomber down. 'There was no way I could keep the airplane on the runway. I ran off the right side and bogged down in the soft earth with no further damage. A reception committee of jeeps, fire trucks and ambulances came roaring up. Colonel Witten's jeep was in the lead, followed by Chaplain Lenahan's; then came the fortunately unneeded rescue equipment.' Once outside Flottorp surveyed the bomber that had brought him and his crew back from Berlin. 'We counted seventeen 20 mm entry holes and there were too many flak holes to count. The No 3 engine had the crank case holed, the oil cooler shot away, a run-away propeller and a fire. The No 4 engine turbo waste gate had been hit and jammed and the top of one cylinder and the valves had been knocked out,' he later wrote. 'The vertical fin had collected seven 20 mm hits that opened up the skin and looked like a Swiss cheese the rats had been at; but the spar structure was not appreciably damaged. The main wing spar on the right had been virtually severed in two places. The right aileron cables were severed but I had not noticed any lack of control and don't know at what point that happened; they may have been only partially cut and failed completely at the end of the flight.' The B-17 never flew again.

Lieutenant Harold Roellig, copilot of B-17 'Mag The Hag II' of the 92nd Bomb Group, recalled his aircraft landed without hydraulics at Podington and ran off the runway into mud. The crew piled out and stood beside the nose looking at the smashed plexiglas. 'Then the top turret gunner bent over and said to me "Lieutenant, look what is stuck in your boot!" He passed me a shell fragment measuring 3 inches by ¾ inch by ½ inch.' After some detective work the crew discovered the tortuous path the fragment had taken: it had sliced through the nose plexiglas, severed one of the hydraulic lines under the cockpit, glanced upwards and pierced the floor between the rudder pedals, then bounced off Roellig's control column before it came gently to rest lodged in his boot.

For one crew, bringing back an almost undamaged aircraft, the most heartrending time came after they were safely down. Lieutenant Bob Shoens landed B-17 'Our Gal Sal' of the 100th Bomb Group at Thorpe Abbotts, one of the few surviving bombers of the ill-fated Low Box of the 13th Wing B Formation. Of the twenty B-17s which had taken off, five had broken off the mission early; and 10 out of the remaining 15 had been shot down. Shoens had returned with another box formation. 'As we circled the airfield alone we could see a lot of empty spaces. We landed and when we taxied to our space we found our squadron commander waiting for us. He was crying. We were stunned to learn that we were the only aircraft of the squadron to return to the field and only one of four to make it back to England. What do you say, what do you do when your squadron commander is crying and wants to know what has happened? You do the same.'

The last bomber to return from the mission was Bernie Dopko's B-17 'Little Willie' of the 388th Bomb Group, which had flown alone at 115 mph at low altitude all the way from Berlin. Dopko reached Knettishall and landed at 5.45 pm, nearly an hour after the last previous aircraft of the group touched down; he had been airborne for 9½ hours. 'Returning crews reported they had seen us bailing out, and upon going to my quarters I found my bed rolled up and all my personal belongings packed ready for shipment to my family,' Dopko remembered. But the biggest shock came when ground crewmen showed him the unexploded 20 mm shell they found lodged in one of the bomber's fuel tanks. 'God, if that thing had exploded we would have been only a flash in the sky!'

The final aircraft to land after the mission, at 5.48 pm three minutes after Dopko's bomber, was Walt Weitner's reconnaissance Spitfire. Carrying the precious photographs of the target Weitner approached his base at Mount Farm near Oxford with plenty of height; his tanks were almost dry but if the fuel ran out he knew he could glide in. The engine kept going as he landed, however. He taxied to his dispersal point then, as he was about to enter it, the Merlin engine sputtered a couple of times then fell silent; the Spitfire rolled to a halt. Walt Weitner's sortie was at an end, just a few feet short of 'according to plan'.

CHAPTER 7

AFTERMATH

It is a classical maxim that it is sweet and becoming to die for one's country; but whoever has seen the horrors of a battlefield feels it is far sweeter to live for it.

John Mosby

In Berlin, as in any city after an attack, the first reaction of the citizens was to engage in a frantic hunt for information on the safety of loved ones. Few felt this need more keenly than Marianne Wittstock, for whom the day should have been one of fulfilment but had turned into a nightmare. At the Rittberg Hospital where she had given birth to her daughter there was now chaos. First there had been the electrical failure which confined her and other patients to the cellars lit only by candles. Then came a new horror. A public air raid shelter in the Rueliplatz nearby had suffered a direct hit which killed many of those inside and injured several others. Wounded men, women and children were brought to the hospital and put down on the ground floor passageways and the floor of the cellar. The shelter's timber supports had shattered under the force of the explosion and some of the groaning injured had long wooden splinters sticking from their bodies. Nobody had time to comfort the frightened young mother sick with worry for the safety of her first-born. 'Worrying about the safety of my husband on the eastern front was one thing, worrying about the safety of my helpless new baby was quite different and far worse,' she remembered. Late that evening her mother was able to pull strings and get into the hospital, and informed her all was well with the baby in the childrens' bunker. The news left Marianne Wittstock weak with relief.*

After the all-clear 37-year-old Foreign Ministry official Arthur von Brietzke set out from his small apartment in the Neukoelln district for Prenzlauerberg to check that his widowed mother was all right. In Neukoelln there had been no damage but he soon learned the streetcars had not resumed running there; he would have to walk the five miles to his mother's. As he crossed the Oberbaum Bridge over the River Spree into the Friedrichshain district he saw the first signs of damage: power lines for the streetcars lying in the street and a lot of smoke and dust blowing from the Weissensee district in the northeast. Becoming more concerned he quickened his pace. Striding along the Elbingerstrasse, at the junction with Greifswalderstrasse, the dust and smoke suddenly thickened and

*The story has a further twist. The new-born daughter, Sabine, is now grown up, married to an American and living in California.

he saw knots of dispirited men, women and children emerge from the semi-darkness like ghostly apparitions. Many were heavily laden with suitcases, bundles of bedding and household items of all kinds. Von Brietzke learned their homes in the Weissensee district had been hit and they were on their way to the well-known Elysium cinema nearby, which had been pressed into use as a reception center. Adding a bizarre touch to the scene was a herd of cows, one of many kept in the city for fresh milk, fleeing from the area; the frightened animals noisily resisted their owner's efforts to move them in the direction he wanted. As the demoralized survivors shuffled past, von Brietzke suddenly caught sight of his brother-in-law, Arthur Schulz. Still badly shaken and with tears in his eyes, Schulz told von Brietzke 'The shit has fallen on us, too!' His home had been wrecked and now he was looking for somewhere to put his wife and two young children. Von Brietzke had himself been bombed out some weeks earlier and had only one small room; he regretted he could not help. Leaving his brother-in-law von Brietzke continued to his mother's apartment in the Schoenhauser Allee and was relieved to find her safe and her home virtually undamaged. Some of the cardboard panels replacing windows smashed during an earlier night raid needed straightening, that was all. When this minor chore was done von Brietzke bade his mother goodbye and set out for the long walk back to Neukoelln.

Housewife Elfriede Grasser, 45, had been visiting friends near the center of Berlin when the attack came and she had taken shelter there. After the all-clear she journeyed by train to the Spandau district where she lived. 'When I arrived at the station friends greeted me with the worrying news that an American bomber had crashed beside our house in the Feldstrasse but the house itself was quite undamaged. At first I was perplexed, I did not like to think what I might find. Eight families were living in the house and in the garden there was only a miserable dug-out shelter.' Elfriede Grasse reached her home to find her husband outside and he took her to see the wreckage. 'With my husband I walked around the smashed aircraft, a sight I shall never forget. From one of the glass turrets there protruded a head with hair encrusted in blood. Close to the wreck lay two more crewmen where they had been thrown clear, their bodies lying on the ground twisted like broken dolls.' The aircraft was B-24 'De-Icer' of the 93rd Bomb Group, shot down by gunners on the Zoo and Humbolthain flak towers.

At his flak battery in the Marienfelde district Dietrich Scheibel and the other boy-gunners were worked hard by the adults at the site, to repair the bomb damage. Not only had the battery to be ready as soon as possible to meet the next attack by the enemy, but nobody wanted to give the youngsters time to brood over the death of the predictor operator. Nevertheless the incident had depressed morale. 'For me it was the first real shock of what war meant, the first sight of a dead comrade. Later I would see far more terrible things but this was the first time and so the shock was all the greater.' During the late afternoon there was a further poignant scene at the gun site: the dead boy's father arrived to call on his son not knowing he had been killed; with him he brought a telegram saying the boy's elder brother had just been killed in Russia.

At Hans Ring's flak battery in the Spandau district four survivors were brought in from one of the crashed American bombers. Ring and the other young gunners clustered around the prisoners. 'They were a great curiosity, almost like men from another planet. We tried to converse with them in our schoolboy English and gave them each a cup of our ersatz coffee. Then, suddenly, the pleasantries ceased when our battery commander saw what was happening. He barked orders telling us to get away from them. It was not proper for German boys to have anything to do with these *amerikanische Gangsters!*' Later a truck arrived to take the airmen away.

In the Zehlendorf district Adolf Echtler watched rescue men burrow deeper and deeper into the house next door searching for the two women who had taken shelter there. When darkness fell the work continued under the harsh glare of arc lamps. In the end both bodies were found and brought out; the women had been killed instantly by the explosion. Later Echtler wrote to his brother describing the damage to his own home:

> In the garden a bomb had exploded leaving a crater 5 meters deep. In the garden opposite is a similar hole with yet another beside the second exit of our shelter. Altogether there are 14 craters in our immediate area. Our house is, of course, severely damaged. The front door has been pushed in, several window frames have been blown away from the surrounding brickwork and so have the bedroom doors. Hardly a single window has survived the blast which seemed to come from all directions. Our garden and drive are covered with bricks and glass splinters. In each room the floorboards have been pushed up and are lying all over the place, mixed with clods of earth blown through the shattered windows.

Like may others in the area Adolf Echtler and his wife spent the afternoon and evening doing what they could to get their home at least partially habitable. They nailed cardboard over the gaping holes where the windows had been, closed those doors which could be made to shut and swept up the broken glass and debris. Even a damaged house was far better than none at all.

Horst Krieger and other apprentices at the Telefunken factory nearby were put to work clearing away the rubble of what had been the works canteen. The building had been flattened by a bomb and the stock, including hundreds of packets of precious cigarettes, lay strewn about in the wreckage. Many of the apprentices smoked when they could get cigarettes, though as boys they were not entitled to any ration. The youngsters pocketed as many packets as they could conceal and continued with the clearing-up operation. Later the cigarettes were smoked by the boys themselves or generously given to friends or relatives. Inevitably, however, the management discovered what had happened and the boyish prank developed into something far more serious: taking the cigarettes amounted to looting; had foreign workers done such a thing they would have been shot out of hand. But it transpired that so many apprentices had been involved the matter could not have been reported to the police without inviting a major investigation, which would certainly have disrupted production. A compromise was found: the boys' fathers would have to pay for the cigarettes and have them deducted from their own ration cards. Then, after stern lectures to the boys, the matter was quietly dropped.

At the Friedrichstrasse railway station Guenther Wolf and Hein Hafemeier were treated like heroes. Still wearing flying suits and carrying helmets and parachutes, after their Messerschmitt 110 night fighter had been shot down by a Mustang, the pair had an hour's wait before the train left for Leipzig; the station had been the radar aiming point for all three American bomb divisions but had escaped without a single hit and was operating more or less normally. The two Luftwaffe airmen went to sit in the station restaurant and immediately became the center of interest. 'Everybody wanted to know how we came to be there in our flying kit. Hein had to explain how his parachute and helmet had become torn and show the 'war wound' to his head. The people wanted to know our life stories, how many missions we had flown, whether we were married, where we were going. Acknowledging the admiring glances from the girls we felt very proud of ourselves,' Wolf recalled. Then someone asked if the pair were going to eat, but though they had money they had no ration cards so were unable to buy anything in the way of food. 'When people heard that they offered us things off their cards. One man let me have a piece of meat off his card, another gave me some bread from his.'

At Wittstock, 50 miles to the northwest of Berlin, Harold Stearns was taken to a school building after his capture and there met two other members of his crew. Here the airmen received a crude and violent interrogation at the hands of their captors. 'I was asked questions by one of the men and when I didn't answer his big stooge would slap me in the face. Then he pulled out a gun and said "I'm going to shoot you!" I said "Go ahead, I don't care!" He called me a "Roosevelt Gangster" and "Murder Incorporated", then punched me in the nose and it started to bleed. I don't know why, I didn't feel a thing, no pain or anything.' Finally Stearns was taken to another room to join his comrades. 'Lieutenant Geisler seemed not to recognize us. We found out later he had been beaten with a rubber hose and was making believe he was incoherent.' Such instances of brutality by officials were rare. The great majority of Americans interviewed by the authors spoke of correct treatment by their captors.

At Salzwedel, 50 miles west of Berlin, Hans Iffland waited anxiously with other pilots of IVth Gruppe of Fighter Geschwader 3 at the operations building as news came in from their comrades. Several had landed at other airfields in the area and as each phoned in there was a cheer: 'Weik has landed at Staaken!' 'Erhardt is at Gatow!' 'Mueller is down at Staaken as well!' 'Stretz landed at Schoenefeld!' Gradually it became clear the Gruppe had lost nobody during this, its first action in the defense of the homeland. When the Gruppe commander, Major Friedrich-Karl Mueller, returned he received from his pilots their formal accounts of the action. Hans Iffland awaited his turn then marched up to the table, clicked his heels and touched his cap in salute then proudly delivered his report: 'Leutnant Iffland begs to submit, returned from the operation with one Fortress destroyed!' Then the German pilot gave details of his victory. *Gratuliere!* said the smiling Mueller. Altogether the pilots made initial victory claims of thirteen B-17s to be submitted to higher authority for confirmation; in fact the actual score was less than half that but it was still a creditable performance for an inexperienced unit. Later in the afternoon, when it was clear there would be no further incursion by the enemy, a beaming Mueller announced 'Boys, tonight we celebrate!'

Some 400 miles away to the west, at the American fighter bases in East Anglia, there was a similar mood. At Leiston the P-51 pilots of the successful 357th Fighter Group had also completed the mission without loss. 'When we got to the debriefing there was a shot of whiskey for each pilot. Then after we delivered our reports we went to our squadron nissen huts where there was a fire going and the pilots who had not been on the mission and the ground officers joined us. There was a lot of back-slapping and boisterousness as people relived the action,' Tom Hayes remembered.

When the bomber crews returned to their operations buildings, more than nine hours after they had left them, there were different feelings. 'Our ten aircrew-members gathered around a table for the debriefing, dog-tired and withdrawn. One or two young intelligence lieutenants asked questions but they didn't ask the right ones and seemed in awe of us. We didn't help them and we didn't volunteer any information,' remembered Les Rentmeester of the 91st Bomb Group at Bassingbourn. ' "Did you see any flak?" "Yes" "Where?" "All over" "Did you see any fighters?" "Yes" "How many?" "Maybe 200" "What kinds?" "All kinds" "Did you see anybody go down?" "Yes" "Who?" "Mason, Tibbetts, Coleman" (a crew was always identified by the first pilot). The frustrated intelligence officer finally let us go.' The men had not always been so tongue-tied during the debriefing: 'For about the first five missions everybody was excited and chattering after the flight was over, describing in detail the events of the past few hours. With each mission the crew became more reticent.'

At Thorpe Abbots, home of the ill-fated 100th Bomb Group, everyone was numb at the loss of 150 crewmen during a single mission. Tired and demoralized, Bob Shoens and his crew shuffled into the room. 'We went to the debriefing room and were the only crew there. They expect you to tell them what the other crews might have told them. It was hard to make any sense of it all.'

At the maternity hospital at Bassum Hermann Reinthaler came out of the anesthetic to find his left arm had been amputated above the elbow. His career as a Luftwaffe fighter pilot was over. Sharing the small ward was Rudolf Sinner who had collected a bullet in the thigh while attacking one of the Fortresses and been forced to bail out of his Messerschmitt. The two men, both Austrians, got to know each other well in the hospital and have been friends ever since.

In the Evangelical hospital at Quakenbrueck Hans-Gerd Wennekers came to, to find his left arm in a sling above his head rigidly bound up with bandages. The operation had saved the arm, after an American bullet had gone through his wrist. Soon afterwards Wolfgang Kretchmer was brought into the ward, his head and arms swathed in bandages which covered the terrible burns he suffered trying to bail out of his Focke-Wulf. There were holes only for his eyes and mouth. Again the two men became good friends and are still in contact.

After about ninety minutes bobbing in their life raft off the Dutch coast, Richard Denton and the two other survivors of B-24 'Major Hoopo' sighted a Royal Air Force high speed rescue launch racing towards them from the west. The shivering airmen were lifted on board and taken below: 'They gave us rum, took off our wet clothes and gave us dry ones, put us to bed and really took good care of us. I had come on board with all of my clothes – they said I was the first man they had ever picked up still with his boots on. So I gave my boots to one of the guys on the boat.' The rescue took place so far out to sea that it would take the motor launch more than five hours to get back to its base at Gorleston.

Orvis Martin was taken to the Royal Navy hospital at Great Yarmouth after he and other survivors from his B-24 had been rescued from the North Sea. 'We were put to bed and covered with the most beautiful white wool blankets I have ever seen. But the care given by those wonderful English nurses, the warm brandy and the thick blankets could not keep me from shaking like an aspen leaf. The shaking went on for most of the night and I got very little sleep.'

At Thorpe Abbots, base of the 100th Bomb Group, there was stunned shock at the day's terrible losses in men and aircraft. 'It was so quiet. The men spoke in low, almost inaudible tones, if they spoke at all. There were many that wandered off by themselves wanting to be alone in their grief. Others, their eyes moist, stood silently. And many drank more than usual that evening. Lieutenant Colonel John Bennett, our squadron CO but now commanding officer of the Group, grasping for some words to say, said the 8th had lost less than ten per cent. But his voice sounded strange and his words trailed off,' remembered Sergeant John Miller, one of the Group's gunners who had not flown on the mission. The chaplains offered prayers for the missing crews, otherwise there was little to break the silence. 'Oh there were some new men that tried, and wanted, to talk. "How was it?" "What happened?" "How many Kraut fighters were there?" "Where was the escort?" "What kind of fighters were they?" "Did they use rockets" "What happened to so and so?" But most of the questions went unanswered. Some missions were just too painful to be relived and discussed.'

Hans Kogler and his radio operator were picked up at Magdeburg by Messerschmitt 108 courier plane and flown back to their base at Wunstorf. There Kogler learned his Gruppe, IIIrd of Destroyer Geschwader 26, had suffered another terrible beating from the American escorts. Of the nine Me 110s which had taken off two had returned early with technical failures, one returned damaged, his own was sitting damaged at Magdeburg and the remaining five were missing. Kogler spent a miserable evening in his office seeking news of those who had not come back and one by one the reports came in of where they had crashed; five of his men had been killed and four wounded. The unit had suffered 50 per cent personnel casualties. And the next day the Gruppe would have to be ready to go into action again.

On the other side of Wunstorf airfield Heinz Knoke sat, similarly dejected, in his Staffel headquarters awaiting news from his missing pilots; he had heard nothing from Wennekers or Zambelli and the day's events had left him mentally exhausted. Knoke broke out the bottle of cognac in his locker; like many Luftwaffe pilots he kept one there so his comrades could drink to him if he was killed. With his friend Johnny Fest he now set about demolishing the bottle, becoming more and more morose as the afternoon wore on. Even the news that Zambelli was safe and Wennekers, though wounded, was in good hands at Quakenbrueck did not lift the gloom. The IInd Gruppe of Fighter Geschwader 11 had started the day with 15 pilots and had lost two killed and one seriously wounded; since a Gruppe had an official establishment of 40 pilots it did not require any great brain to work out where things were leading. And the new pilots coming from the training schools were too few and insufficiently trained to replace those being lost.

At Salzwedel the victory party was getting into its swing. Fighter Geschwader 3 had been partnered with the giant Henkell wine company, a cosy arrangement which guaranteed the unit a plentiful supply of drink throughout the war. After dinner at the *Kasino* the officers gathered for a pleasant evening of drink and chatter punctuated with nostalgic German songs played by one of them on the guitar; as time wore on they sang with increasing fervor and rather less unison, *'Es ist so wunder wunder schoen, hoch in den blauen Luftigen Hoehen . . .'* *'Oh, du schoener We-e-sterwald . . .'* *'Auf der Lueneburger Heide, in dem wunderschoenen Land. . . .'* The party lasted almost till midnight, then Mueller brought it to a close: 'Boys that's enough. Tomorrow we have to be ready again . . .'

At Leiston in England the pilots of the 357th Fighter Group enjoyed a similar evening though with less drink. 'In the evening there was a celebration in the Officers' Club where we were allowed two or three beers. Everything was carefully controlled by the flight surgeons, they were the 'keepers of the keys' of the booze cupboard and the Group had to be in shape to fight the next day,' remembered Tom Hayes.

Late that night Heinz Knoke, weary and not a little drunk, left Wunstorf and in the darkness cycled the mile to the nearby village of Poggenhagen, where his wife Lilo and two-year-old daughter were staying in a guesthouse. 'It was a crazy kind of war to be in, when afterwards you went home to bed with your wife,' he commented. When Knoke got to their room Lilo was already in bed and asleep. He undressed and climbed into bed beside her. She wakened a little and turned to greet him, then caught the whiff of cognac. 'You've been drinking! What have you been up to?!' she murmured. He had been close to death three times that day but could not burden her with that. 'Oh, we had a busy day,' he mumbled. She rolled over and went back to sleep.

The crews of the four American bombers which landed in Sweden all received good treatment, including those on board B-17 'Liberty Lady' of the 306th Bomb Group who came down on Gotland and thought they had been captured by the Germans. 'That evening we were taken to a restaurant in the small town nearby and given a meal. There was no black-out which struck us as strange, the lights were shining just as in an ordinary American town,' recalled Don Courson. 'The next day we were put on a ship for the mainland. Only when we arrived at the other end and saw a huge neon sign saying 'Stockholm' did we realize we were in Sweden.' Few of the airmen interned in Sweden after the 6 March action would spend the rest of the war there; the first were back in England before the end of July 1944.

Altogether more than four hundred American airmen survived the destruction of their aircraft over enemy territory, though by nightfall only a small proportion of these were still at liberty. For those who came down in Germany, where the population was almost uniformly hostile, the chances of avoiding capture were slim and the authors have found nobody shot down on 6 March who succeeded. There were, however, some spirited attempts.

In the sparsely inhabited area 60 miles to the west of Berlin Wallace Beyer, Hubert Peterson and John Frawley, all fugitives from the same B-17 of the 91st Bomb Group, went on their separate ways to walk to one of the Baltic ports, France and Switzerland, respectively. Beyer lasted the longest. In spite of snow and intense cold, no food and a testicle that swelled almost to the size of a baseball after it had been crushed by his parachute harness, he remained free for four days before he was forced to give himself up. Peterson was captured after three days. Frawley was picked up the following morning.

Lieutenant Edward Jones of the 401st Bomb Group, whose B-17 was shot down to the east of Berlin, avoided capture for a week before he gave himself up weak from hunger and with frostbitten toes.

For those who came down in Holland the chances of escape were higher, though it was still not easy. Soon after Lowell Watts of the 388th Bomb Group landed, a couple of Dutch civilians saw him and said he was 4 kilometers inside Holland but were unwilling to help further. 'I lay in the ditch until after sunset, when it got dark I started to walk. My escape kit with the map and money, sewn in the leg of my flying suit, had blown off so I wasn't sure where I was. I walked southwest, came to a railroad track and followed it west.' The American pilot then made a wide detour of a guard station on the line, the whole time making his way southwest. After remaining free that night and most of the following day, Watts was picked up just before nightfall by armed German civilians. 'What I didn't know was that I had landed just north of the point where the German border jutts westwards into Holland. So my walking had simply taken me into Germany! It was a year before I figured that one out!'

Monty Givens, Ken Betts and Dan Walstra, part of the crew of B-17 'Suzy Sagtitz' also of the 388th, had been taken to a farmhouse and given bread and coffee and were wondering what was going to happen to them. Then a Dutchman in his early twenties came into the house and in broken English told the airmen they had better get out quickly. There was a heated argument in Dutch and one of the older farmers grabbed an axe and forced the young man to leave the house, then beckoned to the Americans to remain seated. Soon afterwards a German soldier arrived to take the airmen into custody. They later learned the farmers had reported them to the Germans for money.

Such stories of non-cooperation or hostility to Allied airmen who came down in Holland are the exception; many Dutch men and women took extraordinary risks to help fugitives escape.

After spending the afternoon and early evening hiding in the snow, Elton Skinner of the 95th Bomb Group returned to the farmhouse he had visited earlier in the day. There he learned that his badly injured bombardier, Rus Allman, had been handed over to the Germans so he could get proper medical treatment. Skinner was taken to the hay loft where he joined his top turret gunner. 'The rest of the night was uneventful with the exception of a few fleeting thoughts of German bayonets probing my hiding place. At least I was out of the cold night and still free.' Skinner and his gunner were passed along the escape line but became separated. In the spring of 1944 these escape lines were under pressure not only from the Germans but also from the Allies: in preparation for the invasion the railway system in the west was being systematically pounded from the air and this made it difficult to move the airmen through France to Spain or Switzerland. Skinner had numerous adventures. 'The resistance took from me everything that would identify me as an American, except for my watch which I insisted on keeping. On one occasion I was standing in a streetcar hanging on a strap with German soldiers on either side of me. I glanced up and suddenly noticed my aircrew watch on my wrist, visible to all. Very slowly, so as not to attract attention, I lowered my arm to my side. Fortunately nobody noticed.' Skinner linked up with American troops when they came through Liege in September.

Alan Willis, his navigator, bombardier and top turret gunner, all from B-17 'Flakstop' of the 452nd Bomb Group, had immediately been picked up by the Dutch resistance and passed along the line. They spent their first night in Holland sleeping comfortably in the house adjoining that of the leading Dutch collaborator in the town of Staaphorst; who would have thought of looking for American airmen there? The fugitives were passed through Belgium and into France, where they were eventually overrun by US troops 80 miles east of Paris the following September. 'The Dutch, Belgians and French who helped us were the bravest people in the world. They knew and we knew that if they were caught they would be shot. I have often asked myself, if the situation had been reversed, whether I would have had the guts to help them the way they helped me,' pondered Willis. 'And I never even knew any of their real names.'

Alvis Roberts of the 389th Bomb Group made it to the windmill 'Arnold' had pointed out and soon afterwards the Dutchman and a friend arrived on bicycles. The other man gave Roberts his cycle and the American rode off following some 200 yards behind 'Arnold'. After about twenty minutes the pair arrived at a farmhouse and Roberts was told to hide in the haystack beside the house. Later that evening he was taken into the house, fed, then went up to the loft to sleep. Outside he could hear German military vehicles frequently passing along the road next to the house. Two days later Roberts was moved and joined his pilot, Ken Griesel, and they were taken through Holland and into Belgium. They joined up with American troops advancing through southern Belgium in September.

Victor Krueger of the 458th Bomb Group waited till it was dark, then broke cover and made his way to the farmhouse he could see on the skyline. There the farmer invited him in and contacted the resistance, one of whose members arrived soon afterwards by bicycle. Krueger was beckoned to sit on the carrier and was ridden to the nearby town of Pummerend. In the days that followed Krueger was passed along the line. 'I stayed in about 35 different homes during my time in Holland. Some of the women were so frightened by my being there – I don't blame them – they couldn't eat or sleep and I would have to leave,' he recalled. 'Any Dutch family caught harboring an Allied flyer was liable to be shot and have their house burned. There just aren't words to describe the bravery of the people who helped us.' Krueger got as far as Amsterdam, then caught rheumatic fever and had to be taken back to Pummerend to recover. For more than six months a middle-aged couple, Martin and Julie Schrieken, nursed him back to health in their home. The airman was still with them in

April 1945 when British troops entered the area.

Probably the luckiest and most successful evaders were four members of the crew of Lieutenant Upson's B-17 of the 92nd Bomb Group, the first aircraft to be shot down during the mission. They bailed out over eastern Holland and managed to link up with the Dutch resistance, which passed them down the escape line through Belgium and into France. In France two of the crewmen, Neal Persons and tail gunner Bishop Standlee, became separated from their guide during an air raid. They made their way to Nancy alone and there tried to link up with the French resistance again, initially without success. So eventually they decided to present themselves to the priest at the Catholic church and put themselves at his mercy. The priest seemed not to understand what they wanted, but ushered the two airmen into a room and left them there alone. Then, Persons later recounted, 'After a bit he came back with two other guys. One went into a corner and sat down, he didn't say a word. We tried to get through to the other two, to explain that we were American aviators who had been shot down, were trying to get to Switzerland and had lost contact with the underground. But they didn't seem to understand what we were saying, it was all very frustrating. After about an hour of this Standlee finally got mad with them,' Persons continued, 'I cannot repeat the swear words he used, but it was typical American cussing and he called them some pretty bad things. He said they were a lot of dumb so and sos who weren't going to help us and we would be better off on our own. At that the little fellow sitting in the corner got up and and came over to us. He shook our hands and said "Well, I can see you guys are Americans!" His English was as good as ours!'

Having established themselves with the underground once again, the two evaders continued down the escape line. Then one evening early in June, just three months after they had bailed out of their bomber, they were taken to a point about a mile short of the Swiss border. 'We were told to wait until a certain time, walk a given number of paces in the direction in which they pointed, wait until another given time, then go ahead and keep walking. Then the guys shook our hands, wished us luck and left us. We did just as they had said and after the stop we walked and walked, we went on for miles. Then we came over a hill and there in front of us was a beautiful little town, all lit up. We had seen nothing like that in England, Holland, Belgium or France. We had to be in Switzerland!'

After they reported themselves to the Swiss authorities Persons and Standlee were handed over to the custody of the US consolate. There the airmen met two other members of their crew, Frank Hilger the co-pilot and Bob Dorgan the bombardier, who had arrived in Switzerland a couple of weeks earlier. With other Americans who had reached Switzerland in the same way, the four were accommodated in hotels and allowed to do whatever they wished except leave the country. The men received their pay, including all due to them during their time on the run. Almost every day became a party.

Then, after all the men had been through, tragedy struck. 'We were staying in a hotel near Montreux and sometimes we would go downtown and perhaps have a little bit too much to drink. It was a small town, the police were very friendly, they would sometimes pick one of us up and let him sleep it off in jail.

The next morning they would let him out; there would be no charge, they wouldn't even take names. The only thing was that at midnight the guard would lock up the cells and go home, and come back the next morning,' Persons explained. 'One night that happened to Bob Dorgan. But he was in bed, a little drunk, and he lit a cigarette and went to sleep. His mattress caught fire, he was unable to get out of his cell and he suffocated. He was the only man in our crew to lose his life, and of all the ways that was how it happened to him.'

CHAPTER 8
THE 6 MARCH ACTION ANALYZED

Most official accounts of past wars are deceptively well written but seem to omit many important matters – in particular, anything which might indicate that any of our commanders ever made the slightest mistake. They are, therefore, useless as a source of instruction.

Field Marshal Lord Montgomery

For the attack on Berlin the 8th Air Force put up a total of 814 heavy bombers, including airborne spares. Thirty-eight of the latter were not dispatched and of the remainder 702 (90 per cent) penetrated enemy territory. Escorting the bombers were 644 fighters drawn from the 8th and 9th Air Forces and the Royal Air Force, which flew a total of 943 sorties of which 832 (88 per cent) penetrated enemy territory.

During the course of the action the raiding force lost 69 bombers and 11 fighters. Of the bombers 42 were certainly or probably lost to fighter attack, 13 to flak, 5 to fighters and flak, 5 were lost in collisions with friendly or enemy aircraft and the causes of the remaining 4 losses are not known. Ten escorts fell in action with enemy fighters and one to flak. Thus one bomber in ten, and one fighter in 75, of those sorties which penetrated enemy territory were lost. Broken down into types, the aircraft which failed to return comprised 53 B-17s, 16 B-24s, 1 P-38, 5 P-47s and 5 P-51s. Of the returning bombers 283 had flak damage only, 23 had damage from fighter attack only, 33 had damage from both flak and fighters and 11 had damage from other causes. Four escorts returned with damage. Four of the damaged bombers and two escorts were not repairable. The only other loss was the B-24 which crashed shortly after taking off.

Of the 701 men on board the US aircraft lost in action 229 were killed or missing, 411 taken prisoner, 13 who came down in Holland evaded capture, 8 were picked up from the North Sea by the RAF rescue service and 40 landed in Sweden and were later repatriated. From the aircraft which returned 3 crewmen were killed, 29 wounded and 4 were taken prisoner (those who bailed out of the 306th Bomb Group Fortress over Holland).

As an attempt to curtail production at the three primary targets the attack was a failure. None was hit effectively. Only the Genshagen aero engine plant was attacked at all, by 50 bombers or less than a quarter of the aircraft assigned to it and most of their bombs fell outside the target area. The Erkner and Klein Machnow plants escaped damage altogether.

Had there been either clear skies over Berlin, or else complete cloud cover, the attack would have been more effective. As it was each bomb division leader committed himself to a visual bomb run on his primary target then, when it was too late to revert to a radar bomb run on the center of Berlin, cloud drifted in to conceal the aiming point. Bomb groups were left to select whatever targets they could find in the city. In practice this meant formation leaders bombed 'holes in the cloud' and hit whatever part of Berlin happened to be underneath. It was an indiscriminate form of attack which hit military targets only by chance. Altogether 379 crews reported they had dropped bombs on Berlin itself. The main damage on targets that could be called 'military' was that at the Falkenhagener Army depot, the Telefunken radar factory and the scattered damage to the city's road and rail network. There were very few service casualties, probably less than ten killed or wounded. The most serious effect on production was the two working hours lost at all plants while the workforce went to and returned from shelter. A further 228 crews bombed targets outside the immediate area of Berlin. Most of the damage caused in and around the capital was to private and civic property. A total of 345 civilians were killed or missing and 363 wounded, in Berlin and the surrounding administrative district; the latter included Templin but not Wittenberge nor Verden which were attacked as 'targets of opportunity'.

By and large the US fighter escort functioned well. Of the 17 groups of fighters (three of which flew twice) and three Royal Air Force squadrons assigned to the escort, only two fighter groups failed to rendezvous with the bombers and on both occasions this was during the early part of the withdrawal when there was little enemy activity.

Before describing the Luftwaffe reaction to the attack on 6 March, the authors would point out that this action was chosen because during it the 8th Air Force lost more aircraft than on any other. So, despite some failings, on this day the German defenses functioned as effectively as they ever would.

To contest the incursion Luftwaffe fighter units flew a total of 528 sorties of which 369 probably made contact with the enemy. In the course of the action 66 German fighters were destroyed or damaged beyond repair. One fighter crashed soon after take-off and two training aircraft were shot down by escort fighters; these will receive little further consideration in this analysis. The German records are not complete and it is possible to determine causes for only about half the fighters lost in action; of these 27 were shot down by escorts, two by return fire from bombers, and three were destroyed in collisions with bombers. Thus one German fighter in five of those which made contact with the enemy was lost. Broken down into types those lost comprised 22 Me 109s, 19 FW 190s, 6 Me 410s, 11 Me 110 day fighters and 9 Me 110 night fighters. Including the pilot in the accident after take-off, 36 German aircrew were killed and 25 wounded; of these 25 of the dead and 21 of the wounded were fighter pilots, among them several experienced and successful ones whose services the Luftwaffe could ill afford to lose.

As might be expected the German twin-engined fighters suffered far higher losses from the escorts than their single-engined counterparts. Seventeen Me 110 and Me 410 destroyers (40 per cent of those which engaged) were shot down. The even-slower Me 110 night fighters, burdened with radar and other equipment, suffered worst of all: nine were shot down (50 per cent of those which engaged). Apart from one which collided with a bomber most, probably all, of the twin-engined fighters lost were shot down by Mustangs in the target area.

Apart from the failure to position Hans Kogler's attack formation accurately for a head-on attack on the 1st Bomb Division, the German fighter control organization functioned efficiently during the action. Although 159 fighter sorties probably failed to make contact with the enemy, a third of these involved aircraft based in France and Belgium which were positioned over Reims in case the raiders unexpectedly swung south to attack a target in central Germany; and many of the remainder were based in central Germany and could not assemble properly because of bad weather. German fighter controllers were instructed to scramble fighters even when there was only a small chance of their intercepting the enemy. In the circumstances it was the correct thing to do, though it resulted in many sorties which failed to make contact.

Flak caused the loss of 13 bombers and a fighter, and shared with fighters in the destruction of five more bombers. A further 316 bombers – nearly half the number which penetrated into occupied Europe – returned with its scars. Nobody who had to face the full ferocity of the Berlin flak defenses is likely ever to forget the experience.

The raiders' route and escort plans held up well during the flights to and from the target. The only major deviation from the planned route was after the lead aircraft of the 1st Bomb Division suffered an equipment failure on the way in and led the front half of the force slightly too far to the south. The deviation from the planned track was never more than 20 miles, not a large error by the standards of the time, and was soon corrected. No blame can be attached to the leader for the terrible hammering suffered by the 13th Combat Wing east of Haseluenne. Had he followed the correct route the two leading wings, the 1st and the 94th, would have been attacked by Rolf Hermichen's formation instead of the 13th. And had all the bombers followed the leader along the incorrect route, Hermichen's formation might have missed the chance of a head-on attack altogether and ended up having to turn and make an astern attack on the rear of the bomber stream.

The 13th Combat Wing flew the correct route, its only failure was that it had dropped back a little and lost contact with the wing in front. It was sheer bad luck that Rolf Hermichen's force ran into it and the German pilot had the skill and experience to lead an exemplary attack. Several survivors from the 100th Bomb Group, part of the 13th Wing, which suffered the heaviest loss during the action have expressed the belief that this was one further result of an alleged long-standing grudge by the Luftwaffe against their particular unit. The group had suffered heavily on previous occasions and bore the grim epithet 'The Bloody Hundredth'. In spite of close questioning of nearly all the Luftwaffe pilots contacted, however, the authors did not find a shred of evidence to support the notion of a grudge against the 100th. No German interviewed attached any significance to the 'D-in-a-Square' tail marking which identified the group's Fortresses. The most common reaction was one of amusement, that anyone should think they would even try to single out one particular enemy unit, given the difficulties of making a head-on attack on a bomber formation. The ex-Luftwaffe pilots' feelings on the matter were summed up by Adolf Galland who commented 'When they reached an American formation my pilots had something better to do than look at the tails of the bombers before they decided whether to attack!'

A further misconception, held by many American crewmen, was that the Luftwaffe fighter force mounted a special defensive effort on 6 March because the target was Berlin. In fact, though on the way in some German fighter controllers suspected the target was the capital, none was certain and it was the usual case of doing the best they could to meet the attack with what was available. Both the large-scale fighter interceptions took place on the way in before the Germans could be sure what the target was. To get to Berlin the raiders had to penetrate deeply into enemy territory and this gave the ground controllers plenty of time to assemble their fighters and direct them into the bomber stream. Had the target been any other deep in northern Germany that day, the reaction of the defending fighters would have been equally venomous.

Many returning US crews reported having met 'yellow-nosed' or 'red-nosed' Messerschmitt 109s and Focke-Wulf 190s, some of which were reported to have a 'brilliant red band' around the rear fuselage; usually there was the implication in intelligence reports that fighters carrying these markings belonged to 'elite' units or were flown by ace pilots. In fact colored nose markings were worn from time to time by all aircraft of various Luftwaffe fighter units, regardless of quality, as an aid to recognition in combat. The red band around the rear fuselage was worn by most German fighters engaged in the 6 March action and showed they were from units belonging to Air Fleet Reich. Moreover, for most of the war there were *no* 'elite' Luftwaffe fighter units; all had to take their share of good and inexperienced pilots (the sole exception was the famous Jagdverband 44 jet fighter unit formed by Adolf Galland early in 1945, whose ranks included a disproportionately high number of ace pilots). It was, however, both natural and understandable that US crews returning from action should report they had confronted 'elite' enemy units: no man wished to admit he had been frightened by anything less than the best the enemy had.

The false rumors of what the enemy was doing were not confined to one side. Several of the German fighter pilots interviewed spoke confidently of B-17 and B-24 'flak-cruisers', carrying no bombs but extra armor and guns, said to guard the front, flanks and rear of American bomber formations. In 1943 the 8th Air Force had experimented briefly with seven converted B-17s in this role; it was found these aircraft were significantly heavier and slower than the normal bombers once the latter had released their bombs and the idea was soon dropped. Yet 'flak-cruisers' continued to be mentioned in German reports for the remainder of the war.

After the action bomber crews claimed 97 German fighters destroyed, 28 probably destroyed and 60 damaged. The escorts claimed 82 destroyed, 8 probably destroyed and 33 damaged. Taken together this meant the raiders thought they had destroyed or damaged 83 per cent of the German fighters which made contact with them! In fact the number of German fighters claimed 'certainly' destroyed, 179, was in exaggeration of the true figure of 66 by nearly three to one.

Immediately following the action German fighter and flak defenses reported 108 bombers and 20 fighters destroyed and 12 bombers and a fighter probably destroyed. These initial claims for bombers and fighters destroyed were in exaggeration by nearly two to one compared with the actual loss of 69 bombers and 11 fighters. The claims had all to pass through the grindingly slow machinery of the Luftwaffe's bureaucratic claims commission before confirmed victories could be allocated to pilots and flak batteries; in some cases this took as long as six months, by which time many of the pilots who had scored the victories were long dead. The final list of confirmed German victories for 6 March 1944 has not survived, but without doubt it was far shorter than the initial submission.

Although the German fighter and flak units destroyed more American bombers on 6 March 1944 than they had ever before, or would ever again, and the raiders inflicted only minimal damage on Berlin, the defenders had gained no more than a Pyrrhic victory. The loss of 46 fighter pilots killed and wounded in a single day was a severe blow to the dwindling Luftwaffe fighter force; at this stage of the war the overstretched, understaffed and underprovided German training schools were quite unable to turn out sufficient new pilots to replace those being lost. The 8th Air Force, on the other hand, had lost fifteen times that number of trained crewmen but was able to fill the gaps in its ranks without difficulty. Similarly the bustling US aircraft factories could furnish 74 new heavy bombers and 13 escort fighters far quicker than the bomb-scarred German plants could turn out 42 single-engined and 25 twin-engined fighters. Such were the resources allocated to the 8th Air Force, not only could it replace losses but also continue its planned program of expansion. Against this background, a lengthy campaign of attrition could have only one ending.

CHAPTER 9

THE MEDIA'S ASSESSMENT

Propaganda, as inverted patriotism, draws nourishment from the sins of the enemy. If there are no sins, invent them! The aim is to make the enemy appear so great a monster that he forfeits the rights of a human being. He cannot bring a libel action so there is no need to stick at trifles.

Sir Ian Hamilton

Having seen in some detail what did happen on Monday 6 March 1944, how accurately were the events reported in each side's news media afterwards?

On the following day the *New York Times* carried a front page account of the action by Drew Middleton, under banner headlines:

800 US BOMBERS SMASH AT BERLIN BY DAY; 68 LOST IN BATTLES, 123 OF FOE SHOT DOWN

Air War At Peak

Fortresses, Liberators, Loose 2,000 Tons on German Capital

Fighters Swarm on Nazis

Three-Hour Combat Over the Reich Gives Major Victory Against Luftwaffe

The war in the air reached a new and perhaps decisive phase yesterday when about 800 American heavy bombers fought their way through the massed strength of the Germans' metropolitan air force to blast factories, airfields and other military installations in the Berlin area.

The air battles that raged around and within the tight, wedge-shaped formations of Flying Fortresses and Liberators were the greatest in history, with American fighters, hundreds of which accompanied the bombers, and the 'heavies' engaged throughout the mission.

Preliminary reports on the American victories said that eighty-three Nazi fighters were knocked down by the Mustangs, Thunderbolts and Lightnings of the United States Eighth and Ninth Air Forces and Royal Air Force that escorted and supported the big bombers.

The total of enemy fighters destroyed by the bombers had not yet been tabulated, but the gunners of one division alone of our 'heavies' destroyed at least forty Nazi planes, boosting the minimum number of enemy aircraft shot down to 123.

In addition to these heavy losses to the Nazi fighter force, already suffering from the effects of two weeks of the Allies' heavy day and night attacks over the Reich, returning pilots reported 'first rate' bombing results in the Berlin district.

[Probably more than 2,000 tons of bombs were dropped on Berlin's vital industrial and military targets, The Associated Press reported.]

American losses in the big blow at the Nazi capital were serious. Sixty-eight heavy bombers and eleven fighters were missing – representing a loss of nearly 700 trained airmen – Lieut. Gen. Carl A. Spaatz's Strategic Air Force headquarters here reported.

The account continued with details of the attack and included several eye witness descriptions from returning airmen, many of whom were not named. As was usual at that time, the news-hungry reporters allowed on the airfields to meet the crews had neither the time nor the background knowledge to assess the accuracy of what they were told. All official communiqués were taken at their face value (the following day, when the raiders' total claim was released of 179 enemy fighters destroyed, 36 probably destroyed and 93 damaged, it too would be published without any critical comment concerning its possible accuracy). It should be pointed out, however, that the US victory claims issued by the military were the same as those received from the returning airmen; the claims had not been inflated before issue to the press. On the other hand a cynic might argue that with figures like that there was no need to embellish them anyway. Moreover the descriptions of the effectiveness and the military nature of the bombing, on 'factories, airfields and other military installations in the Berlin area', as usual went far beyond what had actually happened and what the 8th Air Force commanders knew had happened.

In one important aspect the US authorities did take a brave line and deserve credit for it: that of accurately giving their own losses even when these were heavy. The figures of 68 bombers and 11 fighters which failed to return omitted one bomber, probably due to an accounting error. But considering it was wartime the figures were remarkably honest.

So much for the accuracy of the official US communiqués. How did they compare with those issued in Germany? In its issue dated March 8 the newspaper *Berliner Lokal-Anzeiger* published the official version of the previous Monday's events under a banner headline:

THE VICTORIOUS AIR BATTLE AROUND BERLIN

Blow Against US Terror
140 Shot Down – Details of the Success of Our Defense

The first great attack by North American bomber units on the Reich capital ended in bitter defeat for the 8th US Air Force, when it attempted to carry out a heavy attack on Berlin at mid-day on Monday. According to reports received so far, 140 enemy aircraft were destroyed including 118 four-engined bombers. During the ferocious action lasting several hours and extending over many hundreds of kilometers, the enemy fighter escort was unable to prevent German fighters from carrying out massed attacks. The vigorous efforts of the German forces secured an outstanding defensive success and thwarted the planned large-scale attack on the capital.

Following the attempt by the US 8th Air Force in England to strike at the Reich capital last Saturday, on Monday morning strong forces again set out from their bases in southeast England. The German air defenses were ready for them. German light and heavy fighters, assisted by heavy fire from the flak artillery, forced the intruding enemy formations into three set-piece battles. As a result many formations were broken up and a considerable part of the force destroyed.

First Air Battle Near Bremen

The first air battle, involving numerous German day fighter Geschwader, took place south of Bremen at noon on Monday and came as a complete surprise to the enemy. Messerschmitt and Focke-Wulf fighters dived like swarms of hornets on the tight US bomber formations. One senior fighter Gruppe leader, already highly decorated for bravery, personally led his units against the enemy. Later he reported that during one brief period while the attack was being pressed home he saw three heavy bombers breaking up and going down one after the other. No crewman escaped from these US bombers, as the pieces of the enemy aircraft crashed to the ground.

Second Air Battle Over the Elbe

In the second large-scale attack over the Elbe region, further powerful forces of German fighters split apart other enemy bomber formations, after which individual US bombers were destroyed by the fighters' guns. As a result only part of the original raiding force succeeded in penetrating to its target.

The Berlin flak units, with numerous heavy and super-heavy batteries, also played a distinguished part in the defense. When the all-clear sounded the Berlin citizens could see many enemy airmen descending slowly to earth by parachute. Most of the men on board the shot-down aircraft were killed, however.

Third Air Battle Over Holland

As the surviving US bombers withdrew, after releasing their bombs on residential areas of the capital, they faced a third concentrated attack by strong forces of German fighters over Holland. Above the Zuider Zee the German fighter Geschwader struck the retreating bombers yet again. Also in this action the enemy escorts were unable to hinder the work of the German fighters.

The loss of 140 enemy aircraft in the course of the first heavy attack on the capital represents the heaviest defeat yet for the US 8th Air Force during its operations over the Reich. It must be pointed out that the actual number of aircraft lost is doubtless even higher, for many of the returning aircraft were badly shot-up and had the greatest difficulty in regaining their bases in England. Furthermore, it is known that yet others were forced to make emergency landings in Sweden.

Apart from the exaggerated claim for the number of aircraft destroyed, the German newspaper version was a moderately accurate short account of the air battle. The initial victory claims from the fighter and flak units had been passed to the media, with the 'certain' and 'probable' claims lumped together to give the overall figure of 140 raiders destroyed. Although this and other German newspapers were quick to point out the absurdity of the 179 defending fighters claimed destroyed by the American airmen, no figure was issued for German aircraft losses during the action. Dr Goebbels's Propaganda Ministry solved that problem by ignoring it!

On the question of bomb damage to Berlin the *Lokal-Anzeiger* gave little away. There was the usual banal statement that most bombs had fallen on

Stalingrad Nr. 2!

Dies ist dem Führer zu verdanken!

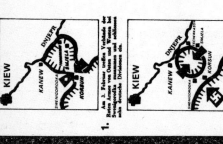
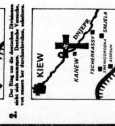

1. Am 3. Februar treffen Verbände der Roten Armee von Osten und Westen bei Swenigorodka zusammen und schliessen zehn deutsche Divisionen ein.

2. Der Ring um die deutschen Divisionen sieht sich zusammen. Deutsche Versuche, ihn zu durchbrechen, scheitern.

3. Am 17. Februar ist die Vernichtung der eingekesselten Divisionen vollendet, den letzten deutschen Durchbruchsversuchen. 27.000 bei Durchbruchsversuchen.

Am 17. Februar wurde die Vernichtung von zehn deutschen Divisionen vollendet, die von der Roten Armee bei Korsun umzingelt worden waren. 55.000 Deutsche fielen in der Einkesselung, 18.200 gerieten in Gefangenschaft. Weitere 27.000 deutsche Soldaten, die zur Armee Generalfeldmarschall Mansteins gehörten, gingen bei den verzweifelten, jedoch vergeblichen Versuchen zugrunde, den Ring der Roten Armee zu sprengen und die eingeschlossenen Kameraden zu befreien.

So erlebte die deutsche Armee ein Jahr nach der grossen deutschen Stalingrad-Katastrophe unter der Führung Adolf Hitlers ein neues Stalingrad.

Wie bei Stalingrad erlebten auch die deutschen Truppen im Ringe von Korsun den Befehl Adolf Hitlers, eine strategisch unmögliche Stellung zu halten.

Wie bei Stalingrad erhielten die deutschen Truppen bei Korsun Adolf Hitlers Versprechen, dass Hilfe und Rettung kommen werde; sie hoffen vergebens.

Wie bei Stalingrad wollten viele deutsche Offiziere an der Front ehrenhafte Kapitulationsbedingungen annehmen; denn sie sagen es vor, das Leben schmausender deutscher Soldaten zu retten, statt sie in hoffnungsloser Lage aufzuopfern. Wie bei Stalingrad werden sie daran durch Hitlers Befehl gehindert.

Wie bei Stalingrad und überall an der Ostfront war die deutsche Strategie von Adolf Hitlers „Intuition" diktiert, auf Kosten schmausender deutscher Mütter, Frauen und Mädchen, deren Söhne, Männer und Verlobte auf russischer Erde für eine längst verlorene Sache umkamen.

Selten hat im Laufe der Geschichte ein militärischer Befehlshaber einen so ungeheuerlichen Fehlschlag wie Hitler bei Stalingrad begangen. Jetzt hat er den Deutschen ein zweites Stalingrad beschert.

WIE VIELE STALINGRADS SOLL ES NOCH GEBEN?

U.S.G. 23.

Stalingrad No. 2!

The Führer can be thanked for this!

On 17 February the Red Army completed the destruction of ten German divisions encircled near Korsun. Of those surrounded 55,000 were killed and 18,200 taken prisoner. A further 27,000 soldiers of Generalfield-marshall Manstein's Army fell during attempts to break through the Red Army encirclement and free their trapped comrades.

So, one year after the great catastrophe at Stalingrad, Adolf Hitler has led the Germany army into another.

As at Stalingrad *the German troops cut off at Korsun had been placed in a strategically impossible position by Adolf Hitler's orders.*

As at Stalingrad *the German troops at Korsun received Adolf Hitler's promises of help and rescue; they waited in vain.*

As at Stalingrad *many front-line German officers wished to open surrender negotiations, to save the lives of tens of thousands of German soldiers instead of sacrificing them in a hopeless situation. As at Stalingrad Hitler's orders prevented this.*

As at Stalingrad *and over the whole of the eastern front, German strategy has been dictated by Adolf Hitler's 'intuition', at a cost to tens of thousands of German mothers, wives and girls of sons, husbands and loved ones who perished on Russian soil for a long lost cause.*

Seldom in history has a military commander had such a run of terrible reverses as that begun by Hitler at Stalingrad. And now he has bestowed upon the German people a second Stalingrad.

HOW MANY STALINGRADS DO THERE HAVE TO BE?

Translation of US leaflet G.28, one of 800,000 copies dropped over Germany on 6 March 1944 and which drew a sharp reaction from the German media. G.28 was one of three leaflet texts dropped that day.

residential districts on the outskirts and the attack caused minimal damage to industry or arms production. Now as it happened the statement was correct concerning the 6 March attack; but Germans interviewed said they had heard the same thing so often before they did not believe it this time.

In a political review broadcast on the German Home service on the evening after the attack, commentator Dr Otto Kriegk discussed the defeat suffered by the American bombers and their crews' exaggerated claims concerning the number of German fighters shot down. Then he continued:

> The commander of the murderous US gangsters sent not only bombs but also leaflets to Berlin. All bombed areas in Germany know these products of Jewish propaganda. There would be no necessity to mention them if it were not possible to draw some interesting political conclusions from these latest products of the Jewish incitement factories in London and Washington. Take one example. How great must be the dependence of the political warfare of Britain and the USA on Bolshevism, if the commanders of the murderous US and British gangsters are forced to take with them leaflets in which Stalin's lie about the alleged encirclement and destruction of German divisions on the southern front is still represented as truth . . .

The offending American leaflet was serial number G.28, 800,000 copies of which were dropped during the attack. The leaflet spoke of the encirclement and destruction of ten German divisions the previous month near Korsun in Russia and a fierce battle in which more than a hundred thousand German troops had been killed or captured. In fact far fewer men had been surrounded and of these two-thirds had managed to fight their way out of the cauldron. Apart from the inelegant wartime clichés used, it is of interest that the German news service should have seen fit to refute what the American leaflet had said: German civilians were strictly forbidden to read leaflets. The broadcast was a tacit admission that many people did risk punishment and steal a glance at the 'poison' from the skies. Perhaps the droppings from the 'Bullshit Bombers' did have some effect.

To sum up the media reports: both sides claimed clear-cut victories for the action on 6 March and greatly exaggerated the number of enemy aircraft destroyed, the American exaggeration being somewhat greater than the German. But while American losses were honestly stated, those of the Luftwaffe were not mentioned by the German media. The German Propaganda Ministry issued an accurate account of the ineffectual bombing of Berlin but few seem to have believed it.

CHAPTER 10
IN RETROSPECT

War is an act of violence whose object is to constrain the enemy to accomplish our will.

von Clausewitz

Having examined the events of 6 March 1944 in some detail, let us look at the importance of the action in the context of the US strategic bombing offensive on Europe, and the bomber offensive in the context of World War II.

Berlin was politically, militarily and industrially the most important city in the Third Reich. It was also the most difficult target for the US bomber crews, shielded as it was by powerful fighter and gun defenses and by its very distance from the US bases in England; a force of heavy bombers endeavoring to attack it had to spend some four hours over enemy territory, subjected to the fury of the German fighter force many of whose aircraft had time to go into action twice. Yet on 6 March 1944 the 8th Air Force demonstrated that even this most difficult of targets was no longer safe from attack by day. In doing so the US force suffered losses which, though high, were tolerable and inflicted losses on the Luftwaffe which, though lower, could not be shrugged off. From now on no worthwhile target anywhere in Germany or occupied Europe could be considered immune from daylight attack.

The 8th Air Force was quick to drive home the lesson. Two days later, on 8 March, it sent another huge force to Berlin and did so yet again on the 9th and the 22nd; and on these occasions cloud did not conceal the capital. Altogether, during the month, the US 8th, 9th and 15th Air Forces mounted 18 large attacks which cost them just over four hundred bombers and fighters. But, thanks to the vast US supply and aircrew training organizations, these could be replaced. During the same period the Luftwaffe units defending the homeland and in the west lost 357 fighters destroyed and 163 damaged; with more difficulty these could be replaced also. The loss of over 300 trained German fighter pilots killed or wounded was quite a different matter however. Already the eastern and southern fronts had almost been denuded of fighter units to strengthen the home defenses; there could be no transfusion of strength from that quarter.

The repeated blows in increasing force on Germany's vitals placed the defending fighter force in a situation it could not control, forcing it to fight when, where and how the enemy chose. The German fighters could not sit on the ground and allow the enemy bombers to carve out their swathes of destruction wherever they wished; but if they rose to engage they now invariably suffered unacceptable losses.

The contest continued with increasing ferocity throughout April, with still greater losses to both sides. By the end of the month the Luftwaffe fighter units in Germany and the west had lost a further 350 pilots killed or wounded. Grimly Adolf Galland reported to his superiors: 'Between the beginning of January and the end of April 1944 our day fighter arm has lost more than 1,000 pilots. They included many of our best Staffel, Gruppe and Geschwader commanders . . .The time has come when our force is within sight of collapse.'

By now the German fighter force could be likened to a badly bleeding boxer being mercilessly beaten, whose own blows were doing little if anything to stem the onslaught. And there was no referee to call 'Enough!' In May Luftwaffe fighter pilot losses topped the 400 mark.

By stopping the production of other types and switching in scarce resources, Reichsminister Albert Speer was able to step up the production of single-engined fighters greatly during the late spring and early summer of 1944, despite the Allied air attacks. Adolf Galland wanted to hold many of the new fighters out of the battle until they and their newly trained pilots were ready to be hurled against an American raiding force in a single co-ordinated blow – *Der Gross Schlag*. But he was never able to do so.

When the Allied troops landed in Normandy in June 1944 the Luftwaffe fighter force in Germany and the west was forced to send almost everything it had to France to contest the invasion and the reserve of fighters was frittered away. Here again they confronted overwhelming Allied strength and suffered terrible losses. The German fighter operations were able to achieve little and without even temporary air superiority over the beachhead German reconnaissance and bomber operations were infrequent, ineffective and costly. Nor did they provide much relief for the savagely pounded German troops, one of whose catchphrases ran: 'If aircraft are camouflaged, they're British; if silver, they're American; and if they aren't there at all, they're German!'

From the end of May 1944 the main weight of the Allied strategic bombing offensive switched to the German synthetic oil industry, with devastating results. From 175,000 tons of aviation fuel produced in April, before this phase of the offensive opened, production fell to 55,000 tons in June, 35,000 tons in July, 16,000 tons in August and a mere 7,000 tons in September. As soon as the plants could be repaired they were wrecked again with new attacks. The effect was immediate. Luftwaffe fighter operations had to be cut back, most bomber and flying training units had to be disbanded and reconnaissance flights were permitted only in 'decisive situations'.

The Luftwaffe never recovered from this cropping of its fuel supplies, which also applied a harsh brake to German operations on land and at sea. During the final seven months of the war the Luftwaffe could never be disregarded from Allied calculations and almost to the end it proved capable of delivering unpleasant surprises. But only once more would it deliver a really heavy blow: on 1 January 1945, when a massed attack by 875 fighters on Allied airfields in France, Holland and Belgium caused the destruction of 144 aircraft and damage to 62 more; the action cost the German fighter force 232 pilots killed, wounded or taken prisoner and never again would it be able to mount more than token air operations.

The subjugation of the German fighter force, and through it the Luftwaffe itself, was a direct result of the large-scale daylight actions fought over Germany mainly by the 8th Air Force in the late winter, spring and summer of 1944. And a significant step in that offensive was the action on 6 March 1944.

What feelings remain, almost forty years later, with those involved in the action on 6 March 1944?

Generalleutnant Adolf Galland, Inspector of Luftwaffe fighters: 'Since this was the first major daylight attack on the capital it was a heavy blow to us, an important milestone in the development of the enemy air offensive. From the beginning of 1944 we knew that some time the Americans would try to attack Berlin by day. They were expected. But when they did come it was still a blow to our morale.'

Lieutenant Les Rentmeester, B-17 pilot, 91st Bomb Group:: 'It was a turning point, similar in some respects to the battles of Vicksburg and Gettysburg during the US Civil War. There had been a long struggle between the two sides for aerial supremacy; after this raid the Allied aircraft roamed the skies of Europe with comparative immunity challenging the Luftwaffe to come up and fight.'

Frau Gertrud Tappert, Berlin housewife: 'I did not think the first daylight air attack on Berlin was significant in itself. I could see the battle fronts falling back and did not think Germany had much chance of winning the war. This was just one more step along that road. We expected things to get a lot worse. And they did.'

Lieutenant Glenn Eagleston, P-51 pilot 354th Fighter Group: 'We were all pretty aroused at the debriefing. We were happy that this milestone was past and we had gone in and bombed Hell out of the German capital, we thought at the time, without too much loss to ourselves. In all we went to Berlin four times that week and I've never been so tired in my life – six-hour missions one right after the other just knocked the coon pee right out of you. I'd swear I could have given you the serial number off my oxygen bottle and dinghy pack by reading it off my left cheek.'

Oberleutnant Heinz Knoke, Me 109 pilot, IInd Gruppe Fighter Geschwader 11: 'It was the most exciting, the most exhausting and the most frightening day's fighting I ever had. Soon after noon I battled with enemy fighters, knocked down a bomber and made a crash-landing on one wheel. Then between sorties, while I was waiting on the ground, my aircraft was shot up and one of my ground crewmen wounded. Later in the afternoon I went into action again, had my wingman shot down and was lucky to escape with my life. All in all it was not a day I shall easily forget.'

Lieutenant Rod Starkey, P-51 pilot, 357th Fighter Group, who scored his first victory that day: 'I think it is a testimony to the kind of training we had that I was able to function at all. Never before in my life had I been so frightened as I was on that day and yet, apparently, I was able to function because of the thoroughness of the training I had received. It was an exciting day and not one I would like to repeat often!'

Lieutenant Thurman Spiva, B-24 navigator, 446th Bomb Group, who returned in one of the bombers straggling behind the main formations: 'Like many other bomber crews before and after 6 March we owed our lives to the courageous fighter pilots who stayed with us that day. We were the lucky ones. They arrived in time and from then on our lives were largely in their hands. You will never find ten more grateful or thankful bomber crew members than we were on that cold winter afternoon.'

Hauptmann Anton Hackl, FW 190 pilot and commander of IIIrd Gruppe Fighter Geschwader 11: 'It was bad enough when a unit lost young pilots, but to lose an experienced older pilot like Hugo Frey was terrible. Inexperienced pilots were replaceable, experienced ones were not. It was a major blow to our Gruppe, like a family that has lost one of its parents.'

Captain Ed Curry, B-17 bombardier, 401st Bomb Group: 'The very name "Berlin" had a horrible, ominous sound about it. When first you saw that long line going right across the briefing map, all the way out and back, it was just scarey as all Hell! You were scared until the combat started. Then you forgot about everything and just did your job. It was only after you got back and were in your sack and started thinking about it, started to wonder about this guy and that guy you had seen go down, that you started shaking.'

Major Hans Kogler, Me 110 pilot and commander of IIIrd Gruppe Destroyer Geschwader 26: 'It was terrible to be in command of a unit with young, idealistic pilots coming in from the training schools and knowing that two or three battles later most would be dead or maimed. And it was terrible for them as well, for they soon learned how slim were their chances of survival.'

Lieutenant Bob Shoens, B-17 pilot, 100th Bomb Group which suffered the heaviest losses during the mission: 'The next day was a stand-down, no mission was scheduled for the 100th. But on 8 March it was back to combat and the target was Berlin again. It would be difficult to describe the feelings everyone had. Do we have to go through it all again? Doesn't anyone have sympathy for what happened? Why Berlin again so soon? Of course, it had to be. There was no time to get caught up in your emotions or self-pity. The war goes on, life goes on. So, the 100th went on. This time we were able to put up only 21 planes and we went to Berlin. And nothing happened. It was a beautiful trip all the way in and all the way out. However, we had ringside seats of another bomb group taking a beating like we had two days earlier.'

POSTSCRIPT

This book would have been impossible without the generous help and encouragement of many good friends. First, the authors wish to thank Roger Freeman, author of *The Mighty Eighth** and foremost expert on the 8th Air Force, for suggesting 6 March 1944 as a subject for a book and for his invaluable advice. Hans Ring made available his superb range of contacts among surviving members of the German fighter force. Bill Hess gave us copies of many of the US fighter combat reports of the action. Arno Abendroth in Berlin made available the fruits of his considerable research into the Allied air attacks on the city. Numerous others kindly let us have material from their collections: Ian Hawkins, Garland Lloyd, Kay Bettin, Gene Munson, Vic Maslen, Bernard Bains, Werner Girbig, A.L. Starcer, Robert Hodges, Tom McHale, Elizabeth Miner Spadaro, Sharon Stillson Dickson, Harry Holmes, Winfried Bock, John Archer, Michael Gibson, Goetz Bergander, James Parton, David McKnight, Ellis Scripture, Walter Hickey, Richard Smith, Ab Jansen, Cliff Hall, Quinten Bland, Jim Walsh, George Hyman, Don Kirkhutt, Donald Sonichsen, Ray Wand, William Cagney, Bryan Schotts and William Bergeron.

We are grateful to the staffs of the following archives for help given: the US Air Force Office of Public Affairs, Magazines and Books Division; the Albert F. Simpson Historical Research Center, Maxwell AFB, Alabama; the US National Archives, Modern Military Records and Missing Aircrew Reports Section; the Bundesarchiv, Freiburg; the Public Records Office, Kew, London; and the British Meteorological Office at Bracknell.

The following US reunion associations gave considerable help in tracking down witnesses of the action on 6 March 1944: the 8th Air Force Historical Society, John Woolnough; 8th Air Force Headquarters, Karl Clement; 1st Air Division Headquarters, Henry Gelula; 2nd Air Division Headquarters, Warren Burman; VIIIth Fighter Command, Ed Creeden; 7th Photo Group, Paul Campbell, Claude Murray; 91st Bomb Group, George Parks; 92nd Bomb Group, Sheldon Kirsner; 93rd Bomb Group, Charles Weiss; 94th Bomb Group, Frank Halm; 95th Bomb Group, Arthur Frankel; 100th Bomb Group, Horace Varian, Storm Rhode; 306th Bomb Group, Russell Strong, William Collins; 353rd Fighter Group, John Balason; 355th Fighter Group, Gordon Hunsberger; 357th Fighter Group, Merle Olmsted; 381st Bomb Group, T. Paxton Sherwood; 384th Bomb Group, Lloyd Whitlow; 388th Bomb Group, Ed Huntzinger; 389th Bomb Group, Earl Zimmerman; 392nd Bomb Group, Gil Bambauer; 401st Bomb Group, Ralph Trout; 445th Bomb Group, Francis DiMola, David Patterson; 452nd Bomb Group, Rom Blaylock; 453rd Bomb Group, Donald Olds.

Several magazines and a newspaper kindly published letters requesting help

*Jane's Publishing Co Ltd, London

to find witnesses, which resulted in several useful contacts. In particular we should like to thank: *Air Mail, Jaegerblatt, Air Force Magazine, Berlin Lokal Anzeiger, the Friends of the Eighth Newsletter,* and the *8th Air Force News.*

We acknowledge permission from Doubleday and Co to quote from the book *Mustang Pilot* by Richard Turner; and *American Heritage Magazine* to quote from Les Rentmeester's memoirs.

Once the documentary framework of the action had been assembled, the bulk of the story told in this book came from the interviews of more than 160 individuals who took part in the fighting or unwittingly became involved in it. These are listed in alphabetical order in the Witnesses section which follows; and to all of them the authors wish to express their gratitude. Special thanks are due to those who kindly wrote for us detailed accounts of their experiences on 6 March 1944: John Miller, Friedrich Ungar, John Flottorp, Rudolf Sinner, Lowell Watts and Bob Shoens. All of the interviews provided useful background information on the action; unfortunately, however, shortage of space and the need to avoid duplication prevented us from drawing on quotations from every one of the interviewees. Alec Lumsden copied the photographs.

When the task of research was complete the authors had a pile of official documents, personal accounts and interview transcripts more than a foot high detailing the part played in the action by almost every unit on either side. Once that was done, all we had to do was write the book.

The Witnesses

In each case the ranks, posts and surnames (of ladies who later married) are those held on 6 March 1944.

Anna Abendroth, housewife, Wedding district, Berlin
Eric Abendroth, AEG electrical company engineer, Wedding district, Berlin
Captain Warren Alberts, 2nd Bomb Division Headquarters, Old Catton, Norwich
2nd Lieutenant Russell P. Allman, B-17 bombardier, 95th Bomb Group, Horham
Captain Sam Arauz, intelligence officer, 384th Bomb Group, Grafton Underwood
Flight Officer Richard Argo, B-17 copilot, 306th Bomb Group, Thurleigh
1st Lieutenant R. Arstingstall, B-17 pilot, 96th Bomb Group, Snetterton Heath
Cees Bakker, schoolboy, Purmerend, Holland
Staff Sergeant Wallace Beyer, B-17 waist gunner, 91st Bomb Group, Bassingbourn
Oberleutnant Dieter Birk, Headquarters Luftwaffe 2nd Fighter Division, Stade near Hamburg
1st Lieutenant Leon Blanding, P-51 pilot, 4th Fighter Group, Debden
Technical Sergeant Norwood Borror, B-17 tail gunner, 401st Bomb Group, Deenethorp
2nd Lieutenant Ralph Bowling, B-17 bombardier, 95th Bomb Group, Horham
Technical Sergeant James Brady, B-17 bombardier, 100th Bomb Group, Thorpe Abbots
2nd Lieutenant August Briding, B-17 bombardier, 95th Bomb Group, Horham
Arthur von Brietzke, Foreign Ministry official, Neukoelln district, Berlin
2nd Lieutenant Charles Bright, B-17 navigator, 385th Bomb Group, Great Ashfield
Leon Butticaz, forced laborer, DWM factory, Reinickendorf district, Berlin
Technical Sergeant Don Chase, B-24 radio operator, 44th Bomb Group, Shipdham
1st Lieutenant Archie Chatterley, P-51 pilot, 4th Fighter Group, Debden
1st Lieutenant Andy Coroles, B-17 bombardier, 94th Bomb Group, Bury St Edmunds
Staff Sergeant Donald Courson, B-17 waist gunner, 306th Bomb Group, Thurleigh
1st Lieutenant Hubert Cripe, B-24 pilot, 453rd Bomb Group, Old Buckenham
1st Lieutenant Elmer Crockett, B-24 pilot, 453rd Bomb Group, Old Buckenham
Captain Harry Crosby, B-17 navigator, 100th Bomb Group, Thorpe Abbots
Captain Ed Curry, B-17 bombardier, 401st Bomb Group, Deenethorp
Staff Sergeant Walter Davis, B-17 tail gunner, 91st Bomb Group, Bassingbourn
Officer Cadet Feldwebel Emil Demuth, FW 190 pilot, Ist Gruppe Fighter Geschwader 1, Twente, Holland
Staff Sergeant Richard Denton, B-24 tail gunner, 446th Bomb Group, Bungay
Leutnant Manfred Dieterle, Me 109 pilot, Ist Gruppe Fighter Geschwader 300, Bonn-Hangelar
Hans-Joachim Dombrowski, schoolboy, Potsdam district, Berlin
Lieutenant General James Doolittle, 8th Air Force Headquarters, High Wycombe
Flight Officer Bernard Dopko, B-17 pilot, 388th Bomb Group, Knettishall
1st Lieutenant James Dye, P-51 pilot, 4th Fighter Group, Debden
1st Lieutenant Glenn Eagleston, P-51 pilot, 354th Fighter Group, Boxted
Briggitte von Elert, housewife, visiting Zehlendorf district, Berlin
Staff Sergeant J. C. Eling, B-17 radio operator, 100th Bomb Group, Thorpe Abbots

2nd Lieutenant Bryce Evertson, B-17 pilot, 91st Bomb Group, Bassingbourn

1st Lieutenant John Flottorp, B-17 pilot, 390th Bomb Group, Framlingham

1st Lieutenant Dick Floyd, B-17 pilot, 92nd Bomb Group, Podington

2nd Lieutenant Cal Ford, B-17 copilot, 95th Bomb Group, Horham

1st Lieutenant Norman Fortier, P-47 pilot, 355th Fighter Group, Steeple Morden

Technical Sergeant John Frawley, B-17 top turret gunner, 91st Bomb Group, Bassingbourn

Staff Sergeant Robyn Fulton, B-17 ball turret gunner, 100th Bomb Group, Thorpe Abbots

Generalmajor Adolf Galland, Luftwaffe General of Fighters, Kladow near Berlin

2nd Lieutenant Earl Gauthier, B-17 bombardier, 92nd Bomb Group, Podington

Colonel Gerald Geerlings, 1st Bomb Division Headquarters, Brampton Grange

2nd Lieutenant Sherman Gillespie, B-17 pilot, 96th Bomb Group, Snetterton Heath

2nd Lieutenant Hank Gladys, B-17 bombardier, 452nd Bomb Group, Deopham Green

Luftwaffenhelfer Gottfried Gottschalk, Light Flak Abteilung 722, Siemensstadt district, Berlin

Elfriede Grasser, housewife, Spandau district, Berlin

Pilot Officer Bill Greenfield, Walrus pilot, No 277 Squadron, Royal Air Force Martlesham Heath

Oberleutnant Hermann Greiner, Me 110 pilot, IVth Gruppe Night Fighter Geschwader 1, Quakenbrueck

Major Anton Hackl, FW 190 pilot, commander IIIrd Gruppe Fighter Geschwader 11, Oldenburg

Leutnant Hermann Hagen, Me 110 pilot, IIIrd Gruppe Night Fighter Geschwader 5, Koenigsburg/Neumark

Lieutenant John Harrison, B-17 pilot, 100th Bomb Group, Thorpe Abbots

Hauptmann Helmut Haugk, Me 110 pilot, IInd Gruppe Destroyer Geschwader 76, Ansbach

Major Tom Hayes, P-51 pilot, 357th Fighter Group, Leiston

Hauptmann Rolf Hermichen, FW 190 pilot, commander Ist Gruppe Fighter Geschwader 11, Rotenburg

Major General James Hodges, 2nd Bomb Division Headquarters, Old Catton, Norwich

Technical Sergeant Louis Holland, B-17 radio operator, 91st Bomb Group, Bassingbourn

1st Lieutenant Billy Joe Holt, B-17 pilot, 390th Bomb Group, Framlingham

1st Lieutenant John Howland, B-17 navigator, 381st Bomb Group, Ridgewell

Leutnant Hans Iffland, Me 109 pilot, IVth Gruppe Fighter Geschwader 3, Salzwedel

Staff Sergeant Russell Johnson, B-17 waist gunner, 401st Bomb Group, Deenethorp

Technical Sergeant Edgar Jurist, B-17 radio operator, 95th Bomb Group, Horham

Reimund Kaluza, Propaganda Ministry official, Central district, Berlin

Ursula Kath, university student, Wilmsersdorf district, Berlin

Norbert Kelling, schoolboy, Eggersdorf near Berlin

1st Lieutenant Joseph Kerch, P-47 pilot, 355th Fighter Group, Steeple Morden

Oberleutnant Ruediger von Kirchmayer, FW 190 pilot, IInd Gruppe Fighter Geschwader 1, Rheine

Niek Klaassen, civil servant, Wormer, Holland

Leutnant Hans Klaffenbach, Me 109 pilot, IInd Gruppe Fighter Geschwader 11, Wunstorf

1st Lieutenant John Klotz, B-17 pilot, 91st Bomb Group, Bassingbourn

1st Lieutenant Dan Knight, B-17 pilot, 401st Bomb Group, Deenethorp

Oberleutnant Heinz Knoke, Me 109 pilot, IInd Gruppe Fighter Geschwader 11, Wunstorf

Major Hans Kogler, Me 110 pilot, commander IIIrd Gruppe Destroyer Geschwader 26, Wunstorf

Oberleutnant Wolfgang Kretschmer, FW 190 pilot, IInd Gruppe, Fighter Geschwader 1, Rheine

Horst Krieger, Telefunken company apprentice, Steglitz district, Berlin

Sergeant Victor Krueger, B-24 ball turret gunner, 458th Bomb Group, Horsham St Faith

Elfriede Kuehn, schoolgirl, Quakenbrueck

Staff Sergeant Lawrence Kunst, B-17 waist gunner, 91st Bomb Group, Bassingbourn

Hauptmann Ernst Laube, Me 109 pilot, Einsatzstaffel Erla, Delitzsch

1st Lieutenant John Lautenschlager, B-17 pilot, 100th Bomb Group, Thorpe Abbots

Staff Sergeant Ed Leighty, B-17 waist gunner, 447th Bomb Group, Rattlesden

Gefreiter Guenther Lemm, Falkenhagener Chaussee Army Depot, Spandau district, Berlin

Unteroffizier Walter Loos, Me 109 pilot IVth Gruppe Fighter Geschwader 3, Salzwedel

Staff Sergeant Edward Ludwig, B-17 top turret gunner, 379th Bomb Group, Kimbolton

1st Lieutentant Kenneth Lyell, B-24 copilot, 446th Bomb Group, Bungay

Staff Sergeant George Madden, B-17 top turret gunner, 100th Bomb Group, Thorpe Abbots

1st Lieutenant William Maher, B-17 copilot, 401st Bomb Group, Deenethorp

1st Lieutenant Cecil Manning, P-51 pilot, 4th Fighter Group, Debden

2nd Lieutenant Herbert Markle, B-17 copilot, 91st Bomb Group, Bassingbourn

2nd Lieutenant Clyde Martin, B-17 navigator, 452nd Bomb Group, Deopham Green

2nd Lieutenant Orvis Martin, B-24 bombardier, 453rd Bomb Group, Old Buckenham

1st Lieutenant Clyde Mason, B-17 pilot, 91st Bomb Group, Bassingbourn

Oberleutnant Walter Matoni, FW 190 pilot, IInd Gruppe Fighter Geschwader 26, Grevilliers

Staff Sergeant Glenn Matson, B-24 tail gunner, 458th Bomb Group, Horsham St Faiths

Captain Jere Maupin, B-17 pilot, 401st Bomb Group, Deenethorp

Technical Sergeant Frank McCauley, B-17 radio operator, 385th Bomb Group, Great Ashfield

Flight Officer Tom McKinney, P-51 pilot, 357th Fighter Group, Leiston

1st Lieutenant Roy Menning, B-17 pilot, 94th Bomb Group, Bury St Edmunds

Staff Sergeant George Meshko, B-17 waist gunner, 96th Bomb Group, Snetterton Heath

Staff Sergeant John Miller, B-17 gunner, 100th Bomb Group, Thorpe Abbots

1st Lieutenant R. B. Miller, B-24 pilot, 389th Bomb Group, Hethel

Lieutenant Colonel Robert Miller, B-24 pilot, 389th Bomb Group, Hethel

1st Lieutenant Samuel Miller, B-24 pilot, 445th Bomb Group, Tibenham

Colonel Ross Miller, B-17 pilot, deputy commander 91st Bomb Group, Bassingbourn

Technical Sergeant Laurence Morel, B-17 tail gunner, 91st Bomb Group, Bassingbourn

Staff Sergeant Dana Morse, B-17 waist gunner, 91st Bomb Group, Bassingbourn

Gert Mueller, Reichs Post Office engineering apprentice, Central district, Berlin

2nd Lieutenant James Muldoon, B-24 pilot, 392nd Bomb Group, Wendling

Staff Sergeant Bert Mullins, B-17 tail gunner, 91st Bomb Group, Bassingbourn

Colonel Harry Mumford, 3rd Bomb Division Headquarters, Elvedon Hall

1st Lieutenant George Neal, B-24 navigator, 389th Bomb Group, Hethel

Captain Carl Norcross, VIIIth Fighter Command Headquarters, Bushey Hall

Private Bill Norko, armorer, 384th Bomb Group, Grafton Underwood

Captain Fritz Nowosad, engineering officer, 384th Bomb Group, Grafton Underwood

1st Lieutenant John O'Leary, B-17 navigator, 91st Bomb Group, Bassingbourn

Brigadier General Earle Partridge, 8th Air Force Headquarters, High Wycombe

Staff Sergeant Neal Persons, B-17 waist gunner, 92nd Bomb Group, Podington

Technical Sergeant Hubert Peterson, B-17 radio operator, 91st Bomb Group, Bassingbourn

1st Lieutenant Myron Pierce, B-17 pilot, 401st Bomb Group, Deenethorp

Technical Sergeant Van Pinner, B-17 top turret gunner, 100th Bomb Group, Thorpe Abbots

1st Lieutenant Peter Pompetti, P-47 pilot, 78th Fighter Group, Duxford

1st Lieutenant Alexander Rafalovich, P-51 pilot, 4th Fighter Group, Debden

Technical Sergeant Robert Ray, B-17 radio operator, 100th Bomb Group, Thorpe Abbots

Oberfeldwebel Hermann Reinthaler, Me 109 pilot, Ist Gruppe Fighter Geschwader 11, Rotenburg

1st Lieutenant Les Rentmeester, B-17 pilot, 91st Bomb Group, Bassingbourn

2nd Lieutenant Earl Richardson, B-17 bombardier, 100th Bomb Group, Thorpe Abbots

Luftwaffenoberhelfer Hans Ring, Heavy Flak Abteilung 437, Spandau district, Berlin

2nd Lieutenant Arval Roberson, P-51 pilot, 357th Fighter Group, Leiston

1st Lieutenant Harold Roellig, B-17 copilot, 92nd Bomb Group, Podington

Technical Sergeant Milton Rudd, B-17 radio operator, 457th Bomb Group, Glatton

Leutnant Lothar Sachs, Me 109 pilot, Ist Gruppe Fighter Geschwader 300, Bonn-Hangelar

1st Lieutenant Paul Saffold, P-47 pilot, 78th Fighter Group, Duxford

Technical Sergeant Raymond Schaaj, B-17 bombardier, 381st Bomb Group, Ridgewell

Oberleutnant Gerd Schaedle, Me 109 pilot, IInd Gruppe Fighter Geschwader 2, Creil

Kriegseinsatzfuehrer Werner Schaeffer, Zoo district flak bunker, Berlin

Luftwaffenhelfer Dietrich Scheibel, Heavy Flak Abteilung 307, Tempelhof district, Berlin

Oberleutnant Herbert Schob, Me 110 pilot, Ist Gruppe Destroyer Geschwader 76, Ansbach

1st Lieutenant Bryan Schotts, B-17 pilot, 401st Bomb Group, Deenethorp

Luftwaffenhelfer Guenther Schulze, Light Flak Abteilung 979, Tempelhof district, Berlin

Oberfeldwebel Leo Schumacher, FW 190 pilot, IInd Gruppe Fighter Geschwader 1, Twente

1st Lieutenant Neal Serkland, B-24 pilot, 445th Bomb Group, Tibenham

1st Lieutenant Ocea Sherman, B-17 navigator, 94th Bomb Group, Bury St Edmunds

1st Lieutenant Bob Shoens, B-17 pilot, 100th Bomb Group, Thorpe Abbots

Hauptmann Rudolf Sinner, Me 109 pilot, commander IIIrd Gruppe Fighter Geschwader 54, Lueneburg

2nd Lieutenant Elton Skinner, B-17 navigator, 95th Bomb Group, Horham

Feldwebel Alois Slaby, Me 410 radio operator, IInd Gruppe Destroyer Geschwader 26, Hildesheim

1st Lieutenant Paul Soffold, P-47 pilot, 78th Fighter Group, Duxford

1st Lieutenant Morgan Spangle, B-17 bombardier, 94th Bomb Group, Bury St Edmunds

1st Lieutenant Fred Sparrevohn, B-24 pilot, 93rd Bomb Group, Hardwick

2nd Lieutenant Thurman Spiva, B-24 navigator, 446th Bomb Group, Bungay

2nd Lieutenant Rod Starkey, P-51 pilot, 357th Fighter Group, Leiston

Technical Sergeant Harold Stearns, B-17 top turret gunner, 100th Bomb Group, Thorpe Abbots

Oberleutnant Fritz Stehle, Me 410 pilot, commander IInd Gruppe Destroyer Geschwader 26, Hildesheim

2nd Lieutenant George Steiger, B-24 copilot, 389th Bomb Group, Hethel

Feldwebel Franz Steiner, FW 190 pilot, Ist Gruppe Fighter Geschwader 11, Rotenburg
Staff Sergeant Leonard Sterle, B-17 waist gunner, 91st Bomb Group, Bassingbourn
Staff Sergeant Thomas Stillson, B-17 ball turret gunner, 306th Bomb Group, Thurleigh
Technical Sergeant Donald L. Stoberl, B-17 radio operator, 303rd Bomb Group,
    Molesworth
1st Lieutenant Paul Sullivan, B-17 navigator, 94th Bomb Group, Bury St Edmunds
Luftwaffenhelfer Werner Synakiewicz, Heavy Flak Abteilung 422, Marwitz
Gertrud Tappert, housewife, Prenzlauerberg district, Berlin
Captain Downey Thomas, B-24 pilot, 448th Bomb Group, Seething
Leutnant Rudolf Thun, Me 110 pilot, IInd Gruppe Night Fighter Geschwader 5,
    Parchim
Feldwebel Friedrich Ungar, Me 109 pilot, IIIrd Gruppe Fighter Geschwader 54,
    Lueneburg
Captain Jordan Uttal, 2nd Bomb Division Headquarters, Old Catton
1st Lieutenant Lowell Watts, B-17 pilot, 388th Bomb Group, Knettishall
Leutnant Hans Weik, Me 109 pilot, IVth Gruppe Fighter Geschwader 3, Salzwedel
Major Walt Weitner, Spitfire reconnaissance pilot, 7th Photo Group, Mount Farm
Feldwebel Hans-Gerd Wennekers, Me 109 pilot, IInd Gruppe Fighter Geschwader 11,
    Wunstorf
Leutnant Gerd Wiegand, FW 190 pilot, Ist Gruppe Fighter Geschwader 26,
    Wevelghem
2nd Lieutenant Alan Willis, B-17 pilot, 452nd Bomb Group, Deopham Green
Police Oberwachtmeister Wilhelm Winkler, Zehlendorf district, Berlin
2nd Lieutenant Robert Wise, P-47 pilot, 78th Fighter Group, Duxford
Luftwaffenhelfer Alexander Witzigmann, Flak Grossbatterie Gross Zeithen, Berlin
Leutnant Guenther Wolf, Me 110 pilot, IIIrd Gruppe Night Fighter Geschwader 5,
    Brandis
Hauptmann Heinrich Wuerzer, Me 109 pilot, commander Ist Gruppe Fighter
    Geschwader 302, Jueterbog
Colonel Hubert Zemke, P-47 pilot, commander 56th Fighter Group, Halesworth
Captain Harding Zumwalt, P-47 pilot, 78th Fighter Group, Duxford

Bibliography

Air Ministry, London: *The Rise and Fall of the Luftwaffe*
Steve Birdsall: *The B-17 Flying Fortress*, Arco Publishing, New York
   The B-24 Liberator, Arco Publishing, New York
Ken Blakebrough: *The Fireball Outfit*, Aero Publishers Inc, Fallbrook, California
Eric Brown: *Wings of the Luftwaffe*, Jane's Publishing, London
W. Craven and J. Crate: *The Army Air Forces in World War II*, University of Chicago Press
Eighth Air Force: *Eighth Air Force Tactical Development*, (unpublished)
Jeffrey Ethell: *Mustang: A Documentary History of the P-51*, Jane's Publishing, London
   P-38 Lightning at War, Scribner's New York; Ian Allan, Shepperton, England
   Escort to Berlin, Arco Publishing, New York
Roger Freeman: *The Mighty Eighth*, Jane's Publishing, London
Adolf Galland: *The First and the Last*, Henry Holt and Co, New York
Werner Girbig: *Im Anflug auf die Reichhauptstadt*, Motorbuch Verlag, Stuttgart
William Green: *Warplanes of the Third Reich*, Jane's Publishing, London
Grover Hall: *One Thousand Destroyed*, Brown, New York
David Irving: *The Rise and Fall of the Luftwaffe*, Weidenfeld and Nicolson, London
Edward Jablonski: *Flying Fortress*, Doubleday and Co, New York
Heinz Knoke: *I Flew For the Führer*, Holt, Rinehart and Winston, New York
Horst-Adalbert Koch: *Flak*, Podzun Verlag, Bad Nauheim, Germany
Len Morgan: *The P-47 Thunderbolt*, Arco Publishing, New York
   The P-51 Mustang, Arco Publishing, New York
Wilbur Morrison: *The Incredible 305th*, Duell, Sloan and Pearce, New York
Ernst Obermaier: *Die Ritterkreuzträger der Luftwaffe*, Verlag Dieter Hoffmann, Mainz
Alfred Price: *Battle over the Reich*, Scribners, New York; Ian Allan, Shepperton, England
   Luftwaffe Handbook, Scribners, New York; Ian Allan, Shepperton, England
   Focke-Wulf 190 at War, Scribners, New York; Ian Allan, Shepperton, England
   World War II Fighter Conflict, Jane's Publishing, London
   The Bomber in World War II, Scribners, New York; Jane's Publishing, London
Josef Priller: *Geschichte eines Jagdgeschwaders*, Kurt Wowinckel Verlag, Neckargemuend,
   Germany
Hans Ring and Werner Girbig: *Jagdgeschwader 27*, Motorbuch Verlag, Stuttgart
Kenn Rust: *The 9th Air Force in World War II*, Aero Publishers, Fallbrook, California
J. R. Smith and Antony Kay: *German Aircraft of the Second World War*, Putnam, London
Swedish Aviation Historical Society: *Flyghistorisk Revy*, Special Issue, November 1976
Richard Turner: *Mustang Pilot*, Doubleday and Co, New York
US Government: *US Strategic Bombing Survey*, Government Printing Office, Washington
   DC

APPENDIX A

Equivalent Ranks

US Army Air Force	*Luftwaffe*
General (Five Star)	Generalfeldmarschall
General (Four Star)	Generaloberst
Lieutenant General	General
Major General	Generalleutnant
Brigadier General	Generalmajor
Colonel	Oberst
Lieutenant Colonel	Oberstleutnant
Major	Major
Captain	Hauptmann
First Lieutenant	Oberleutnant
Second Lieutenant	Leutnant

Non-commissioned	
Flight Officer	Stabsfeldwebel
Master Sergeant	Oberfeldwebel
Technical Sergeant	Feldwebel
Staff Sergeant	Unterfeldwebel
Corporal	Unteroffizier
Private 1st Class	Gefreiter
Private 2nd Class	Flieger

APPENDIX B

The Striking Force, 6 March 1944

The order of the attacking force was as follows: 1st Bomb Division, 3rd Bomb Division, 2nd Bomb Division. In each case the number of aircraft in each unit which took off is given then, in brackets, the number which penetrated enemy territory.

1st BOMB DIVISION. PRIMARY TARGET: VKF BALL BEARING WORKS, ERKNER

Order of the wings in the formation: 1st Combat wing in the lead, 94th flying abreast and to the left of it; 4 minutes (12 miles) behind the 1st came the 41st, with the 40th abreast and to the left of it; 4 minutes behind the 41st came the composite 40th-41st Combat Wing Formation.

1st Combat Wing
Lead Box	2	(2)	B-17s of the 482nd (Pathfinder) Bomb Group, Alconbury
	18	(16)	B-17s of the 91st Bomb Group, Bassingbourn
Low Box	21	(21)	B-17s of the 381st Bomb Group, Ridgewell
High Box	12	(11)	B-17s of the 91st Bomb Group, Bassingbourn
	9	(9)	B-17s of the 381st Bomb Group, Ridgewell

94th Combat Wing
Lead Box	1	(1)	B-17 of the 482nd (Pathfinder) Bomb Group, Alconbury
	23	(18)	B-17 of the 401st Bomb Group, Deenethorp
Low Box	21	(20)	B-17s of the 351st Bomb Group, Polebrook
High Box	21	(18)	B-17s of the 457th Bomb Group, Glatton

41st Combat Wing
Lead Box	1	(1)	B-17 of the 482nd (Pathfinder) Bomb Group, Alconbury
	18	(17)	B-17s of the 379th Bomb Group, Kimbolton
Low Box	20	(20)	B-17s of the 303rd Bomb Group, Molesworth
High Box	7	(7)	B-17s of the 303rd Bomb Group, Molesworth
	5	(4)	B-17s of the 379th Bomb Group, Kimbolton
	6	(5)	B-17s of the 384th Bomb Group, Grafton Underwood

40th Combat Wing
Lead Box	1	(1)	B-17 of the 482nd (Pathfinder) Bomb Group, Alconbury
	20	(16)	B-17s of the 92nd Bomb Group, Podington
Low Box	20	(20)	B-17s of the 306th Bomb Group, Thurleigh
High Box	14	(11)	B-17s of the 92nd Bomb Group, Podington
	7	(6)	B-17s of the 306th Bomb Group, Thurleigh

Composite 40th-41st Combat wing
Lead Box 18   (17)   B-17s of the 305th Bomb Group, Chelveston
Low Box   18   (18)   B-17s of the 305th Bomb Group, Chelveston
High Box 18   (0)   B-17s of the 384th Bomb Group, Grafton Underwood
                      (failed to assemble with Division)

Escort for 1st Bomb Division
Penetration Support
          53   (51)   P-47s of the 359th Fighter Group, East Wretham
                      Made rendezvous with bombers near Dutch coast
          49   (45)   P-47s of the 358th Fighter Group (IXth AF), Raydon
                      Made rendezvous with bombers near Dutch coast
          35   (32)   P-47s of the 56th Fighter Group, Halesworth
                      Made rendezvous with bombers near Lingen
          36   (36)   P-47s of the 78th Fighter Group, Duxford
                      Made rendezvous with bombers near Dummer Lake

Target Support
          35   (25)   P-51s of the 4th Fighter Group, Debden
                      Made rendezvous with bombers northeast of Brunswick
          47   (31)   P-38s of the 55th Fighter Group, Nuthamstead
                      Failed to rendezvous with bombers

Withdrawal Support
          47   (32)   P-47s of the 355th Fighter Group, Steeple Morden
                      Made rendezvous with bombers northwest of Hanover
          39   (37)   P-47s of the 361st Fighter Group, Bottisham
                      Made rendezvous with bombers near German border
           9   (8)   P-51s of the 361st Fighter Group, Bottisham
                      Made rendezvous with bombers near German border

Total strength 1st Bomb Division, 301 (259) B-17s including Pathfinders.
Total strength escort, 350 (297) P-38s, P-47s and P-51s.

3rd BOMB DIVISION. PRIMARY TARGET: ROBERT BOSCH
ELECTRICAL WORKS, KLEIN MACHNOW

Planned order of wings in formation: 4th Combat Wing A Formation in the lead,
B Formation echeloned to the left of it; 4 minutes behind the 4A Formation came the
13th Combat Wing A Formation, with the B Formation echeloned to the left of it; 4
minutes behind the 13A Formation came the 45th Combat Wing A Formation, with the
B Formation echeloned to the left of it. During the form-up the 45th Combat Wing, A
and B Formations exchanged places and flew the mission in those positions.

4th Combat Wing, A Formation
Lead Box   2   (2)   B-17s of the 482nd (Pathfinder) Bomb Group, Alconbury
          19   (15)   B-17s of the 385th Bomb Group, Great Ashfield
Low Box   21   (18)   B-17s of the 447th Bomb Group, Rattlesden

4th Combat Wing, B Formation
Lead Box   21   (21)   B-17s of the 94th Bomb Group, Bury St Edmunds
Low Box   6   (6)   B-17s of the 94th Bomb Group, Bury St Edmunds
            5   (5)   B-17s of the 385th Bomb Group, Great Ashfield
            9   (9)   B-17s of the 447th Bomb Group, Rattlesden

13th Combat Wing, A Formation
Lead Box   1   (1)   B-17 of the 482nd (Pathfinder) Bomb Group, Alconbury
          23   (20)   B-17s of the 390th Bomb Group, Framlingham
Low Box   23   (21)   B-17s of the 95th Bomb Group, Horham

13th Combat Wing, B Formation
Lead Box   15   (15)   B-17s of the 100th Bomb Group, Thorpe Abbots
            7   (6)   B-17s of the 390th Bomb Group, Framlingham
Low Box   20   (17)   B-17s of the 100th Bomb Group, Thorpe Abbots

45th Combat Wing, A Formation
Lead Box   21   (19)   B-17s of the 388th Bomb Group, Knettishall
Low Box   12   (11)   B-17s of the 388th Bomb Group, Knettishall
            9   (9)   B-17s of the 452nd Bomb Group, Deopham Green

45th Combat Wing, B Formation
Lead Box   27   (21)   B-17s of the 96th Bomb Group, Snetterton Heath
Low Box   23   (21)   B-17s of the 452nd Bomb Group, Deopham Green

Escort for 3rd Bomb Division
Penetration Support
          16   (16)   P-47s of the 365th Fighter Group (IXth AF), Gosfield
                      Made rendezvous with bombers near Dutch coast
          34   (31)   P-47s of the 353rd Fighter Group, Metfield
                      Made rendezvous with bombers near Dummer Lake

Target Support
          45   (34)   P-51s of the 354th Fighter Group (IXth AF), Boxted
                      Made rendezvous with bombers near Magdeburg
          30   (23)   P-38s of the 20th Fighter Group, Kings Cliffe
                      Made rendezvous with bombers northwest of Berlin

Withdrawal Support
          32   (32)   P-47s of the 78th Fighter Group, Duxford
                      Failed to rendezvous with bombers
          48   (47)   P-47s of the 352nd Fighter Group, Bodney
                      Made rendezvous with bombers near Dummer Lake

Total strength 3rd Bomber Division, 264 (237) B-17s including pathfinders.
Total strength of escort, 205 (183) P-38s, P-47s and P-51s.

2nd BOMB DIVISION. PRIMARY TARGET: DAIMLER BENZ AERO ENGINE WORKS, GENSHAGEN

Order of wings in formation: 2nd, followed at 2-minute (6-mile) interval by the Composite 14th-96th Wing, followed at a 2-minute interval by the 20th Wing.

2nd Combat Wing

Lead Box	2	(2)	B-24s of the 482nd (Pathfinder) Bomb Group, Alconbury
	25	(18)	B-24s of the 445th Bomb Group, Tibenham
Low Box	28	(23)	B-24s of the 453rd Bomb Group, Old Buckenham
High Box	26	(20)	B-24s of the 389th Bomb Group, Hethel

Composite 14th-96th Combat Wing

Lead Box	1	(1)	B-24 of the 482nd (Pathfinder) Bomb Group, Alconbury
	27	(23)	B-24s of the 392nd Bomb Group, Wendling
Low Box	28	(23)	B-24s of the 44th Bomb Group, Shipdham
High Box	33	(20)	B-24s of the 458th Bomb Group, Horsham St Faiths

20th Combat Wing

Lead Box	1	(1)	B-24 of the 482nd (Pathfinder) Bomb Group, Alconbury
	26	(25)	B-24s of the 446th Bomb Group, Bungay
Low Box	31	(30)	B-24s of the 93rd Bomb Group, Hardwick
High Box	21	(20)	B-24s of the 448th Bomb Group, Seething

Escort for 2nd Bomb Division
Penetration Support

50	(50)	P-47s of the 362nd Fighter Group (IXth AF), Wormingford Made rendezvous with bombers over Zuider Zee
35	(34)	P-47s of the 56th Fighter Group, Halesworth Made rendezvous with bombers near Meppel

Target Support

48	(33)	P-51s of the 357th Fighter Group, Leiston Made rendezvous with bombers northeast of Magdeburg

Withdrawal Support

39	(32)	P-38s of the 364th Fighter Group, Honington Made rendezvous with bombers northwest of Berlin
49	(42)	P-47s of the 356th Fighter Group, Martlesham Heath Made rendezvous with bombers northwest of Hanover

Total strength of 2nd Bomb Division, 249 (206) B-24s including pathfinders.
Total strength of escort, 221 (191) P-38s, P-47s and P-51s.

GENERAL WITHDRAWAL SUPPORT

48	(44)	P-47s of the 359th Fighter Group, East Wretham Made rendezvous with bombers near Dummer Lake, fighters on their second sortie of the day
49	(49)	P-47s of the 358th Fighter Group (IXth AF), Raydon Made rendezvous with bombers east of Zuider Zee, fighters on their second sortie of the day
43	(42)	P-47s of the 362nd Fighter Group (IXth AF), Wormingford

                  Made rendezvous with bombers over the Zuider Zee,
                  fighters on their second sortie of the day
27   (26)   P-51 Mustangs of Nos 19, 65 and 122 Squadrons, Royal Air
                  Force, Gravesend. Made rendezvous with bombers north of
                  Hanover

Total strength of General Withdrawal Support, 167 (161) P-47s and P-51s

Post-Strike Reconnaissance
         1   (1)   Spitfire XI of the 7th Photographic Group, Mount Farm

GRAND TOTAL STRENGTH OF STRIKING FORCE

     814   **(702)**   B-17s and B-24s
     943   **(832)**   P-38, P-47 and P-51 escort sorties
       1   **(1)**   Spitfire post-strike reconnaissance

 1,758 **(1,535)** aircaft sorties

APPENDIX C

Fighter Units Available for the Defense of Germany, 6 March 1944, and Aircraft Serviceable

Authors' note: this table was based on official German records which were almost complete; in the few cases where there were gaps or probable errors in the records, figures based on the best available information have been inserted.

1st Fighter Division, Headquarters Doeberitz near Berlin

Fighter Geschwader 3

Stab	Me 109	3	Salzwedel
I Gruppe	Me 109	23	Burg
II Gruppe	Me 109	19	Gardelegen
IV Gruppe	Me 109	13	Salzwedel

Fighter Geschwader 301 (single-engined night fighters)

III Gruppe	Me 109	21	Zerbst

Fighter Geschwader 302 (single-engined night fighters)

Stab	Me 109	1	Doeberitz
I Gruppe	Me 109	8	Jueterbog
II Gruppe	Me 109	8	Ludwigslust

Sturmstaffel 1	FW 190	7	Salzwedel

Destroyer Geschwader 26

II Gruppe	Me 410	12	Hildesheim
III Gruppe	Me 110	9	Wunstorf

Industrial Fighter Units

Ago	FW 190	3	Oschersleben
Erla	Me 109	6	Delitzsch
Arado	FW 190	4	Tutow

Airborne Tracking Detachment

	FW 190	5	Parchim

Night Fighter Geschwader 5

Stab	Me 110	1	Doeberitz
I Gruppe	Me 110	11	Stendal
II Gruppe	Me 110	13	Parchim
III Gruppe	Me 110	16	Brandis, Koenigsberg/Neumark
IV Gruppe	Me 110	10	Erfurt-Bildersleben
V Gruppe	Me 110	14	Insterburg, Powunden

Night Fighter Gruppe 10 (tactical development unit)

	Me 110 ⎱		
	Ju 88 ⎰	12	Werneuchen
	He 219		
	Me 109		

Air Observation Staffel 1

	Ju 88	3	Neuruppin

2nd Fighter Division, Headquarters Stade near Hamburg

Fighter Geschwader 11

Stab	Me 109	4	Rotenburg
I Gruppe	FW 190	14	Rotenburg
II Gruppe	Me 109	15	Wunstorf
III Gruppe	FW 190	19	Oldenburg
10 Staffel	Me 109 ⎱ FW 190 ⎰	10	Aalborg
11 Staffel	Me 109	10	Lister

Fighter Geschwader 54

III Gruppe	Me 109	20	Lueneburg

Trials Detachment 25

	FW 190	15	
	Me 109	10	
	Me 410	5	Achmer
	Ju 88	8	
	He 177	4	

Industrial Fighter Units

Neumuenster	Me 109	4	Neumuenster
Fieseler	FW 190	3	Kassel-Rothwesten
Focke-Wulf	FW 190	4	Langenhagen

Night Fighter Geschwader 1

10 Staffel	Me 110	7	Quakenbruek
III Gruppe	Me 110	2	Wittmundhafen

Night Fighter Geschwader 3

Stab	Me 110	1	Stade
I Gruppe	Me 110	14	Vechta
II Gruppe	Ju 88, Do 217	12	Schleswig
III Gruppe	Me 110	7	Stade
IV Gruppe	Me 110, Ju 88	14	Westerland

Night Fighter Geschwader 7

I Gruppe	Ju 88	10	Muenster-Handorf, Hopsten

Air Observation Staffel 2

	Ju 88, Me 110	3	Stade

3rd Fighter Division, Headquarters Deelen near Arnhem, Holland

Fighter Geschwader 1

Stab	FW 190	3	Rheine
I Gruppe	FW 190	19	Twente

| II Gruppe | FW 190 | 19 | Rheine |
| III Gruppe | Me 109 | 13 | Moenchen Gladbach |

Fighter Geschwader 300 (single-engined night fighters)

Stab	Me 109	2	Deelen
I Gruppe	Me 109	10	Bonn-Hangelar
II Gruppe	FW 190	5	Rheine

Night Fighter Geschwader 1

Stab	Me 110	1	Deelen
I Gruppe	He 219	3	Venlo
II Gruppe	Me 110, Do 217	9	St Trond
IV Gruppe	Me 110	11	Leeuwarden

Night Fighter Geschwader 2

Stab	Me 110, Ju 88	3	Deelen
II Gruppe	Ju 88	13	Deelen
III Gruppe	Me 110, Ju 88	6	Twente

Air Observation Staffel 3

| | Ju 88 | 3 | Venlo |

4th Fighter Division, Headquarters Metz, France

Fighter Geschwader 2

Stab	Me 109	1	Cormeilles
II Gruppe	Me 109	23	Creil
III Gruppe	FW 190	19	Cormeilles

Fighter Geschwader 26

Stab	FW 190	1	Lille-Nord
I Gruppe	FW 190	24	Lille-Nord, Florennes, Wevelghem
II Gruppe	FW 190	16	Epinoy, Grevilliers
III Gruppe	Me 109	32	Vendeville, Denain, St Dizier

Night Fighter Geschwader 1

| III Gruppe | Me 110 | 12 | Chenay |

Night Fighter Geschwader 4

Stab	Me 110	1	Chenay
I Gruppe	Me 110, Ju 88, Do 217	5	Florennes
II Gruppe	Me 110, Do 217	14	Coulommiers

7th Fighter Division, Headquarters Schleisheim near Munich

Fighter Geschwader 3

| III Gruppe | Me 109 | 20 | Wiesbaden-Erbenheim |

Fighter Geschwader 5

| I Gruppe | Me 109 | 20 | Herzogenaurach |

Fighter Geschwader 27

I Gruppe	Me 109	33	Fells am Wagram
II Gruppe	Me 109	27	Wiesbaden-Erbenheim
III Gruppe	Me 109	19	Seyring
IV Gruppe	Me 109	26	Graz

Fighter Geschwader 53
II Gruppe   Me 109   15   Frankfurt-Eschborn

Fighter Geschwader 300 (single-engined night fighters)
III Gruppe   Me 109   4   Wiesbaden-Erbenheim

Fighter Geschwader 301 (single-engined night fighters)
I Gruppe   Me 109   19   Leipheim
II Gruppe   Me 109   7   Seyring

Destroyer Geschwader 1
II Gruppe   Me 110   26   Wels

Destroyer Geschwader 76
Stab   Me 110   1   Ansbach
I Gruppe   Me 110   19   Ansbach
II Gruppe   Me 110   14   Ansbach
III Gruppe   Me 110   6   Oettingen

Industrial Fighter Units
Messerschmitt   Me 109   4   Regensburg-Obertraubling
Messerschmitt   Me 109   3   Weiner Neustadt

Fighter School Operational Staffeln (flown by instructors)
FG 104   Me 109   8   Fuerth
FG 108   Me 109   7   Voeslau

Night Fighter Geschwader 6
I Gruppe   Me 110   14   Mainz-Finthen
II Gruppe   Me 110   14   Echterdingen

Night Fighter School Operational Staffeln (flown by instructors)
NFG 101   Me 110   4   Ingolstadt, Munich-Reim
NFG 102   Me 110   9   Kitzingen

APPENDIX D

The Defensive Reaction, 6 March 1944

Authors' note: this table was based on official German records which were almost complete; in the few cases where there were gaps or probable errors in the records, figures based on the best available information have been inserted.

Abbreviations used:

FG   - Fighter Geschwader
DG   - Destroyer Geschwader
NFG - Night Fighter Geschwader

Air Obs Staf - Air Observation Staffel
Air Tr Det   - Air Tracking Detachment
Ind Ftr U   - Industrial Fighter Unit

Where applicable the Gruppe number is given in Roman numerals in front of the Geschwader number, thus III/FG 3 denotes the IIIrd Gruppe of Fighter Geschwader 3.

	Take-off Time	Airfield	No	Type	Unit	Remarks
1.	10.45	Twente, Holland	16	FW 190	I/FG 1	Assembled with attack formation over Lake Steinhuder, went into action against bombers over Haseluenne at noon.
2.	10.59	Ansbach	24	Me 110	I and II/DG 76	Assembled with attack formation over Magdeburg, went into action against bombers over Tangerhuette at 12.42
3.	11.00	Wunstorf	15	Me 109	II/FG 11	As 1. This Gruppe provided top cover for the attack formation.
4.	11.04	Oldenburg	18	FW 190	III/FG 11	As 1.
5.	11.05	Rheine	22	FW 190	Stab, II/FG 1	As 1.
6.	11.09	Rotenburg	4	Me 109	I/FG 11	As 1.
			13	FW 190		

No.	Time	Location	Count	Type	Unit	Remarks
7.	11.18	Grevilliers, France	6	FW 190	II/FG 26	After take-off patrolled in the Reims area in case the bomber stream turned south. Failed to make contact with the enemy, landed at airfields in the Wiesbaden-Mannheim area.
8.	11.20	Epinoy, France	5	FW 190	II/FG 26	As 7.
9.	11.20	Wevelghem, Belgium	7	FW 190	I/FG 26	As 7.
10.	11.21	Creil, France	22	Me 109	II/FG 2	As 7.
11.	11.22	Lueneburg	20	Me 109	III/FG 54	As 1.
12.	11.25	Hildesheim	10	Me 410	II/DG 26	As 2.
13.	11.26	Wunstorf	9	Me 110	III/DG 26	As 2.
14.	11.27	Cormeilles, France	13	FW 190	III/FG 2	As 7.
15.	11.30	Stade	1	Ju 88	Air Obs Staf 2	Observation aircraft, joined the bomber stream north of Hanover and tracked it from there eastwards.
16.	11.35	Burg nr Magdeburg	23	Me 109	I/FG 3	As 2. This Gruppe provided top cover for the attack formation.
17.	11.36	Gardelegen	16	Me 109	II/FG 3	As 2.
18.	11.37	Salzwedel	16	Me 109	Stab, IV/FG 3	As 2.
19.	11.37	Salzwedel	7	FW 190	Sturmstaffel 1	As 2.
20.	11.37	Jueterbog	8	Me 109	I/FG 302	As 2.
21.	11.45	Parchim	5	FW 190	Air Tr Det	Observation aircraft, joined the bomber stream west of Berlin and tracked it through the target.
22.	12.04	Parchim	9	Me 110	II/NFG 5	Vectored on to the rear of the bomber stream, to engage stragglers.
23.	12.10	Stendal	2	Me 110	I/NFG 5	As 22.
24.	12.13	Koenigsburg/Neumark	3	Me 110	III/NFG 5	As 22.
25.	12.15	Epinoy, France	5	FW 190	II/FG 26	As 7.
26.	12.24	Wiesbaden-Erbenheim	15	Me 109	III/FG 3	Failed to make contact with bomber stream.
27.	12.24	Wiesbaden-Erbenheim	31	Me 109	II/FG 27 and III/FG 300	As 26.
28.	12.25	Oschersleben	3	FW 190	Ind Ftr U Ago	As 2.
29.	12.35	Rechlin	2	Me 110		Aircraft from the Luftwaffe Trials Establishment at Rechlin.
			1	Me 109		

No.	Time	Location		Aircraft	Unit	Remarks
30.	12.42	Brandis	4	Me 110	III/NFG 5	As 22.
31.	12.45	Quakenbrueck	1	Me 110	IV/NFG 1	Oblt Greiner, shot down B-17 immediately after take-off.
32.	12.50	Parchim	1	Me 110	II/NFG 5	Observation aircraft, joined bomber stream west of Berlin and tracked it westwards.
33.	12.55	Delitzsch	2	Me 109	Ind Ftr U Erla	As 2.
34.	1.00	Herzogenaurach	6	Me 109	I/FG 5	Failed to make contact with the bomber stream.
35.	1.00	Parchim	3	FW 190	Air Tr Det	Second sorties by observation aircraft, tracked bombers westwards
36.	1.01	Oldenburg	7	FW 190	III/JG 11	Second sorties, probably failed to make contact with the bomber stream.
37.	1.05	Sorau	1	FW 190	Air Tr Det	As 35.
38.	1.25	Quakenbrueck	2	Me 110	IV/NFG 1	
39.	1.30	Biblis	2	FW 190		
40.	1.35	Gardelegen	7	Me 109	II/FG 3	Second sorties, failed to intercept.
41.	1.40	Bonn-Hangelar	10	Me 109	I/FG 300	Went into action against the bomber stream in the Lingen area, about 2.50.
42.	1.40	Wiesbaden-Erbenheim	21	FW 190	II/FG 26	Second sorties, as 41.
43.	1.40	Wiesbaden-Erbenheim	17	Me 109	II/FG 2	Second sorties, as 41.
44.	1.45	Biblis	6	FW 190		
45.	1.46	Mannheim-Sandhofen	10	FW 190	III/FG 2	Second sorties, as 41.
46.	1.48	Rotenburg	13	FW 190	I/FG 11	Second sorties, as 41.
47.	1.56	Florennes, Belgium	13	FW 190	I/FG 26	As 41.
48.	1.56	Burg nr Magdeburg	4	Me 109	I/FG 3	These may have been the fighters which attempted to intercept Major Weitner's Spitfire west of Berlin
49.	2.00	Stade	1	Me 210	Air Obs Staf 2	Observation aircraft, joined bomber stream near Hanover and tracked its movement westwards.
50.	2.00	Wunstorf	5	Me 109	II/FG 11	Second sorties, engaged by escorts near Nienburg before they could reach the bombers.
51.	2.00	Quakenbrueck	2	Me 110	IV/NFG 1	Oblt Greiner, flying one of these aircraft, shot down a bomber near Uelzen.
52.	2.08	Deelen, Holland	2	Me 109	Stab/FG 300	As 41.
53.	2.09	Lueneburg	7	Me 109	III/FG 54	Second sorties, as 41.

No.	Time	Base	No.	Aircraft	Unit	Notes
54.	2.20	Rheine	4	FW 190	II/FG 1	Second sorties, as 41.
55.	2.29	Oldenburg	4	FW 190	III/FG 11	Second sorties, as 41.
56.	2.43	Ansbach	15	Me 110	I and II/DG 76	Second sorties, failed to intercept.
57.	3.05	Bonn-Hangelar	4	Me 109	I/FG 300	As 56.
58.	3.20	Rheine	3	FW 190	II/FG 1	As 56.

APPENDIX E

US Combat Losses, 6 March 1944

1st BOMB DIVISION
91st Bomb Group

1.	B-17G 42-97483 Destroyed	2nd Lt B. Everton	Damaged by fighter attack north of Magdeburg at approximately 12.45, continued to target but caught fire after bombing. Crashed at Wilmersdorf near Bernau, northeast of Berlin. All crew bailed out and taken prisoner.
2.	B-17G 42-31079 Destroyed	1st Lt P. Coleman	Shot down by German fighters north of Magdeburg, 12.45 possibly by Lt Iffland of Fighter Geschwader 3. Right stabilizer shot off, reported by other US bombers. Four killed, six bailed out and taken prisoner. Aircraft crashed near Gardelegen.
3.	B-17G 42-31578 'My Darling Also' Destroyed	1st Lt B. Tibbetts	Rammed by German fighter north of Magdeburg, approx 12.50, 8 crew killed, 2 bailed out and taken prisoner.
4.	B-17G 42-31869 'Hell and High Water' Destroyed	1st Lt C. Mason	Shot down by German fighters north of Magdeburg, approx 12.45. Two crew killed, eight bailed out and taken prisoner. Aircraft crashed near Trebbin, south of Berlin.
5.	B-17G 42-31911 Destroyed	1st Lt D. Harding	Shot down by German fighters north of Magdeburg at 12.49. All crew bailed out and taken prisoner. Aircraft crashed at Ramstedt, 13 miles N Magdeburg.

| 6. | B-17G
42-38118
Destroyed | 2nd Lt B. Fourmy | Hit by flak west of Hanover at approx 12.30, left formation and descended to low alt. Engaged by Oblt Greiner of Night Fighter Geschwader 1 at 12.46 over Quakenbrueck airfield. Engaged by Light Flak Abteilung 844; crash landed 7 miles SW Quakenbrueck. Two killed, eight taken prisoner. |

Seventeen aircraft of the 91st Bomb Group returned with light and moderate damage.

92nd Bomb Group

7.	B-17G 42-97527 Destroyed	1st Lt R. Townsend	Shot down by 10.5 cm guns of Heavy Flak Abteilung 231 at Oythe near Vechta, at 2.31 pm. Aircraft broke up in the air and only the tail gunner, S/Sgt O. Maiocco, bailed out and taken prisoner. Remaining crewmen killed.
8.	B-17G 42-31503 Destroyed	1st Lt F. Krizan	Believed shot down north of Magdeburg by fighters, at approx 12.50. All crew bailed out and taken prisoner. Aircraft crashed at Brachwitz, SW of Berlin.
9.	B-17G 42-31680 Destroyed	1st Lt E. Cooper	Believed shot down by fighters during the return flight, at about 2.50 pm. One killed, remainder of crew bailed out and taken prisoner. Aircraft crashed near Plantleunne. Loss links with a claim by Major H. Baer of Fighter Geschwader 1.
10.	B-17G 42-40052 Destroyed	1st Lt W. Upson	Aircraft hit by heavy flak near German-Dutch border at about 11.30 on the way in. Incendiary bombs caught fire and it left the formation heading west. Five crew bailed out and taken prisoner. Five bailed out over Holland and evaded capture. Returned with serious flak damage.
11.	B-17 42-97479 Seriously Damaged		

Seventeen other aircraft of the 92nd Bomb Group returned with light or moderate damage.

303rd Bomb Group

| 12. | B-17
42-31213
'Pistol Packin Mama'
Seriously Damaged | | Aircraft returned with serious flak damage. |

13. B-17
42-31055
'Aloha'
Seriously Damaged — Aircraft returned with serious damage following flak and fighter attack.

Twenty-two other aircraft of the 303rd Bomb Group returned with light or moderate damage.

305th Bomb Group

Twenty-three aircraft of the 305th Bomb Group returned with light damage.

306th Bomb Group

14. B-17G
42-40006
'Liberty Lady'
Landed in Sweden,
set on fire by crew — 1st Lt C. Smith — Damaged by flak over Berlin, two engines knocked out. Landed on the Island of Gotland, Sweden, where the crew set fire to the aircraft. Crew interned.

15. B-17
Damaged — Lt A. Adams — Damaged by flak over Berlin, two engines knocked out. Attacked and further damaged by fighters during the return flight. Four crewmen bailed out over Holland and taken prisoner.

Seventeen other aircraft of the 306th Bomb Group returned with light or moderate flak damage.

351st Bomb Group

Eleven aircraft of the 351st Bomb Group returned with light or moderate damage.

379th Bomb Group

16. B-17G
42-31555
Destroyed — 1st Lt W. Hendrickson — Probably shot down by fighters north of Magdeburg at about 12.50. One killed, remainder of crew bailed out and taken prisoner. Aircraft crashed at Ochsenmoor near Kiepholz.

17. B-17G
42-37764
Damaged beyond repair — Damaged beyond repair during attack by fighters. Returned to England.

Fifteen aircraft of the 379th Bomb Group returned with light or moderate damage.

381st Bomb Group

18. B-17G
     42-31448
     Destroyed

     2nd Lt M. Fastrup

Forced to leave the formation, by fighter attack between Magdeburg and Berlin at about 1.05 pm. Finished off by Oberleutnant W. Matoni of Fighter Geschwader 26 near Juelich at 3.05 pm. Crashed near Etzweiler/Rheine. All crew taken prisoner.

19. B-17
     42-31553
     Destroyed

     1st Lt E. Naushalter

Shot down by fighters NE of Magdeburg at about 1.10 pm. Five crewmen bailed out and taken prisoner, five killed. Aircraft crashed 2 miles S of Wernsdorf.

20. B-17
     42-3125
     Destroyed

     2nd Lt R. Coyle

Probably shot down by fighters NE of Magdeburg at about 12.50. Two killed, eight bailed out and taken prisoner.

Fifteen other aircraft of the 381st Bomb Group returned with light damage.

384th Bomb Group

Three aircraft of the 384th Bomb Group returned with light flak damage.

401st Bomb Group

21. B-17
     42-38136
     Destroyed

     2nd Lt C. Kolb

Damaged during attack by fighters NE of Magdeburg at about 12.50. Finished off by 8.8 cm guns of Heavy Flak Abteilungen 326 and 605 over Berlin. All crew bailed out and taken prisoner. Aircraft crashed at Biesow, E of Berlin.

Thirteen other aircraft of the 401st Bomb Group returned with light or moderate damage from flak.

457th Bomb Group

22. B-17
     42-31595
     Destroyed

     2nd Lt E. Whalen

Rammed by Me 410 piloted by Fw W. Bonnecke of Destroyer Geschwader 26. Bomber then swung sharply across the formation and rammed another B-17. All crew killed. Wreckage scattered over 4 miles, to SW of Berlin.

23. B-17G 42-31627 Destroyed   2nd Lt R. Graves   Rammed by aircraft No 22. Only the tail gunner, Sgt E. Williams, survived, taken prisoner. Aircraft crashed 4 miles N of Treuenbriezen, SW of Berlin.

Five other aircraft of the 457th Bomb Group returned with light damage.

2nd BOMB DIVISION
44th Bomb Group

Three aircraft of the 44th Bomb Group returned with light or moderate flak damage.

93rd Bomb Group

24. B-24J 42-109832 'De-Icer' Destroyed   1st Lt J. Harris   Destroyed over Berlin by guns of Heavy Flak Abteilungen 123, 224 and 513. Crashed in Spandau district, Feldstrasse. Seven killed, three bailed out and taken prisoner.

One other aircraft of the 93rd Bomb Group returned with moderate damage, following a fighter attack.

389th Bomb Group

25 B-24J 42-100424 Destroyed   1st Lt K. Griesel   Forced to leave the formation after being hit by flak near Vechta, crew bailed out over Holland, aircraft crashed near Hoogeven. All crew survived; 8 taken prisoner, 2 evaded capture.

Thirteen other aircraft of the 389th Bomb Group returned with minor damage from flak.

392nd Bomb Group

26. B-24H 42-7598 'Flak Ducker' Destroyed   1st Lt E. Hestad   Aircraft seen to leave formation at about 2.15 pm, N of Hanover. Crashed 10 miles SE of Amersfoort in Holland. All crew survived, taken prisoner.

27. B-24 Destroyed   1st Lt P. Shea   Crashed immediately after take-off from Wendling. All crew killed.

445th Bomb Group

28. B-24H
42-7586
'God Bless our Ship'
Destroyed

1st Lt G. Lymburn

Shot down at about 1.40 pm over Berlin by guns of Heavy Flak Abteilungen 211, 437 and zbV 5552. One killed, rest bailed out or crash landed in aircraft and taken prisoner. Aircraft crash landed near Neuruppin, NE of Berlin.

29. B-24J
42-109796
'Balls of Fire'
Destroyed

1st Lt N. Serkland

Failure of electrical system of left inboard engine, forced to leave formation and abort mission. Shot down by fighter 8 miles NE Furstenau. Three killed, remainder bailed out and taken prisoner.

Twelve other aircraft of the 445th Bomb Group returned with light or moderate damage from flak.

446th Bomb Group

30. B-24J
42-100288
Destroyed

1st Lt Paltz

Damaged by fighter attack west of Berlin, one engine knocked out and forced to abort mission. Returned at low altitude but suffered further damage from flak and fighters. Ditched in the North Sea. Three crewmen rescued, remaining seven drowned. Seriously damaged during attack by fighter.

31. B-24
42-7649
Seriously Damaged

Six other aircraft of the 446th Bomb Group returned with light or moderate damage from flak.

448th Bomb Group

32. B-24H
41-29191
'Hello Natural'
Landed in Sweden

2nd Lt C. York

Damaged by flak over Berlin, aircraft landed in Sweden and all crew interned. Pilot returned July 1944, remainder of crew returned September 1944. Aircraft returned to USA in 1945.

Two other aircraft of the 448th Bomb Group returned with light or moderate damage.

453rd Bomb Group

33. B-24H
42-64457

1st Lt E. Crockett

Damaged by flak over Berlin and forced to leave the formation. Suffered further damage from fighters during the return flight.

No.	Aircraft	Status	Crew	Details
		Destroyed		Crew bailed out over the North Sea 5 miles off Yarmouth, 4 rescued and 6 killed. Aircraft crashed in sea.
34.	B-24H 42-64460	Destroyed	1st Lt P. Tobin	Shot down by fighters near Plantleunne, at about 2.50 pm during the return flight. Four bailed out, remainder killed when the aircraft blew up.
35.	B-24H 42-52191	Destroyed	2nd Lt H. Meek	Aircraft ditched in North Sea. Only one survivor.
36.	B-24H 42-52226	Destroyed	1st Lt H. Cripe	Shot down by fighter over Holland during the return flight. Crew bailed out over Zuider Zee, 3 rescued and 7 drowned. Aircraft crashed 2 miles NE Edam.
37.	B-24 42-52299	Seriously Damaged		Returned with serious flak damage.
38.	B-24 41-28654	Seriously Damaged		Returned with serious flak damage.

Thirteen other aircraft of the 453rd Bomb Group returned with light or moderate damage from flak.

458th Bomb Group

No.	Aircraft	Status	Crew	Details
39.	B-24H 41-29286	Destroyed	Capt J. Bogusch	Brought down by fire from guns of Heavy Flak Abteilungen 185 and 601, at Bramsche. Also engaged by Light Flak Abteilung at Nordhorn. Aircraft crashed near Tubbergen, Holland, at 3.02 pm. Six survived, four killed.
40.	B-24H 41-29299	Destroyed	2nd Lt T. Hopkins	Aircraft crashed near Nijkerk, Holland. All ten crewmen survived, taken prisoner.
41.	B-24H 42-52306	Destroyed	2nd Lt J. McMains	Shot down by Oblt Greiner of Night Fighter Geschwader 1 at about 2.10 pm, crashed beside the Army munitions factory at Muensterlager near Ueltzen. Two crew killed, 8 taken prisoner.
42.	B-24H 42-52450	Destroyed	2nd Lt B. Ballard	Badly damaged by flak over Berlin. Aircraft crashed at approx 3.17 pm at Purmerend, Holland. Three killed, nine taken prisoner. Ball turret gunner, Sgt Krueger, evaded capture for 14 months.

43. B-24H
42-52515
Destroyed | 2nd Lt G. Clifford | Shot down by flak over the target. Crashed near Petzow, just to the west of Berlin, at 1.45 pm. Eight killed when aircraft exploded; two bailed out and taken prisoner.

Three aircraft of the 458th Bomb Group returned with minor damage.

3rd BOMB DIVISION
94th Bomb Group

44. B-17G
42-38022
Destroyed | 1st Lt C. Johnston | Shot down by fighter over western Germany, at about 2.30 pm. Eight bailed out and taken prisoner. Two killed. Aircraft crashed 2 miles south of Wieste, near Plantleunne.

Sixteen aircraft of the 94th Bomb Group returned with light or moderate flak damage.

95th Bomb Group

45. B-17G
42-97495
Destroyed | 1st Lt J. Conley | Shot down by fighter attack near Haseluenne at approx 12.00. Some of crew bailed out near Barnstorf. All crew survived, taken prisoner.

46. B-17G
42-31251
Destroyed | 1st Lt T. Keasbey | Shot down by fighters near Diepholz at approx 12.20. Aircraft crashed 8 miles S of Bremen. All crew bailed out and taken prisoner.

47. B-17G
42-31299
'Junior'
Destroyed | 1st Lt L. Garland | Shot down by fighter at about 2.50 pm, over Beilen, Holland. All crew bailed out. Aircraft crashed 9 miles SW Assen. Pilot evaded capture for four months, but all eventually taken prisoner.

48. B-17G
42-32002
'Berlin First'
Destroyed | 2nd Lt T. Barksdale | Shot down by fighter near Quakenbrueck at approx 12.10. Aircraft crashed near Barnstorf. All ten crewmen bailed out and taken prisoner.

49. B-17G
42-38024
Destroyed | 1st Lt M. Russell | Shot down by fighter near Quakenbrueck at approx 12.15. Aircraft crashed near Colnrade. Nine bailed out, taken prisoner, one killed.

No.	Aircraft	Pilot	Details
50.	B-17G 42-39793 Destroyed	1st Lt R. Read	Seen to go down after fighter attack near Quakenbrueck at about 12.10. All crew survived, taken prisoner.
51.	B-17F 42-29943 'Situation-Normal' Destroyed	2nd Lt A. Mailman	Shot down by fighter attack near Haseluenne at approx 12.00. Aircraft crashed near Barnstorf. Five killed, five bailed out and taken prisoner.
52.	B-17G 42-3529 Destroyed	2nd Lt F. Frantz	Damaged by flak, finished off by fighter attack north of Magdeburg on the return flight at about 1.55 pm. One killed, nine bailed out and captured.
53.	B-17 42-38151 Seriously Damaged		Seriously damaged by flak and fighter attack. Returned to England.

Eleven other aircraft of the 95th Bomb Group returned with light or moderate damage.

100th Bomb Group

No.	Aircraft	Pilot	Details
54.	B-17G 42-97491 'Ronnie R' Destroyed	1st Lt D. Radtke	Shot down during fighter attack near Haseluenne at approx 12.00. Aircraft crashed near Twistrigen. One killed, other nine bailed out of aircraft and taken prisoner. Finished off by Ofw Reinthaler of Fighter Geschwader 11.
55.	B-17F 42-30170 Destroyed	1st Lt C. Montgomery	Shot down during fighter attack near Haseluenne at approx 12.00. Aircraft crashed near Colnrade. One killed, other nine bailed out and taken prisoner.
56.	B-17G 42-97482 'Terry and the Pirates' Destroyed	1st Lt W. Terry	Shot down during fighter attack near Haseluenne at approx 12.00. Aircraft crashed near Quakenbrueck. Seven killed, three bailed out and taken prisoner.
57.	B-17F 42-30278 Destroyed	2nd Lt Z. Kendall	Probably shot down during fighter attack near Haseluenne at approx 12.00. No survivors.
58.	B-17G 42-31051 Destroyed	2nd Lt R. Koper	Shot down during fighter attack near Haseluenne at approx 12.00. Aircraft crashed at Jump near Oldenburg. Seven killed, three bailed out and taken prisoner.

No.	Aircraft	Pilot	Notes
59.	B-17G 42-31731 Destroyed	1st Lt A. Amiero	Shot down during fighter attack near Haseluenne at approx 12.00. Aircraft crashed near Quakenbrueck. Nine killed, only the left waist gunner survived.
60.	B-17G 42-31735 Destroyed	1st Lt G. Brannan	Shot down during fighter attack near Haseluenne at approx 12.00. Aircraft crashed at Hausstette near Bakum. Two killed, eight bailed out and taken prisoner.
61.	B-17G 42-31800 Destroyed	2nd Lt S. Barton	Aircraft failed to return, all crew survived and taken prisoner.
62.	B-17G 42-38011 Destroyed	1st Lt E. Handorf	Shot down by an Me 109 at about 2.20 pm near Diepholz. Aircraft blew up. Only two bailed out, both taken prisoner.
63.	B-17G 42-38044 Destroyed	1st Lt M. Rish	Shot down during attack by fighters near Haseluenne at about 12.00. Aircraft crashed, disintegrating, near Quakenbrueck. Three killed, seven bailed out and taken prisoner.
64.	B-17G 42-38059 Destroyed	Capt D. Miner	Shot down during attack by fighters near Haseluenne at about 12.00. Aircraft crashed near Quakenbrueck. Four killed, six bailed out and captured.
65.	B-17G 42-38197 'Half and Half' Destroyed	1st Lt J. Lautenschlager	Shot down during attack by fighters near Haseluenne at about 12.00. Aircraft crashed at Halterm near Visbeck. One killed, other nine bailed out and taken prisoner.
66.	B-17G 42-39872 'Rubber Check' Destroyed	1st Lt F. Granack	Damaged by flak over Berlin and forced to leave the formation. Finished off by fighter. Crashed near Ostpriegnitz at about 2 pm. Two killed, eight bailed out and taken prisoner.
67.	B-17G 42-39994 'Barrick's Bag' Damaged, landed in Sweden	1st Lt S. Barrick	Damaged during attack by fighters near Haseluenne at about 12.00. Landed in Sweden, all crew interned until September 1944, then returned.
68.	B-17F 42-30799 Destroyed	1st Lt W. Murray	Shot down during attack by fighters near Haseluenne at about 12.00. Aircraft went down with tail on fire. Three killed, seven bailed out and taken prisoner.

No.	Aircraft	Pilot	Details
69.	B-17 'Nelson King' Seriously Damaged	1st Lt J. Swartout	Collided with, or rammed by, FW 190 during attack near Haseluenne at 12.00. Much of the fin and rudder knocked off. Continued with mission.

Eleven aircraft of the 100th Bomb Group returned with light or moderate damage.

385th Bomb Group

Nine aircraft of the 385th Bomb Group returned with light or moderate flak damage.

388th Bomb Group

No.	Aircraft	Pilot	Details
70.	B-17G 42-31135 'Suzy Sagtitz' Destroyed	1st Lt M. Givens	Shot down by fighter over western Holland, possibly by Hptm Frey of Fighter Geschwader 11. Aircraft crashed near Oud Schoonebeek. One killed, nine bailed out and taken prisoner.
71.	B-17G 42-31163 'A Good and Happy Ship' Landed in Sweden	2nd Lt C. Wallace	Damaged in action with fighters near Lingen at about 2.50 and left formation, landed in Sweden and the crew interned. All repatriated to England in November 1944. Aircraft later served with the Swedish airline ABA.
72.	B-17G 42-31194 Destroyed	1st Lt C. Grindley	Shot down by fighter near Dutch border at about 2.50 pm. Crashed at Schoeningsdorf. Two killed, one later died of wounds. Seven taken prisoner.
73.	B-17G 42-31240 Destroyed	2nd Lt J. McLaughlin	Shot down by fighter attack south of Bremen at about 2.50. Crew bailed out and aircraft flew for about half an hour on autopilot before it crashed at Soltau, south of Hamburg. All crew taken prisoner.
74.	B-17G 42-37886 'Blitzin Betsy' Destroyed	1st Lt L. Watts	Shot down by fighter near Dutch border at about 2.50 pm. Pilot held aircraft steady for crew to bail out but it collided with No 75 and both aircraft went down. Four killed, six bailed out and taken prisoner. Aircraft crashed S of Klazienaveen, Holland.
75.	B-17G 42-40054 Destroyed	Capt P. Brown	Rammed by No 74 and went down steeply. Three killed, one later died of wounds, six bailed out and taken prisoner. Aircraft crashed near Coevorden, Holland.

76.	B-17G 42-38177 'Shack Rabbits' Destroyed	2nd Lt A. Christiani	Shot down by fighter near German-Dutch border at 2.50 pm. Aircraft crashed near Bentheim. Five crew killed, five bailed out and taken prisoner.

Twenty aircraft of the 388th Bomb Group returned with light or moderate damage.

390th Bomb Group

77.	B-17G 42-31935 Destroyed	1st Lt R. Starks	Shot down by fighter during the attack near Quakenbrueck at about 12.15. Aircraft crashed at Hemmelte, SW Cloppenburg. Three killed, other seven bailed out and taken prisoner.
78.	B-17G 42-39876 Damaged beyond repair	1st Lt J. Flottorp	Returned to England, damaged beyond repair as a result of attacks by fighters.

Eighteen other aircraft of the 390th Bomb Group returned with light or moderate damage.

447th Bomb Group

79.	B-17G 42-31227 Damaged beyond repair	1st Lt A. Socolofsky	Aircraft severely damaged over Berlin by two flak shells which burst immediately under it. Radio operator was blown out of the top hatch of his position without a parachute. Aircraft returned damaged beyond repair.

Twenty-three other aircraft of the 447th Bomb Group returned with light or moderate flak damage.

452nd Bomb Group

80.	B-17G 42-31337 Destroyed	2nd Lt H. Sweeny	Aircraft forced to leave formation after being engaged over Berlin by Heavy Flak Abteilung 437. Finished off by guns of the 15th Flak Brigade, Hanover. Aircraft crashed 2 miles south of Fassberg, came down on the gun testing range of the Rheinmetall Borsig factory. All crew bailed out and taken prisoner, one died of wounds shortly after capture.
81.	B-17G 42-31373	2nd Lt C. Wagner	Shot down by fighter near the German-Dutch border at about 2.50 pm. Aircraft crashed near Staphorst, Holland. Four crew

killed, one taken prisoner, five evaded capture.

82. 'Flakstop' Destroyed
B-17
42-31919
Damaged beyond repair — 2nd Lt R. Schimmel — Suffered severe damage from attack by fighters and flak. Crash landed in England. Damaged beyond repair.

Eleven other aircraft of the 452nd Bomb Group returned with light or moderate damage.

PATHFINDER AIRCRAFT

482nd Bomb Group

83. B-17GSH
42-3491
Destroyed — Colonel R. Wilson — Shot down by guns of the Heavy Flak Abteilungen 126 and 307 over Berlin at 1.26 pm. Aircraft broke up and crashed near Lake Harvel. Six killed, four prisoners.

Nine other aircraft of the 482nd Bomb Group returned with light or moderate flak damage.

8th AIR FORCE FIGHTER UNITS

4th Fighter Group

84. P-51B
43-6887
Destroyed — 1st Lt C. Manning — Hit by return fire from an Me 110 during a combat to the west of Berlin. During the return flight the oil pressure dropped and the engine caught fire. Pilot bailed out near Sogel and taken prisoner.

85. P-51B
43-6630
Destroyed — 1st Lt R. Messenger — Shot down in combat near Berlin, pilot bailed out and taken prisoner.

86. P-51B
43-6690
Destroyed — Major H. Mills — Shot down in combat near Berlin, pilot bailed out and taken prisoner.

87. P-51B
43-6899
Destroyed — 1st Lt E. Whalen — Reported by US pilots to have been hit by debris from an exploding Me 110.

Three aircraft of the 4th Fighter Group returned with light or moderate damage.

56th Fighter Group

88. P-47D
42-75397
Destroyed   2nd Lt A. Stauss   Shot down in Haseluenne action at about 12.15. This loss, or No 90 links with claim by Oberst W. Oesau of Fighter Geschwader 1.

Two aircraft of the 56th Fighter Group returned with light damage.

78th Fighter Group

89. P-47D
42-7983
Destroyed   F/O E. Downey   Shot down in the Haseluenne action at about 12.15. Loss links with the claim by Fw H. Wennekers of Fighter Geschwader 11, at this position and time. Pilot killed.

90. P-47D
42-7998
Destroyed   2nd Lt G. Turley   Shot down in action near Haseluenne at about 12.15.

Two aircraft of the 78th Fighter Group returned with light or moderate damage.

353rd Fighter Group

91. P-47D
Damaged beyond repair   Lt Ireland   Aircraft crash landed at its base, pilot seriously injured.

356th Fighter Group

92. P-47D
42-75255
Destroyed   1st Lt M. Erickson   Shot down in combat in the Lingen area at approx 2.45 pm. Pilot bailed out east of Almelo, Holland and taken prisoner. This loss links with the claim by Ofw A. Heckmann of Fighter Geschwader 26, at this position.

93. P-47D
42-74711
Seriously Damaged   Lt N. Farmer   Returned seriously damaged due to enemy action, landed at the emergency airstrip at Woodbridge.

Two other aircraft of the 356th Fighter Group returned with light or moderate damage.

359th Fighter Group

94. P-47D
Damaged beyond repair

Returned damaged beyond repair. Unit engaged in withdrawal support.

361st Fighter Group

95. P-47D
Seriously damaged

Returned seriously damaged due to enemy action, belly landed at base.

364th Fighter Group

96. P-38J
42-94965
Destroyed

2nd Lt L. Ferguson

Shot down in action west of Berlin at about 2.10 pm. Pilot bailed out but killed when parachute failed to open.

9th AIR FORCE FIGHTER UNITS

354th Fighter Group

97. P-51B
43-12446
Destroyed

1st Lt R. Donnell

Shot down during action west of Berlin. Pilot taken prisoner.

362nd Fighter Group

98. P-47D
42-75635
Destroyed

Major F. Nelander

Aircraft hit by fire from Light Flak Abteilung 667, during attack on the airfield at Twente in Holland after breaking off support during the penetration phase. Pilot bailed out and taken prisoner.

APPENDIX F

German Combat Losses, 6 March 1944

Fighter Geschwader 1

1.	1st Gruppe	FW 190A 340003 Destroyed	Fw W. Dotzauer	Shot down at approximately 3 pm, aircraft crashed 2 miles northwest of Dalen in Holland. This loss and No 2 link with claims by Capt R. Sedman and 2nd Lt W. Moore flying P-47s of the 361st Fighter Group. Pilot killed.
2.	1st Gruppe	FW 190A 340002 Destroyed	Uffz A. Haupt	Shot down at approximately 3 pm, aircraft crashed near Steenwijk in Holland. See above. Pilot killed.
3.	1st Gruppe	FW 190A 642558 Destroyed	Off Cdt Fw E. Demuth	Shot down in action near Haseluenne at approximately 12.10 pm, by 2nd Lt J. Icard flying a P-47 of the 56th Fighter Group. Pilot bailed out with serious burns. Aircraft crashed near Minden.
4.	1st Gruppe	FW 190A Destroyed		Destroyed in action.
5.	1st Gruppe	FW 190A Destroyed		Destroyed in action.
6.	1st Gruppe	FW 190A Damaged		Damaged during a combat sortie, not as a result of enemy action.
7.	IInd Gruppe	FW 190A 430680 Destroyed	Ofw D. Lueth	Destroyed in action near Haseluenne at approximately noon, aircraft crashed at Eydelstadt south of Barnstorf. Pilot killed.
8.	IInd Gruppe	FW 190A 463000 Destroyed	Oblt W. Kretschmer	Shot down near Quakenbrueck at approximately noon by Colonel H. Zemke flying a P-47 of the 56th Fighter Group. Pilot bailed out with serious burns.

No.	Gruppe	Aircraft	Pilot	Remarks
9.	IInd Gruppe	FW 190A Damaged	Ofw Haninger	Damaged in action, this aircraft crash landed 4 miles south of Bremen at 12.10 pm.
10.	IInd Gruppe	FW 190A Damaged	Lt L. Schumacher	Damaged in action with bombers near Zwolle in Holland at approximately 3 pm, made normal landing at Rheine.
11.	IInd Gruppe	FW 190A Damaged beyond repair		Damaged beyond repair during noon action near Haseluenne.
12.	IInd Gruppe	FW 190A Damaged beyond repair		

Fighter Geschwader 2

No.	Gruppe	Aircraft	Pilot	Remarks
13.	IInd Gruppe	Me 109G 27033 Destroyed	Uffz G. Sens	Shot down near Lingen at approximately 2.55 pm by Capt W Koraleski flying a P-47 of the 355th Fighter Group. Pilot bailed out with minor wounds.
14.	IInd Gruppe	Me 109G 10232 Destroyed	Ofw W. Morzinek	As above. Pilot wounded.
15.	IInd Gruppe	Me 109G Destroyed	Oblt G. Schaedle	Shot down after a long chase at low altitude, at approximately 3 pm by Capt W Koraleski, Flt Off C. Barger and 1st Lt N. Fortier flying P-47s of the 355th Fighter Group. Aircraft wrecked when crash landed in a field near Hopsten.
16.	IInd Gruppe	Me 109G Damaged		Damaged in action.
17.	IInd Gruppe	Me 109G Damaged		Damaged in action.

Fighter Geschwader 3

No.	Gruppe	Aircraft	Pilot	Remarks
18.	Staff	Me 109G Destroyed		Destroyed in action in Berlin area at approximately 1 pm.

No.	Gruppe	Aircraft	Pilot	Notes
19.	IInd Gruppe	Me 109G 411348 Destroyed	Uffz. E. Britzlmair	Shot down during action north of Magdeburg at approximately 12.45 pm, pilot bailed out wounded. Aircraft crashed at Moeckern near Magdeburg.
20.	IInd Gruppe	Me 109G Destroyed		Destroyed in action in the Berlin area at approximately 1 pm.
21.	IVth Gruppe	Me 109G Destroyed		Destroyed in action in the Berlin area at approximately 1 pm.

Fighter Geschwader 11

No.	Gruppe	Aircraft	Pilot	Notes
22.	Staff	Me 109G 27126 Destroyed	Ofw H. Reinthaler	Shot down east of Haseluenne at approximately 12.10 pm by 2nd Lt R. Wise flying a P-47 of the 78th Fighter Group. Pilot was shot through the left elbow and bailed out. Aircraft crashed at Buente near Bassum. Later pilot's left forearm was amputated.
23.	Ist Gruppe	FW 190A 642523 Destroyed	Fw F. Steiner	Shot down near Haseluenne at approximately noon by Major J. Stewart flying a P-47 of the 56th Fighter Group. Pilot bailed out and dislocated his right knee when he struck the tail of the aircraft.
24.	Ist Gruppe	FW 190A 430467 Destroyed	Fw H. Neuendorf	Shot down near Haseluenne at approximately noon by Major J. Stewart flying a P-47 of the 56th Fighter Group. Pilot killed, aircraft crashed near Cloppenburg.
25.	Ist Gruppe	FW 190A Destroyed		Destroyed in action.
26.	Ist Gruppe	FW 190A Damaged		Damaged in action.
27.	Ist Gruppe	FW 190A Damaged		Damaged in action.
28.	IInd Gruppe	Me 109G 410222 Destroyed	Fw H. G. Wennekers	Shot down near Quakenbrueck at approximately noon by 1st Lt W. Tonkin flying a P-47 of the 78th Fighter Group. Pilot shot through left wrist, bailed out
29.	IInd Gruppe	Me 109G 410819	Uffz. P. Reinhardt	Shot down near Haseluenne at approximately noon, pilot killed. Loss links with claim by Colonel H. Zemke flying a

No.	Gruppe	Aircraft	Pilot	Remarks
30.	IInd Gruppe	Destroyed Me 109G 20049	Fw M. Hauptmann	P-47 of the 56th Fighter Group. Shot down 10 miles north of Nienburg at approximately 2.50 pm and pilot killed, by 1st Lt R. Janney flying a P-47 of the 359th Fighter Group.
31.	IInd Gruppe	Destroyed Me 109G Destroyed	Uffz F. Zambelli	Shot down near Nienburg at approximately 2.50 pm by Capt W. Bolefahr flying a P-47 of the 359th Fighter Group. Pilot bailed out.
32.	IInd Gruppe	Me 109G Damaged	Oblt H. Knoke	Damaged in combat with enemy formation east of Haseluenne at approximately 12.10 pm. Right landing gear shot away. Landed at Wunstorf on remaining gear leg.
33.	IInd Gruppe	Me 109G Damaged	Oblt H. Knoke	Shot up on the ground at Wunstorf at approximately 1.45 pm when about to take off for a combat sortie, by 1st Lt J. Carder flying a P-51 of the 357th Fighter Group.
34.	IInd Gruppe	Me 109G Damaged	Lt H. Klaffenbach	Damaged by bombers' return fire, in action east of Haseluenne at approximately 12.10 pm.
35.	IIIrd Gruppe	FW 190A Destroyed	Hptm H. Frey	Shot down by return fire in action against B-17s of the 452nd Bomb Group over Coevorden at 2.48 pm. Pilot killed, the aircraft crashed near Sleen in Holland.
36.	IIIrd Gruppe	FW 190A Destroyed	Uffz Gluttig	Destroyed in action. Pilot killed.
37.	IIIrd Gruppe	FW 190A		Destroyed in action.

Fighter Geschwader 26

No.	Gruppe	Aircraft	Pilot	Remarks
38.	Ist Gruppe	FW 190A 642987 Destroyed	Ofw H. Heitmann	Pilot seriously wounded in right arm during action near Osnabrueck at approximately 2.30 pm and bailed out. Aircraft crashed near Haste.

Fighter Geschwader 54

No.	Gruppe	Aircraft	Pilot	Remarks
39.	IIIrd Gruppe	Me 109G 410557 Destroyed	Hptm R. Sinner	Pilot seriously wounded by return fire while engaging a straggling B-17 near Bassum at approximately 12.15 pm. Bailed out.

40.	IIIrd Gruppe	Me 109G 440135 Destroyed	Uffz H. Rosenberg	Missing following action with enemy formation near Cloppenburg. Pilot killed.
41.	IIIrd Gruppe	Me 109G 440118 Destroyed	Uffz W. Straub	Missing following action with enemy formation south of Oldenburg. Pilot killed.
42.	IIIrd Gruppe	Me 109G 440139 Destroyed	Uffz E. Louis	Aircraft crashed at Borstel 6 miles east of Sulingen. Pilot killed.
43.	IIIrd Gruppe	Me 109G 44080 Damaged	Fw F. Ungar	Pilot wounded in foot east of Haseluenne at approximately 12.15 pm, during engagement by 2nd Lt B. Casteel flying a P-47 of the 56th Fighter Group. Pilot forced landed in a field near Homfeld.
44.	IIIrd Gruppe	Me 109G 15864 Damaged	Uffz E. Mueller	Pilot wounded in combat, forced landed near Aumuehle.
45.	IIIrd Gruppe	Me 109G 411922 Destroyed	Oblt G. Loos	Shot down near Rheinsehlen at approximately 1.50 pm by Lt J. Carder flying a P-51 of the 357th Fighter Group. Pilot bailed out but his parachute harness came open and he fell to his death.

Fighter Geschwader 300

46.	Staff	Me 109G Damaged		Damaged in action.
47.	Staff	Me 109G Damaged		Damaged in action.
48.	Ist Gruppe	Me 109G Destroyed	Off Cdt Fw K. Neumann	Crashed shortly after taking off from Bonn-Hangelar for a combat mission, at 1.47 pm. Ran into the slipstream of another aircraft during formation assembly, spun out of control and crashed into a house just outside the airfield. Pilot and four civilians killed.
49.	Ist Gruppe	Me 109G Destroyed		Destroyed in action.

No.	Gruppe	Aircraft	Status	Pilot	Notes
50.	1st Gruppe	Me 109G	Destroyed		Destroyed in action.
51.	1st Gruppe	Me 109G	Destroyed		Destroyed in action.
52.	1st Gruppe	Me 109G	Damaged	Lt L. Sachs	Engine damaged by return fire from a B-17 of the 306th Bomb Group, made wheels-down landing at Twente in Holland.
53.	1st Gruppe	Me 109G	Damaged	Lt M. Dieterle	Damaged by return fire from a B-17 formation, made wheels-down landing at base.
54.	IInd Gruppe	FW 109A	Destroyed	Uffz A. Roth	Shot down in combat at about 3 pm, pilot killed and aircraft crashed at Oldebroek in Holland. Loss links with claim made by] 1st Lt B. Hill flying a P-47 of the 355th Fighter Group.

Fighter Geschwader 302

No.	Gruppe	Aircraft	Status	Pilot	Notes
55.	1st Gruppe	Me 109G 411256	Destroyed	Fw E. Buhrig	Shot down in action in the Berlin area at about 1 pm, pilot bailed out and died later of wounds. Aircraft crashed near Hohenlobbese, east of Magdeburg. Loss links with claim by Colonel Bickell flying a P-51 of the 354th Fighter Group.
56.	1st Gruppe	Me 109G 410697	Destroyed	Uffz K. Pelz	Shot down at about 1.40 pm as it came in to land at its base at Stendahl, by Major T. Hayes flying a P-51 of the 357th Fighter Group. Pilot killed.
57.	1st Gruppe	Me 109G	Damaged		Damaged in action.
58.	1st Gruppe	Me 109G	Damaged		Damaged during a combat sortie, not as a result of enemy action.

Sturmstaffel 1

No.	Gruppe	Aircraft	Status	Pilot	Notes
59.		FW 190A 642962	Destroyed	Lt G. Dost	Crashed into the ground turning to avoid being hit by Capt G. Davis and 1st Lt T. Harris, flying P-51s of the 357th Fighter Group, who were chasing. Aircraft crashed near Salzwedel at approximately 1.45 pm. No rounds fired at the FW by the P-51s. Pilot killed.

No.	Unit	Aircraft	Crew	Notes
60.		FW 190A Destroyed		Destroyed in action.

Destroyer Geschwader 26

No.	Unit	Aircraft	Crew	Notes
61.	IInd Gruppe	Me 410A Destroyed	Fw W. Bonnecke	Collided with, or rammed, B-17 of the 457th Bomb Group which then collided with another B-17 and all three aircraft went down. Me 410 crashed at Luette south of Brandenburg, both crew killed, at approximately 12.45 pm.
62.	IInd Gruppe	Me 410A Destroyed	Lt W. Kutscher	Shot down during action north east of Magdeburg at about 12.45 pm. Both crew bailed out. Aircraft crashed near Doeberitz. Both crew wounded.
63.	IInd Gruppe	Me 410A Destroyed	Uffz W. Penekamp	Shot down during the action northeast of Magdeburg at about 12.45 pm. Pilot wounded, both crew bailed out. Aircraft crashed near Magdeburg.
64.	IInd Gruppe	Me 410A Destroyed	Fw H. Schneider	Shot down during the action northeast of Magedburg at about 12.45 pm. Pilot wounded, both crew bailed out. Loss links with claim by 1st Lt A. Chatterley flying a P-51 of the 4th Fighter Group. Aircraft crashed near Brandenburg.
65.	IInd Gruppe	Me 410A Destroyed		Destroyed in action.
66.	IInd Gruppe	Me 410A Destroyed		
67.	IInd Gruppe	Me 410A Damaged		Damaged in action. radio operator killed. Pilot made an emergency landing at Schwanebeck bei Bernburg.
68.	IIIrd Gruppe	Me 110G 500014 Destroyed	Oblt W. Meltz	Shot down during action north east of Magdeburg at about. 12.45 pm. Radio operator killed, pilot bailed out near Koethen with wounds.
69.	IIIrd Gruppe	Me 110G 130039 Destroyed	Lt H. Freiberger	Shot down during action north east of Magdeburg at about 12.45 pm. Radio operator killed, pilot bailed out with wounds.
70.	IIIrd Gruppe	Me 110G	Gefr H. Hillringhaus	Shot down during action north east of Magdeburg at about

No.	Gruppe	Pilot	Aircraft	Serial	Status	Remarks
				130038	Destroyed	12.45 pm. Both crew killed, aircraft crashed near Hoersingen.
71.	IIIrd Gruppe	Lt K. Burckhardt	Me 110G	130062	Destroyed	Shot down during action north east of Magdeburg at about 12.45 pm. Both crew bailed out, pilot wounded.
72.	IIIrd Gruppe	Uffz Rischke	Me 110G	500001	Destroyed	Shot down during action north east of Magdeburg at about 12.45 pm. Radio operator killed, pilot bailed out near Gardelegen.
73.	IIIrd Gruppe	Major H. Kogler	Me 110G		Damaged	Badly damaged northeast of Magdeburg at about 12.45 pm by Flt Off T. McKinney flying a P-51 of the 357th Fighter Group. Pilot made single-engined landing at airfield at Magdeburg.

Destroyer Geschwader 76

No.	Gruppe	Pilot	Aircraft	Serial	Status	Remarks
74.	Staff	Ofw W. Haugk	Me 110G		Destroyed	Shot down during action north east of Magdeburg at about 12.45 pm. Radio operator killed. Pilot bailed out, wounded. Aircraft crashed near Calvoerde.
75.	Ist Gruppe	Oblt H. Schob	Me 110G	120036	Destroyed	Shot down by P-51s during action north east of Magdeburg at about 12.45 pm. Both crew wounded, bailed out and landed 1 mile south of Letzlingen.
76.	Ist Gruppe	Lt H. Bogatzki	Me 110G	120043	Destroyed	Shot down during action north east of Magdeburg at about 12.45 pm. Both crew killed. Aircraft crashed 3 miles southwest of Greienthal.
77.	Ist Gruppe	Uffz W. Handrick	Me 110G	210091	Destroyed	Shot down during the action north east of Magdeburg at 12.45 pm. Both crew wounded, bailed out. Aircraft crashed at Ursleben near Hanover.

Night Fighter Geschwader 5

No.	Gruppe	Pilot	Aircraft	Serial	Status	Remarks
78.	Ist Gruppe	Oblt H. Jankowski	Me 110G	720259	Destroyed	Shot down by P-51s near Berlin. Aircraft crashed 5 miles southwest of Eberswalde, both crew killed.
79.	Ist Gruppe		Me 110G		Destroyed	Shot down near Berlin at about 1.50 pm.

No.	Gruppe	Aircraft	Status	Pilot	Details
80.	IInd Gruppe	Me 110G 5444	Destroyed	Oblt V. Sorko	Shot down by P-51s near Berlin at about 1.50 pm. Both crew killed. Aircraft crashed just to north of Bernau.
81.	IInd Gruppe	Me 110G 720660	Destroyed	Ofw W. Kammerer	Shot down by P-51s near Berlin at about 1.50 pm. Both crew killed. Aircraft crashed 6 miles south of Straussberg.
82.	IInd Gruppe	Me 110G	Destroyed		Shot down near Berlin at about 1.50 pm.
83.	IIIrd Gruppe	Me 110G	Destroyed		As above.
84.	IIIrd Gruppe	Me 110G 5680	Destroyed	Lt H. Muth	Pilot killed during attack by P-51 over Berlin at about 1.50 pm. Radio operator bailed out, wounded. Aircraft crashed at Spreenhagen.
85.	IIIrd Gruppe	Me 110G	Destroyed	Lt H. Hagen	Aircraft set on fire during attack by P-51 flown by Capt J. Broadhead of the 357th Fighter Group. Pilot made a belly landing at Kagen near Erkner, where the aircraft burned out on the ground.
86.	IIIrd Gruppe	Me 110G	Damaged	Lt G. Wolf	Shot down near Berlin by 2nd Lt L. Ruder flying a P-51 of the 357th Fighter Group, at about 1.50 pm. Pilot crash-landed aircraft near Bernau.

Luftwaffe Test Establishment, Rechlin

No.	Aircraft	Status	Pilot	Details
87.	Me 110G 210010	Destroyed	Ufiz E. Waechter	Shot down during air combat. Pilot killed, radio operator bailed out wounded. Aircraft crashed near Pritzwalk. This loss links with the claims of 1st Lt E. Hunt of the 354th Fighter Group, and 1st Lt D. Bochkay and 2nd Lt Pagels of the 357th Fighter Group, all flying P-51s; these relate to an Me 110 shot down northwest of Berlin at about 1.25 pm.

Miscellaneous German Losses

88. Pilot Training School B. 17 — Heinkel 111H Destroyed — Fw Hohfell — Shot down by enemy action, aircraft crashed near Halberstadt. All 5 on board killed. This may have been the 'Ju 88' reported shot down near Magdeburg by 1st Lt B. McGrattan flying a P-51 of the 4th Fighter Group.

89. Pilot Training School A. 42 — Arado 96 964237 Destroyed — Gefr W. Brommbach — Hit by enemy fire and crashed near Helmstedt, pilot killed.

90. Paratroop Replacement Unit — Heinkel 111J 2304 Damaged — Hit on the ground at Stendahl, during a strafing attack by P-51s of the 357th Fighter Group at about 1.40 pm.

INDEX